THE EARTHEN GATE

Jia Pingwa is a formidable cultural figure in China, where he is widely regarded as one of the most important writers of his generation. Born in 1953, his early stories dealt with the countryside around his home city Shangluo in the Shaanxi region. In the 1990s, however, his novels, short stories, poetry and non-fiction became more overtly political, outspoken and challenging to the prevalent climate of censorship, leading to his 1993 novel *The Abandoned Capital* being banned for 17 years by the State Publishing Administration, ostensibly for explicit sexual content.

As his writing became more confrontational, his audience grew exponentially. He also gained critical acclaim from the literary establishment, including winning the Mao Dun Literary Prize, one of the most prestigious writing awards in China, for *Shaanxi Opera* in 2008. Aside from writing, he is a talented professional calligrapher and artist.

This book is part of Shaanxi Stories, a series of translated works by acclaimed authors from the Shaanxi province of China, produced by Valley Press in collaboration with Northwest University, Xi'an. The series editors are Hu Zongfeng and Robin Gilbank. Other books in the series:

MOUNTAIN STORIES, Ye Guangqin
HOW OLD DAN BECAME A TREE, Yang Zhengguang
THE BLOOD RED SUN, Wu Keijing
THE HOWL OF THE WOLF, Hong Ke
THE WILD LAND, Jia Pingwa
IRRATIONAL THINGS, Mu Tao
SUN PALACE, Ye Guangqin
THE HOUR OF THE LOCUST, Yang Zhengguang

The Earthen Gate

JIA PINGWA

translated by Hu Zongfeng
and He Longping

VP

Valley Press

Second Edition published in 2022 by Valley Press
Woodend, The Crescent, Scarborough, YO11 2PW
www.valleypressuk.com

ISBN 978-1-912436-69-9
Cat. no. VP0192

Text and cover design by Peter Barnfather.
Cover art: *China-Aster And Fuchsia* (1847) by James Ackerman.
Series edited by Hu Zongfeng and Robin Gilbank.

Chapter One

When A-Bing was dragged down and barked out a *wow*, how many ages passed by in an instant! From that moment onwards, the dog and I both found ourselves incapable of ever cherishing a sense of belonging.

Just then, the crowd squeezed urgently towards me and I could only crick my back in resistance, bearing the onslaught of that pressure which surged like high banks of waves. Did the willow rod used to prop up the tilting wall in my courtyard suffer in this way? Did the ghost-shaped legs of that ceramic tripod in Old Ran's collection share the same feeling?

One moonless gusty night fifty years ago, the old buffalo belonging to Grandpa Cloud Forest's family wrestled free from its tether and approached the entrance of the village. Unexpectedly, it ran into a leopard and the two engaged in a fierce duel. The leopard's forepaws gouged into the buffalo's shoulders and the buffalo head-butted the leopard's belly. Neither of these adversaries could outflank the other and neither of them dared to pause for breath. At the break of day – after a nightlong tug-of-war – both of the beasts expired from fatigue at the foot of the tall stony weir.

I couldn't bear it, I really couldn't bear it any longer; my back ached and my bosom felt painfully swollen. I knew that once my knees gave way and I fell flat on the ground, I would be trampled by thousands of men's and women's feet. "Who is this?" folks would ask. "She can't be scooped up and she can't be swept aside. Instead, she has to be shovelled away together with the earth and dirt. Who does this meat pie belong to?"

Good! The ferocious-looking policeman ran over with a nightstick! His legs were stumpy and dark sweat stains seeped through the canvas uppers of his rubber shoes. He didn't raise his baton and his gaping mouth closed again, leaving only a red tongue licking his parched, chapped lips.

The crowd leaned backwards. As long as there is wind to blow it, any small blade of grass or young wood will sway. Still, the present disturbance was soundless; only A-Bing woofed another two times after making that *wow*. He reminded me of a toothless old crone who would blurt out one word loudly then slip into a murmur, her voice feeble, like helpless sighs. How grateful I felt for the lingering sound of those two woofs, which did not make the momentary silence any more horrible. I shrugged my shoulders and stood steady.

The endless hot lines of July steam once again appeared before my eyes and the water and sky mingled into one colour. Yep, water and sky were the same colour.[a] But far away there were not only single cells and distant shadows.[b] Outside the square, the buildings composed of steel and concrete metamorphosised in the midst of these hot lines of steam. They contorted and twisted like drunkards. The vehicles, which passed one after another, became so soft it was as though they had lost their edges and corners and seemed ready to melt away at any time.

Forty metres away on the first floor of the nearest building, the family had, rather surprisingly, erected a small fence woven out of broken bamboo struts scavenged from scaffolding on a deserted building site. Enclosed within this were vegetables and sundry sunflowers. The sunflowers dazzled golden yellow. Van Gogh! Of course, I knew of him – an ugly Dutch man who lopped off his own ear. His oil painting looked something like this. Did he lose his mind over the summer? Did the summer sun cause people to become insane more easily?

Fan Jingquan once flew in an aeroplane and was given a bird's-eye view of the whole city. "Do you know?" he related. "The Western Capital is built in the shape of a spider." Which part of the spider corresponded to this square? This square was huge and, emulating the design of foreign countries, had been sowed over with grass seed. Even so, the lawn was not all of a piece – with one patch green and the other yellow. Some parts were even naked with the dirty tawny earth exposed. It was a mottled surface, somewhat like Father's mangy head.

Father had passed away by then. His work permit still lay in an old camphor wood box which bore a bronze boss. Three words had been scrawled in the column headed 'Birthplace': *Benevolent Lenient Village*.

A railway worker who had reached the four corners of the country, he retired that summer and came back to his home village. Barely had his buttocks touched the threshold, when he took off his cap to kill an itch by scratching it downwards and then pulled down his socks to kill it by scratching upwards, saying: "Huh, this is still the most beautiful place!" Grandfather, who was turning the windlass handle on the well head, sniggered: "Son, now you finally know your homeland!" Grandfather let go and the handle swirled; *thump*, the bucket plunged to the bottom of the well and shattered into smithereens.

Father was an ancient tree and, come what may, the leaves of that tree would return to their roots. But I, being a weak sapling at best, was destined to be uprooted and have the clinging soil shaken away until I appeared as clean as if I'd been washed by water.

Five years ago, when the square was being built, our fellow

villagers peeled away the surface of their fields to dig out the sand enthusiastically from underneath. Every night they would transport it on horse-drawn carts and sell it at the eastern gate of the old city, feeling content that they could make a packet. The Mayor named the plaza the 'City Square' and explained on the TV how the name symbolised the process of urbanisation. We too visited the square and flaunted it to our relatives from far away in much the same manner as we showed off the *Drum Music of the Ming Emperor* performed in the village Bodhisattva Temple fair. However, with the expansion of the capital city over the past few years, buildings to the left-hand side and to the right-hand side of Benevolent Lenient Village merged like molten lead – those on this spot joined with those on that spot or those on that spot merged with these on this patch. It appeared that after having dreamed a dream, we had woken from our slumber and become citizens of the Western Capital. We were living in the Western Capital, but we led a life akin to pathetic stray dogs.

Look; Tibetan mastiffs, Saint Bernards, Japanese akitas, sheepdogs, Alaskan malamutes. Since they won the favour of human beings, they found themselves with masters but no home. Yet, are human beings reliable? Is the Western Capital reliable?

An official ordinance was posted to prohibit the raising of dogs without a licence. Strays were being hunted down throughout the city. What must flash before the eyes of these dogs as they were lynched on the cement pillar? Did they envisage the snowy Hokkaido Canyon with its stretches of black pine woods or the expansive Swiss grasslands? Or, did they picture shimmering wall lamps and soft sofas in luxurious living rooms?

No longer did wheat waves roll on June days. No more did persimmon trees stand serene and solemn like the one-thousand-handed bodhisattva. There were no more crows swooping over to foretell death, no magpies dropping by to announce good tidings. No more did we harvest shepherd's purse with bamboo baskets in our hands while the grass-hoppers took wing from the top of our feet, and there were no sour date trees to prick our fingers bloody. Today, neither of us – neither man nor dogs – warranted a hometown.

Pressing against me in the crowd was a podgy woman. Her thick coating of powder and rouge had been leeched away by her sweat, making her face look like it was painted, and her sodden dress made of pure silk had become sticky against her body, revealing the contours of her pendulous breasts and protruding belly. Is an older woman composed only of stinky flesh? I tried to force my way past her and, on raising my head, found that a man not so far away was fixing me with his hot stare. His eyes had been glued to me for a long time. I glared at him, but he continued to stare intently at me, brave like a fly. What a rascal! How could he manage to have those kinds of thoughts in a place such as this?

As I cursed in my mind, I saw several green-headed flies take off from the cement pillar and hover above our heads before one of them finally landed on the fat woman's left earlobe. I knew from my experience in Benevolent Lenient Village that one can never find a fly even if you are in the wilderness. However, if you've emptied your bowels they are bound to materialise. When Brow and I would go over to tidy up Grandpa Cloud Forest's house, the old man would show his masterly move of catching flies in mid-air with chopsticks. Not wanting to vex us, he would say with a smile: "This was one I raised myself!"

Flies are forever hiding somewhere in the world, so in which part of the city did this fly usually hide? The Western Capital was built during the Wanli period of the Ming Dynasty. If flies were also raised at that time (*buzz buzz, buzz buzz*), does it mean they had been flying on from the Ming Dynasty right down until the present day?

"Hey, haul it up, Fatty, pull the rope taut!"

"His old lady's...; I can't undo the noose!"

"Keep it clean, Fatty, use civilised language."

"His mother's *reproductive organ*! The collar is made of genuine leather!"

"Use your knife to cut it!"

Chow!

The collar was sliced in two and, in the sunshine, a set of dog reins exquisitely woven out of silk and hempen strands was lobbed in my direction with a swoosh. I bent to pick them up and saw the words on the cloth tag hanging from the ring: *German Wolfhound*. I had collected almost a dozen sets of dog reins with all kinds of names attached to them. Many other rein-gatherers squinted at me with envious eyes. They must have thought the officer was trying to flatter me because I was a woman. They weren't to know that Fatty was a close acquaintance of Brow's, whereas I'd only seen him once at her home.

Fatty looked in my direction with one eye narrowed and shot me a grin that exposed his white teeth.

"He knows you?" the podgy woman asked with a stiff voice.

"I know him. He is the guy credited with cracking the 28/11 murder case."

"Then he is something of a celebrity."

Fatty ought, indeed, to have been a celebrity. For months, the Western Capital was abuzz with talk of the murder.

People had installed burglar-proof windows and doors, which they thought made their residences as safe as they could be. Nevertheless, all four members of an artist's family were stabbed to death in their home. Notices proclaiming a 200,000-yuan reward for information leading to an arrest were posted on the streets. These stirred many citizens' hearts; it's said that fifteen individuals made reports, though they all turned out to be worthless lies.

Just as the cops were at their wits' end, Fatty inadvertently winkled out a confession when he was interrogating a suspect for another case. The murderers – two moneyless junkie crooks – shacked up on the opposite side of the street to where the artist's studio was located and they knew his colleagues. The investigation team, which consisted of more than one hundred members, busied themselves for a month together with their police dogs, yet still no lead was found. The criminals even went down to watch the clamorous scene and, patting a police dog, said: "This guy must have eaten too much meat."

However, one of the gang was hauled in over another burglary case. When the policemen took turns to cross-examine him for two days and two nights, his withdrawal symptoms flared up. Nasal mucus and tears began to stream down and his body shivered like bran being sifted.

Fatty, a parcel of white powder in his hand, promised: "Own up and you can have this."

The drug was passed over to the criminal. "Do you know how much this parcel is worth?" the captured man asked.

"How much?"

"200,000 yuan! I'm going to give you 200,000 yuan!"

Fatty still didn't know what he was driving at.

"Now my habit is getting worse," wailed the suspect. "But

I have no dough to buy it with. Even when I have enough, it's getting harder and harder for me to lay my hands on the stuff and, what's more, the drug is probably fake. I hate to death those guys who make the fakes!"

Gnashing his teeth for a while and calling the policeman 'Brother Fatty', the criminal gave out a *hee-hee*. "Thank you for your white powder, but I don't want to live, really, I don't want to. Your brother will learn from Lei Feng and help you render an outstanding service." Next, he told Fatty how they committed the 28th November murder. Maybe he had made up his mind to die, so he didn't give a damn. Or maybe, owing to the effects of the drugs, confessing to the murder became a show of bravado. Either way, he had concealed two knives on his person and, with the first oblique thrust, sent a blade into the lower portion of the artist's son, who was sleeping soundly. He didn't even bother to withdraw it as the lad's fleshy member fell from his body and bounced on the floor. The artist's daughter was stabbed to death in the doorway of her small bedroom. Upon hearing the commotion, the artist came out from another room in a pair of baggy shorts, with one foot bare and one in a slipper. They bumped into each other and wrestled. The second criminal snatched up an ink slab and pounded the artist's head with it before delivering another stab to his victim's belly. His intestines slithered out with a gurgling sound. Next, the lady of the house was threatened at knifepoint to surrender her money. She wouldn't. The knife was dug into every joint and twisted around.

"These were my first killings, Brother Fatty. I sat on the floor paralysed after killing that old woman, my pullover and woollen trousers wet through with sweat. Then, I spotted a dog – a local breed. A very fine animal. Standing watching at the toilet doorway, it must have been frightened silly. I said: 'You saw everything, you fine animal?' and pounced with the knife raised. The dog, however, crawled into another room and used its body to slam the door shut. It barked loudly. We then opened the front door and ran like the clappers."

His description concurred with the murder scene, though the large investigation team had always thought that the murderer was a lone wolf and a professional killer. How were they to believe that it was this skinny man of no more than five foot one in front of them? When they caught his accomplice, however, their confessions were identical and the murder case was cracked. Fatty took the primary credit. He was a lucky dog: he sent the murderers to the execution ground and they sent him 200,000 yuan (perhaps they owed him this huge sum in their previous lives).

Panting heavily, Fatty now placed the thick rope noose around the neck of the German wolfhound. His pudding face beneath the police cap dripped with beads of perspiration and his belt was cinched loosely; because of his expansive belly, the waist of his trousers hung low at the front and his buttocks were wrapped tight at the back. The noose was being drawn tighter and tighter and the wolfhound found itself being towed towards the cement pillar. The already-strangled dogs lay in a disorderly pile, clearly visible to the living animals.

Right now, the German wolfhound ought to be passing out through fear. It didn't bark and only dug in its four limbs stiffly out of instinct, engaging in a tug-of-war with Fatty. One moment it was towed forwards and another moment Fatty was dragged backwards. The crowd let out a chuckle. Their subdued laughter made Fatty shamefaced and a policeman standing below the cement pillar came up. He took over the other end of the rope and they dragged the wolfhound forwards. A stupid dog, which was strangled earlier, lay there paralyzed after it was pushed down from the carriage of the vehicle and Fatty was forced to raise the cheap animal by grasping its collar while runny waste dripped down from between its two hind legs. Dog shit is very stinky and that foul smell was especially repugnant in the baking sun. This must have been the under-boss's watchdog. A small bronze bell forged in the early years of the Republic of China was still fastened to its collar.

A garrotted Alaskan malamute was said to have been the pet dog of the biggest boss at a company. Having bitten a dozen or more people, it was the number one most wanted in the hunt for unlicensed dogs. Of a Belgian breed, strong and brassy-yellow-haired, the heroic way in which the dog accepted its execution shocked everyone present. Not having to be dragged to the cement pillar, it trotted there, raised its head for the noose and then let out a garrulous sound like a big-shot delivering a speech.

The German wolfhound turned out to be the polar opposite of its dead peers. When Fatty and the other policeman dragged it forward, each of its four feet left a furrow behind in the lawn. What a fate for this dog; it was not destined to be hanged on the cement pillar but to be strangled to death in full view of the capacity audience. When Fatty and the officer pulled the rope taut on both sides, I could see it plainly dangling in mid-air. Its long tongue lolled out. Three flies zoomed over straightaway and one of them landed on the tip of its black nose.

Fatty, obviously exhausted and thinking that the dog had been throttled to death, relaxed his hands. Hardly had he done that when the wolfhound stirred, rolled then sprang to its feet and raced to the other side of the square with the rope trailing behind. Evidently unable to sprint fast and its forelegs giving way after twenty metres, it tumbled down, though it struggled to its feet again and resumed its escape attempt.

This turn of events stupefied the audience and the policemen alike. After about a minute, the officers all pounced and began to chase the dog in circles around the square. When the hound wheeled around and charged back to break through the crowd, the spectators stepped backward in unison to give way. The other end of the rope leading from the dog's neck struck at Fatty's feet, causing him to stumble, but Fatty always enjoyed good luck and, as he tripped over the rope, the dog again fell to the ground. I could see blood spurting out of its mouth and nostrils, splashing everywhere and forming a reef of pink cloud in the sunshine. Fatty seized the rope with both hands and the dog was dragged to the cement pillar again. Having made an exhibition in front of the audience, the policemen took out their hatred tenfold on the dog. Fatty and a pimply-faced policeman pulled the long thick rope taut. Acne Mug shouted: "Water! Water! Stifle it!"

A policeman sidled over with a plastic bottle of mineral water and tipped it into the dog's mouth. The water went down with a gurgling sound, and was again spurted out, once more creating a reef of pink cloud. I had never seen such a tall column of water spewed out of anybody's mouth and certainly not so evenly-scattered; in the sunshine, there was the flicker of a rainbow. The dog's four limbs twitched and then dangled feebly. Scarcely had Fatty let go with his hand, when the ferocious-looking policeman shouted: "Don't lay it down! Not until it is cold through and through. A dog can't be allowed to touch the earth. Dogs belong to the earth; if they touch the earth, they spring back to life. Haul it up! Haul it up!"

I didn't know why, but once spoken I could never forget these words.

My arm had a scar on it. Mother once told me that it would disappear when I grew up. Still it remained. One day when I was six, I watched Grandfather smoking his water pipe. When he smoked his water pipe, he never used a papery taper because he could grab a live cinder as quick as lightning from the brazier and press this into the bowl of the pipe. While drawing on his pipe – *slurp slurp* – he would tell me things about Great-grandfather's West Guanzhong Academy and the old-fashioned private school where he used to give lectures, and he would teach me to recite:

To have a prosperous family, one should store up virtues and do good.

To be a good child, one should work the land and read books.

Unable to understand what he meant, I followed suit and reached out a hand to catch a red hot cinder, but was burnt, so cried out and flung it away. It landed on my arm by accident. Grandfather's response was: "Well done! From now on my words will be branded in your mind."

Grandfather passed away long ago. As I grew up, the scar grew longer. In that winter when the final piece of farmland in the village was requisitioned, we slaughtered our last ten oxen. Our share of the beef made Brow and me wild with joy. We cooked sliced beef with shredded carrots. Next, we prepared beef seasoned with soy sauce and then we went to Uncle Six Pounds' home to show off our cooking skills. A mound of cow dung was being dried in Uncle Six Pounds' courtyard and the foul smell was downright nasty. He was burying his share of beef in front of the steps, cursing loudly:

"What an evil thing! Pigs and sheep are born for the plate, but an ox is never supposed to be eaten. Is a beef-eater still a man? I can't see any benevolent leniency in these Benevolent Lenient Village folks." He roared at us with his waist bent, his slobber flying and his eyeballs bulging out as glossy as two bronze bells.

Panic set in after Brow and I came back home, knowing that some retribution was awaiting us since we had eaten the flesh of an old ox who had toiled for us its entire life. As expected, a patch of fine, soft, yellow hair erupted out of our arms and what made it especially bad for me was that the hair formed a halo around my scar. After she got to know that salesman, Brow used imported hair remover to get rid of hers. Mine still persisted and was to become the only hallmark that betrayed my peasant origins to others.

The German wolfhound left me deeply saddened, and I even hated it because of those stupid exploits before its death. Then I got to thinking about how the loss outweighed the gain brought by his death struggle. If, on the other hand, it was acting out of instinct, why did the other dogs not do likewise? What hint was it trying to drop for me? Anyhow, I now regretted having come to the City Square to watch this scene. I began to squeeze backwards. Some took the chance to try and snatch the dog leash from my hands and that rascal even gave my waist a pinch. I flicked my hand furiously, bound all the strands around my middle, and left with a fuzzy mind. I was heading off towards the Institute of Agricultural Science and Technology in the southern corner of the city to look for Old Ran.

Old Ran's colleague, Fan Jingquan, was as per usual sitting in his dorm room. The white-haired young man majored in agriculture but his hobby was writing novels. His works had never been published and he liked reciting his newest piece for Old Ran's ears as he sat listening quietly with closed eyes.

When I came in, Fan stopped reading and asked: "Feeling sleepy, Ran?"

Old Ran answered: "I am listening, go on." His eyes were still shut.

"Listening, my arse! You didn't even notice that Plum had come in and you still claim to be listening to my novel?"

Fan was as shrewd as a monkey and could detect the scent of a woman. I was standing at an oblique angle to the glass door, tidying up my hair. My wet fringe was sticky against my forehead. Upon hearing his words, I smiled. Every time I came here, I pretended to be a casual passerby. I had come running in here so many times saturated in black sweat and bumped into Fan Jingquan at the gate of the courtyard. I would turn a blind eye to him, strut past with my head held high and my chest sticking out and not come in unless he shouted loudly at me.

Old Ran opened his eyes and, after catching sight of me, sprang to his feet. He swore: "Tomorrow I shall also write a novel and read it out loud so you know what it is like to be forced to listen."

Fan said, "Thi, thi, this Ran" in embarrassment and after a while he laughed. "Plum, are you here for love or learning?"

Fan was the tutor for my correspondence courses.

I replied that I was looking for both.

Fan's small eyes blinked. "Got it. You two get busy," he said and left.

Old Ran and I stayed and he became hospitable in a solicitous way. He still hadn't replaced his pair of old myopic glasses and their sides continued to be held on with adhesive tape. Still wearing the sloppy trousers that I disliked, he ran in and out on his two wiry legs buying all kinds of snacks for me. Was I still a child? Why not buy some bubble gum?

"You don't look OK, Plum. What's wrong?" asked Old Ran.

I explained about how dogs were being strangled in the square and that more than one hundred had been killed.

Old Ran didn't seem to feel grief-stricken but removed his glasses to wipe them. His bulging fish eyes were gleaming. When the German wolfhound was finally hanged on the cement pillar, its tongue lolled out and its eyes popped out like two glass balls dangling on strings.

"Put your glasses on!" I ordered him. "When you take them off I don't recognise you."

Old Ran replaced his glasses and became his former self.

He remarked: "I have acquaintances in the police bureau and I will obtain a dog pelt to put on my bed. That should stop you from getting bronchitis in the winter."

I let out an '*hmm*' and, feeling unable to go on talking with him, lay down ready to sleep face-up on his small, squeaky bed.

Old Ran related how he had laid his hands on another piece of Ming or Qing Dynasty furniture locally. Called a *wuzi* – a square stool – and made of sandalwood, it could be placed on the bed and used as a seat or a pillow or a back rest. The ancients knew how to enjoy life, that's for sure.

But today Ming or Qing furniture was not on my mind.

I bent my legs to sleep on one side and my sandals dropped down. Old Ran no longer rattled on about furniture but complained about how hot it was. His head was all sweaty, yet his glassy eyes remained riveted on my bare feet. "Your feet look so pleasant."

I disliked my feet most of all – five toes in a bolt straight row, so fleshy, unlike Brow's slender toes that could be slipped into pointy leather shoes. I withdrew my feet and tucked them under the quilt.

"Really, your toenails are just like porcelain plates." Old Ran rolled on and once more took off his glasses to wipe them. The dog reins woven out of colourful silk and hempen strands hung on the back of the chair. My eyes were now merely slits, and I listened to Old Ran who, in the midst of rapid breathing, stuttered out his sweet words. He asked me when I would give him my hand, whether we should entertain the guests at home or book tables in a restaurant in the city. I still paid no attention to him. He bit his tongue for a while and a pool of spittle could be heard gargling about his mouth. He then proceeded to close the curtains and drew cautiously over to paw my feet, legs and then abdomen and breasts. He was stealthy like a thief.

The sunlight from the window hadn't been entirely blocked out and the golden rays that seeped through a gap were reflected in a bedside mirror so as to leave a white patch on the ceiling. There was a saying from a book, which stated: "When you play mahjong, you forget about reading and when you read, you forget about mahjong." What about now? Fondled by Old Ran, I was as quiet as a kitten and tried my level best not to recall the goings-on in the square. Yet, in my confusion, I sensed that some pedestrian had paused outside and was at present listening all-ears to the squeaking sound of the wooden bed and was peeping in through the cat's eye.

That peeping Tom must be a burglar and was bound to sneak in with a knife. First, he would stab Old Ran, thrusting the knife into his joints before my very eyes and rotating the handle. Old Ran would perish, his high-magnification myopic glasses tumbling down and his mouth and nostrils thick with bloody soap-sud-like foam. Next, the murderer would clutch at my neck with both hands and lift me in a chokehold before planting me down and seizing my ankles, seeming to say: "I won't let you touch the ground. You little bitch!"

Spasms wracked my whole body. Old Ran, however, had mounted me and was kissing my neck and face like crazy. My mind stopped functioning. Now only Old Ran could be my saviour. Old Ran! Old Ran! My Old Ran! I pushed him aside to undress myself. My upper garment was a big-collared, flaxen cloth blouse and, as I peeled it off, it masked my face.

"Come on!" I groaned. But a woman is a woman; no matter how headstrong she might be, she can only be saved by a man in the end. I knew that wantonness must be written all over my face, but I no longer cared. "You wanna do that, let's do it well. I'm yours. You can screw me senseless; you can fuck me to death."

Poor Old Ran slipped momentarily into a trance. He had not been expecting that I, who had always guarded my body like jade, would suddenly become a slut. He acted all wanton and lustful only when I refused, but became panic-stricken when I seized the initiative.

I flicked my blouse to one side and he still stood there frozen. I gasped: "I want it." Brought up sharp, he suddenly touched my frame as though kneading cold bean-starch noodles. His face was full of shyness as he dragged over the quilt to hide my body and murmured that he couldn't do it now. I reached out a hand to give his crotch a grope. It was soft and withered with a dash of exotic, slippery wet stuff. He had come while he was caressing and kissing me.

Chapter Two

I was often bleary-eyed at that time and, from winter to summer, my exhaustion grew more acute by the day. Every morning, even though I had slept for an age, my mind was still in a state of confusion after I got up and it would take five or ten minutes to become clear. Next, I would feel cheerful for no reason or else inexplicably annoyed. I couldn't explain why, but the mood would dog me throughout the day. Maybe it was my inheritance from Benevolent Lenient Village since, back then, Grandfather was affected by the same thing. He used to sit placidly outside the courtyard on the ancient horse-mounting stone as the raw grassy odour from the fields outside the village was blown into the lanes. The stench of cow shit and pigswill – two scents which would easily make people sober up – floated past from who knows where. Grandpa would massage his knees for half a day then stand up, nip off a flower from the adobe wall and go into the main room to brew tea, asking: "Hasn't Plum got up yet?"

Brow and I slept on the *kang* and, through the crack between the door panels, could spy how he drank three mugs of tea, brewed so strong that when poured the liquid resembled a dangling thread. We could also spot the pale-coloured flower that was pinned behind the bolt of my bedroom door. Later, Grandfather passed away and so did Father and Mother. The blossoms still exploded into bloom on the wall of the courtyard, but nobody would nip them off and pin them behind the bolt for me to wear after combing my hair.

Brow and I slept together for another ten years until we both became fully-mature maidens. The villagers all gossiped that we were ripe persimmons that would ooze juice the moment they were touched. Nonetheless, maturity brought with it more vexations. Every day after we had woken up, Shaved Head from the grocery store would play his two-stringed *erhu* under the peach tree in his back courtyard. The bowed music swung back and forth and we shut our eyes again, visualising in our minds a huge bird landing from the sky with its wings outstretched. Then we drifted off again until a crocodile of children chanted loudly outside our window: "Such a big window and such a big gate, such a grown-up woman but she doesn't have a mate!" We giggled away on the *kang*.

The bright red sun peeped in through the latticed window and illuminated our red quilt, together with the exposed halves of our bodies.

Brow observed: "The sun is one pole-length from the ground."

I retorted: "The height to your arse!"

We still didn't get up, instead plucking the hairs from one another's forehead. Brow claimed that I looked like my grandfather. Really, with my oblong face and long pleats of nostril, I did take after Grandpa. When Brow said this, she was back-handedly gloating about her own beauty. I was not as attractive as her, but felt proud that I had the bearing of one of my elders. I started to recite the couplet composed by my great-grandfather when he was lecturing in the West Guanzhong Academy:

Orphaned when young, I boarded at the River Wei and, saddened that I had achieved nothing although so old, I wanted to light candles and read at night.

Now I have established a lecture hall here for the ignorant children in the hope that they will study hard and cherish time like me.

Pointing at Grandfather's own couplet, which hung on the back wall of the main chamber, I intoned:

Possess not half a mu of farmland but worry about the whole world.
Read ten thousand volumes and befriend the ancients spiritually.

After my recitation, a crestfallen Brow bleated in a weak voice: "Sister Plum, you are sure to go to university in the future." Then, we held our tongues. This uncomfortable silence was an increasingly common occurrence. In the end, I failed the college entrance examinations. Brow, meanwhile, grew more and more glamorous and inevitably we became estranged. Did we no longer romp playfully together because each of us had found our love? Those who are in love are lonely, lonely like tigers or pigs. Brow was as stupid as a pig!

For dozens of years, the city dwellers maligned our village, saying: "Their persimmons are bitter, their walnuts have hard shells, their women are stunted and their girls are swarthy." It was not easy for Benevolent Lenient Village to produce an enchantress like Brow. But she changed after falling in love with the agent who sold fitness equipment as part of a pyramid scheme. We two grew apart and she started to tell lies. Honestly, she did. Whenever I invited her to sleep over at my place, she would always bemoan how her mother had just suffered another asthma attack and she needed to go back home and look after her. But when I ran into her mother later, she would be in the pink, saying she had taken three doses of Uncle Cloud Forest's medicinal herbs and the disease hadn't visited her throughout the winter.

What is more, Brow's mother nagged about when we were going to get married because Brow always told her how she stayed with me every day. "Best if you two sisters marry two brothers. Then you needn't live apart." I knew straightaway that Brow was bunking up with the bushy-bearded pyramid salesman every night.

On the day when two new patients boarded at my home, Old Ran entrusted Fan Jingquan to deliver a couple of tutorial books for the correspondence courses to me. We chit-chatted about rice, noodles and the weather, then our topic wandered to Grandpa Cloud Forest's medical skills. Of course, Grandpa Cloud Forest's medical skills were wonderful, perhaps even unbelievable. He only had one eye and, at an early age, had been a victim of infant paralysis. Heaven knows where he had learned medicine. Yet, when he treated any difficult disease, especially hepatitis B, the remedies he prescribed almost always worked like a charm. If he had been a self-employed doctor like those living downtown, he would have become the wealthiest man in the capital city. Nonetheless, he still lived in three adobe rooms behind the old shrine and his furnishings consisted of a plank-built cabinet, an eight-bushel urn and a chest (but never any modern appliances with their flashing lights). He had no children and no wife, and lived a solitary life as simple as could be.

Patients thronged to our village and he took in and treated eighty-four of them every month – in other words, around three a day. Each household in the village had registration cards issued by him. A patient didn't go to see Grandpa Cloud Forest directly. Instead they registered with a certain family who would then take care of their meals and boarding and buy the necessary medicines. A mildly-ill patient needed to stay for eight to ten days and a seriously-ill one, a month or two. This way, every patient would pay the host hundreds or even thousands of yuan, yet Grandpa Cloud Forest only charged two yuan to cover the grain and dishes.

Folks in Benevolent Lenient Village lived a well-off, harmonious life, all thanks to Grandpa Cloud Forest. "Grandpa Cloud Forest is our Gandhi," I declared. I had read books on Gandhi and meant that with all sincerity. But someone interjected at the door: "Why don't you sing *The East Is Red*?"[c] It was Brow's voice. I brushed her aside, eyeing her gorgeously-dressed body and the hirsute man behind her. I knew Bushy Beard was the agent with the pyramid sales scheme – a woman's senses don't make mistakes in that regard – but I also understood immediately that Brow had come here to show off. I didn't expose her lies and only laughed on purpose like a quacking duck.

"Sister Plum! What are you laughing at?"

"The head has become the face and the face has become the head."

The selling agent's face was now scarlet. Did it redden because of my words or did his skin look like a roasted chicken's to start with?

Brow, of course, knew I was mocking her and, nostrils twitching, felt surprised that her friend didn't permit her a little glory upon meeting her lover for the first time. Fan Jingquan muttered in a low voice: "Plum, you are not as refined as Brow." Did he also loathe how I had overstepped the mark? Fan, however, went on: "Brow's view of love is that it should diversify the breed. You are sweet on Ran and your child will still be a little Bleary Eyes."

"Beat it! Beat it!" I yelped. I sat up on the bed and, again, gawped at the selling agent while howling with laughter.

Brow wrenched my shoulders and noted: "Sister Plum, there's a piece of leek in your teeth." My laughter died and I scooped up a mirror to take a look. There was no leek there. It was their turn to hoot at me as I was put in an awkward position.

That was when our relationship soured. Especially when Brow told me, after we had quieted down, that she had found a new job and was no longer a waitress at the bar of a hotel. Instead, she was a clerical worker in a real estate development company. The boss of the company was Bushy Beard Shao's friend. She invited me to go along too and boasted how she could give me a recommendation for a job as a salesgirl in the marketing department. I was infuriated! There were so many real estate companies in the capital city that kept on claiming they would renew the old city and expand the new metropolis. Our village faced being boxed in by cement and then dwindling away or even being wiped off the surface of the earth. Our fellow villagers all harboured a grudge against the ferociously-expanding Western Capital as well as those powerful and influential dirty rich real estate bosses. They were fighting a war to the bitter end to protect our homeland. And yet Brow wanted to be a traitor!

I was exasperated that she had changed so fast, just for the sake of love. Now, love can make a person relegate their parents into second place, but how could somebody sell out their land and kin? We argued there and then. I tried to save her by pointing out how dangerous her actions were and insisting that she would become a *persona non grata* in Benevolent Lenient Village. I even deliberately related the story of Liu Rushi, which I had learned from my correspondence courses. I told her about this Ming Dynasty singer who persuaded her newly-married husband, Qian Qianyi, to commit suicide when performing his official duty as the Qing army flooded southward. Brow didn't know who this Liu Rushi was. She maintained that she was unwilling to think about the situation and that she wanted to be on the up-and-up, living in clover. Why then shouldn't she go and work in that company? What *was* the so-called homeland when it was at home? Only a sparrow pays attention to its nest. Had I ever seen a tiger's lair?

The more I tried to reason with her, the more insufferable I felt her snobbery was becoming. I said that she didn't look like a peasant. Brow snapped: "If it were still the period when 'in agriculture we learn from Dazhai Village,'[d] I could go and become an *iron lady*. But now I am a company secretary and I should live like a lady." I could find no words to reason with her and we parted company unhappily. After seeing her off, I walked along the village lanes to let go of my depression.

I caught sight of a herd of people squatting down below the courtyard wall at the entrance to the lane. Men and women, old and young, they were eating out of huge bowls and nattering. I suddenly found the words with which to persuade Brow. *A peasant, no matter how good they are, is still a peasant.* They should still find their homes to return to at the sunny foot of their courtyard wall in the countryside. Brow never came to my home again. She still lived in the village, with the neighbours belittling her all the while. Her beauty used to be the apple of our eye. Now, however, when she flounced back home along a village lane after work, few were willing to greet her.

One day, the wind blew down a piece of Bolt's washing that was hanging out to dry, carrying it out of the courtyard and depositing it in the lane. Brow picked it up and knocked at the gate of Bolt's courtyard, calling: "Hey, one of your clothes has been blown outside and I've hung it on the latch of your gate." Bolt stood in the courtyard. "Thank you. Who are you?" She answered: "This is Brow." "Brow? Who is Brow? I don't know her." At that precise moment, I was hitching up my trousers in the latrine and, from over the privy wall, saw her face burning with embarrassment. Despite having a smidgen of sympathy for her, I squatted down once again, snorting and smiling coldly, taking pleasure in her misfortune.

That morning, in the midst of my dream, I detected a faint booming sound, like magma surging within the depths of the earth. Mornings were serene in Benevolent Lenient Village and this was the first time that serenity had been broken by such a strange noise. This took me a little off guard but did nothing to dispel my drowsiness. Where was the lingering *erhu* music? Chaotic footsteps could be heard outside the window and many people were shouting abuse, sighing and chirping gossip. Finally, I worked it out. The old buildings on that stretch of low-lying land near our village were being replaced and the bulldozers from a real estate company had come to raze them. I heaved a sigh and sank into a bad mood, knowing that from now on I could kiss goodbye to my tranquil mornings. Now the adjacent low-lying land was being cleared, our village must be next on the agenda. Gloomily, I went to the privy with the piss basin in my hands and my hair dishevelled. The patient who was afflicted with ascites and boarding in my lean-to was squatting inside and his wife was taking care of him. Hearing my footfall, she came out and asked me apologetically to wait a while longer. We stood chatting under the pomegranate tree just outside the privy.

"Big sister, we have brought you too much trouble," she said. "He has tight bowels. Such a big man, but he shits like a lamb."

The pomegranate tree was a riot of flowers. This sallow-faced soul of a wife – had she been infected too?

"No hurry," I reassured her. "How is he after three doses of the herbal medicine?"

"Miraculous! He's been disease-ridden for three years and attended all kinds of hospitals, but in vain. He takes medicine by the gunny sackful and all the meat in his body has turned sour. At night, the mosquitoes bite me but not him. After he took those three doses, I dared not entertain much hope and try to treat the dead horse as if it were alive. We never expected he would pass the ascites."

A dull collapsing sound came again. The privy walls were made of mud bricks and, after standing there for so many years, had grown rotten at the base. Would a single kick send them tumbling down?

"Grandpa Cloud Forest is a miracle worker. Feel free to stay here and be treated for a spell. I am sure he will heal."

The woman, her face creasing into a chrysanthemum shape, nodded her head repeatedly.

"Yeah, yeah. On first catching sight of my husband, he said: 'Disease-ridden for three years? Your liver has become swollen and reaches beyond the rib cage a distance of two fingers' width.' I thought you'd told him about it. But yesterday he predicted that the ascites had been passed out and today dogs would be slaughtered on the square and asked me to collect the piss of a white dog to kickstart the medicine. See, that old man is a cripple. How could he know dogs would be slaughtered on the square? I went there with a tea mug, but couldn't squeeze my way to the front. When

I'd finally made it, the dogs had all been lynched. Where could I get the piss? And a white dog's piss for that matter. But who could have known that a woman from your village by the name of Brow had adopted a white dog? At first light today, I went to look for her. I wanted to ask you to accompany me, but you were still in bed. The herbs are being decocted. Say, is that a miracle or what?"

I had witnessed Grandpa Cloud Forest perform miracles too many times to be astonished. What did astonish me was Brow fetching back a white dog. Among that truckload of dogs being transported to the square to be hanged, there were many white ones. Nonetheless, when I left, the only white mutt left alive belonged to a local breed. Later on, we would name it A-Bing. How could Brow bring A-Bing back home? As far as Brow was concerned, I despised her from the bottom of my heart, but she had saved a pathetic dog from the square and that stirred up some warm feelings towards her. Looking skyward, I smiled.

"She saved a dog as well as herself."

"She saved my husband."

"She is still a member of Benevolent Lenient Village."

"Just as she always was."

I didn't offer an explanation, immediately going to Brow's home to look for her. She wasn't there. Outside the courtyard, a clutch of old ladies was playing sliver cards with their grandchildren in their arms, grumbling about how no rain fell last year and how it had become hot so early this summer. How could the five types of grain run to seed? (Where were the five grains?) Next, they commented on what a pity it was that Old Granny Qi, who lived on the low-lying land, had moved away. She could no longer find partners to play sliver cards with. Their eyes were moist. They blew their noses and flung big handfuls of snivel on the ground.

"You are asking about Brow?" they clucked. "She's brought back a dog, a very charming beast. And she took A-Bing to get registered early this morning."

"Who is this A-Bing?"

"You don't know A-Bing?"

They then told me that Liuhe's family hen had laid an egg which was a double-yolker, Shaved Head's wife had chipped a front tooth yesterday while eating and that A-Bing was the name Brow had given to the dog.

"Plum, here is a riddle for you. *You use it when young, but you don't when you are grown up; a husband has it but his wife uses it; a monk has one, but he doesn't use it at all.* You've received a schooling, so can you get it?"

I left them and went to the village to look for someone else. On my way, it suddenly clicked: the answer to the riddle was *a name*? These old ladies must have felt sad about their own lives. After marrying, they just became known as their husband's woman, now even a dog was entitled to have a name of its own.

Once again, I congratulated Brow and felt duty-bound to advertise my friend's chivalrous deed. However, whenever I saw a fellow villager the first thing they talked about was Brow and A-Bing. They even shamed me by asking why I had not gone to the square. Why had I not brought A-Bing back home? They rattled on, saying that so many dogs had been hanged, kishus, German wolfhounds, Afghan hunting dogs, local dogs, whippets, stupid dogs. When it was the turn of A-Bing – the local animal – he let out a bark as he was dragged down from the vehicle, a very pitiable bark. All the people heard it and fixed their eyes on him and everyone was simultaneously taken aback by his beauty. He was a big, sixty-pound, seventy-centimetre-tall hound, the lower half of his body fine-coated and the upper half wire-haired.

When he was led through the sunshine to the cement pillar, he walked as the crow flies, his head slightly raised and his mouth half shut. His small nose was beige and the rims of his eyes were dark. It seemed as though he was demonstrating his charms for one last time. For a moment, the audience forgot they were watching a massacre. Instead they remained agog with bated breath as if they were appreciating a famous model's catwalk show.

As he was being led step by step past that massive pile of dog corpses to the cement pillar, the people, finally remembering what was to come next, started to sigh and stiffen. The policemen stiffened worse than anyone else. Fatty unconsciously stroked his back and, while leading the way, even his walking posture became deformed. Acne Mug, the water-pourer, massacre director and team leader all froze, their eyes glistening before his beauty. At long last, the team leader declared for the entire audience to hear: "It's really such a beautiful dog."

Fatty queried: "Boss, should this one be hanged as well?"

The team leader asked: "What do you think?"

"It is the artist's dog, which was adopted by his neighbour."

"Then why didn't he get him registered?"

Fatty released an "Ah?". The two whispered in each other's ears, blah-blahhing. Fatty sidled over, stared at the crowd for quite a long while and asked: "Who here lives in the 'burbs?"

Brow raised her hand and called out loudly: "I live in the southern suburbs."

Fatty let out a laugh. He waved at Brow to approach the lawn and proclaimed: "Remember, take the animal away and don't stay within the city limits. Can you guarantee that?"

Brow left with A-Bing shortly afterwards.

"Just think, so many dogs have been strangled to death and he alone is still alive. He must possess some magical power within his body."

"That dog enjoys an enviable karma. The criminals didn't kill him and the policemen didn't hang him."

"Sure, the dog must have been a temptress in its previous life. Who could raise a knife to such a beauty?"

"It's a male. A male dog."

"What is destiny? This is destiny. But there are so many people here, how come Brow should be the lucky one?"

I knew why. Fatty was Brow's friend and as he stared at the crowd, he must have glimpsed her. Brow's eyes talked to him and Fatty asked her to bring A-Bing away on purpose.

Chapter Three

Whatever there was to be said about the matter, our fate is the fate of the dog. We have forged an inexplicable bond with canines, or else in a previous incarnation we were ourselves dogs.

While Chivalry was still in the village, he liked lecturing others and swore blind that each man had a soul and, moreover, the matter of whether a soul is great or negligible had nothing to do with the body. The body only provided a boarding place for the soul. An imposing body might house a despicable soul and an ugly body might house a lofty one. When the body, like a vehicle of iron and wood or a hempen sack, was ready to decompose and rot, the soul floated up to the sky, where similar souls were floating everywhere, gathering, converging and dispersing like the clouds. The saying that *birds of a feather flock together* referred to this.

The souls ambled at leisure in mid-air. If, on their way, a bee happened to be carrying the pollen it had collected to the heart of another flower and that flower was able to bear fruit, a soul would land there. From then on, that fruit would contain a soul. Or, if a man and a woman were copulating, a soul may land there and the baby that was in the process of being conceived would possess that soul. It was not only humans, therefore, who had a soul, but also animals, grasses, trees, flying birds, swimming fishes and stones. What about man? Well, consider this: although you were a father in this life, in the next you might be the child of your child.

I brayed with laughter when Chivalry outlined his theory.

"If this were the case," I exclaimed, "there is no distinction between nobility and lowliness."

Chivalry replied: "Right. Emperors and beggars stand on the same line and so do generals and whores."

I relayed his words to Grandpa Cloud Forest and he smiled, reflecting: "Chivalry will become a wanderer."

As expected, Chivalry was not to be seen in Benevolent Lenient Village for a few years. Needless to say, when I encountered A-Bing again, Chivalry's words leapt into my mind and I sensed the dog must have been a glamorous woman in his previous life. Full mourning attire makes a woman beautiful. The dog was silvery white all over, with not even one hair of a different hue. Despite boasting such a huge build, he nevertheless had four tiny paws, which left behind mume-blossom prints on the ground when he padded over (you could almost smell their faintly hidden aroma). His eyes were like deep water, slightly tinged with light blue and outlined in a much darker shade. I dare say I couldn't apply eyeliner with such finesse and nor could Brow, even though she was so particular about her looks.

There is a proverb to the effect that ugliness can ward off evil spirits and things that are too beautiful easily breed disaster. Notwithstanding, on that night dimly-lit by the moon, when A-Bing appeared at the doorway of the toilet, the armed murderer hesitated. Before the cement pillar, Fatty's eyes sparkled and beauty again overcame death. A-Bing, having conquered death twice, must have been a small animal transmogrified into a spirit. Later on, I dared not be alone with him. I came to fear a sort of demonic aura.

Brow's courtyard wasn't large. Back when her mother was still alive, she was a hotbed of diseases, inflicted not only with asthma but also rheumatoid arthritis, making the joints of her four limbs go all cockeyed. A hive of bees sheltered under the grape trellis in the small courtyard. Every day when the dappled sunshine sifted through the vines, Brow and I would harvest the bees to sting her joints. The buzzing insects wanted to fly away and a ball of splendid illusory light flashed behind their yellowish wings. We had to pinch their wings and press their tiny arses against a joint for their poisonous stings to dig in. With each sting, her mother would suck in a breath of cold air to help withstand the pain. What a pity that a bee must die after having inflicted just one sting. "I don't want to live, don't want to live," her mother gasped. "How many bees must die for me to live?" She refused the venom therapy and one night silently opened the beehive to let the swarm free.

After her mother died, Brow lived with me until we went our separate ways. Her house no longer looked the same. The clay brick walls had been whitewashed with lime and papered over. Curtain boxes and trailing curtains had been installed. The architraves and the foot of the walls were skirted with Chinese ash boards. A TV, a VCR and a stereo system stood on the squat cabinet. There was a sofa chair crafted from scented rosewood and behind the sofa chair stood an upright lamp with a slim stem and a massive shade.

"Ha!" I gaped from the threshold, half-shocked by and half-blustering at the ornaments in her room. "Brow has become a citizen of modern society. What's this? Slippers? Slippers made from leather. On boiling hot days like this, you wear leather slippers? Let me have a try."

Brow was stock-still.

That face of hers had become a canvas for colours to be smeared on. Old Ran once asked why he never saw me in make-up. I, at least, had the courage to present myself before others without plastering on any slap.

Brow immediately became the dutiful hostess and helped me to try on the slippers. She told me how it was cool to wear leather slippers in summer and that a cowhide mattress provided padding on the bed. I chortled at my own rustic ignorance.

"All bought by Old Shao." Brow became Brow again after composing herself. Back on form, she forgot to pour me a cup of tea. On top of that, she failed to bring out sweets and fruit. Rather she flung open wide the three doors of the wardrobe. Hanging inside were styles for all the four seasons. Among these was every kind of leather shoe. These alone must have totalled more than thirty pairs – high-sided, low-sided, pointy-toed, round-toed, square-heeled and conical-heeled. She took out a greyish silk top and a pair of trendy trousers for me. I didn't have egret legs like her and couldn't squeeze into the trousers. She went in there again and foraged out a sports blouse with a design of small grey and black checks. She threw it on me, shut the door, filleted me out of my floral-patterned dress and gave me a pleated one, shouting that it would suit me the best.

"Brow," I twisted my waist in front of the mirror. "Will you pardon your ugly elder sister's past deeds? I have massive hips. They make this dress stretch out like a mortar bucket for pounding rice. Before I came along today, I was really afraid that you would give me the cold shoulder."

Reflected in the looking glass, I could see a framed photograph on the windowsill of Brow taken with the help of a lambency mirror.

"Really? A-Bing didn't bite you when you came in."

A-Bing was busy with a pair of leather stilettos behind the door, grabbing one and depositing it on the rosewood sofa and then grabbing its counterpart and doing the same thing.

"It seems the dog knows me. We are destined to be sisters."

"A-Bing is a male!"

"Then he is Shao's younger brother."

Upon hearing my words, A-Bing quit his horseplay and stood up on his hind legs. His forepaws were wrapped softly around his belly like the old ladies who loitered at the entrance to the village waiting for their family to come back home and share a meal. Nestled among his pure white body hair at the bottom of his hind legs, a shaft of red meat dangled spiritlessly. Whenever Old Ran smiled, it was humbly and with embarrassment. When he had teeth, he had no hard flatbreads to gnaw on and when he had hard flatbreads, he was toothless.

"Brow, don't you realise that his whip is on full display?"

"That's his only flaw. Maybe he picked up a disease after the horrid experience at the square."

We didn't continue with this topic. Brow was still busy removing small novelties from the drawers – a *Louis Vuitton* travel bag, a certificate bag, a coffee-coloured *Ferrari* wallet, a portable, leather, zippered *Guerlain* toiletry bag. She also wanted to give me a bottle of *Estée Lauder* skin crème. What was wrong with her? Had my arrival moved her or was she showing off? I hated the spices of envy produced in my heart and reminded myself secretly that Brow and I have divergent interests. After all, I am a woman and no matter how independent a woman might be, she can never shake off the shackles of men and clothes. I couldn't redress my mental imbalance.

Brow's Bushy Beard Shao had first been introduced to me by A-Shun's maternal uncle-in-law. I already had Old Ran, so I asked Brow to go instead. Old Shao was made of money, but he was divorced and had a son. My jealousy drove me to ask how Old Shao's son was. Brow answered me with a serious face and continued to list the fine qualities of the *Estée Lauder* skin crème. Again, I felt I was being base.

"I want none of these," I declared. "Really. A heap of English letters – I don't want any of them. Do you know that our fellow villagers are being nice to you again? Are you still working at that company? No matter how well you marry and what kind of life you lead, you are still a member of this community and your house still stands here."

"I know this," Brow replied. "Sister Plum, the villagers treated me differently and I've cried many times. I still work at that company. They might level houses here and there, but they will never come to Benevolent Lenient Village. I've told our old Village Head this and many folk in the village know it too. I never expected that A-Bing would bring me good luck. I saved him, but in fact he saved me. A-Bing, A-Bing!"

A-Bing had gone out to take a leak under the grape trellis, his tail wagging gently. He raised one of his hind legs and rested it on the entwined grape roots. I again caught an eyeful of that exposed whip. Brow said that man has a soul and dogs have half a soul. After having stayed with her for only one or two days, A-Bing had already started to protect her. If Old Shao were to lay a finger on her, he would bite him. If I didn't believe that, I could try myself.

"Ah," I said in my mind. "If he really were so loyal, why didn't he bite the criminals when they were murdering the artist?" I didn't try to take A-Bing in my arms, nor did I try to play with him. I only hung the dog reins I brought at the head of the bed. Anyhow, after hearing a bang on the gate, A-Bing retreated in a panic, his piss staining his tracks. He crawled on to my chest and fixed his black eyes on me.

Seven or eight of our fellow villagers entered together with Shao. The villagers knew I had come to Brow's home and felt satisfied with her compromise, but still thought it embarrassing to visit her. So, they cooked up the excuse of searching for me and of wanting to look at A-Bing.

At the entrance to the lane, they ran into Bushy Beard and shouted that they wanted to have a drink. They bought several parcels of freshly stir-fried peanuts and came along together. Feeling flattered at being honoured with the sudden presence of so many guests, Brow hastily picked up a mirror to survey herself. She neatened her hair with two swishes of the comb and again took out the lipstick.

I cursed her: "Preening!"

She, however, said in a low voice: "Remove your hairpin. With your fringe pinned back you look older than you are."

I was so angry I brushed her off, but she had already lifted the door curtain and was standing outside greeting all-comers with smiles, not even asking them to take off their shoes. Seven or eight pairs of shoes then left muddy prints on the carpet.

Bushy Beard opened a small bedside cabinet, took out a bottle of *L'Or de Martell* and decanted it into high-stemmed glasses for them to drink. These village bumpkins; it's not that they had never drunk foreign alcohol before, but this time they acted the fool and asked what liquor this was, in which country it was produced and how one should drink it.

I became a little angry, thinking the flattery had gone too far. Besides, Brow had been the one to offend Benevolent Lenient Village. Now we were being nice to her because she had behaved well and our presence showed off our broad-mindedness. Still, for the sake of a bottle of *L'Or de Martell* should one stoop so low?

What really depressed me was that Gao Feng from the front lane was wearing a pair of rangy leather boots like those worn by American soldiers. He must have been showing off. The weather was hot but he didn't give a damn. Was it that he didn't want Bushy Beard to laugh at his shabbiness and rustic crudity? He asked what Bushy Beard's "Comfortable Safe Healthy" body builder was. Bushy Beard invited him to lie face-up on the carpet and to rest his feet in the swaying stirrups. Poor Gao Feng, when he took off his American-soldier boots, it was revealed that one of his dirty socks had a hole in it and the foul smell emanating from it reeked to high heaven.

"So far this is the most up-to-date, the most scientific and the most convenient body builder. It was invented by a Japanese scientist and is based on the principle of fish swimming by swaying their spines. Why is it that fish never catch intestinal diseases or diseases of the stomach? This machine can cure any liver or lung ailment and all the disorders of the five solid and six hollow internal organs. It can also be used for weight-loss. Ask Brow how many kilos she has shed. Swaying here for one minute is equivalent to jogging fifteen kilometres, without the heart palpitations, the panting and the exhaustion. You can fall asleep as snug as a bug in a rug! Close your eyes. How do you feel? Tell the others what you feel."

"Hey." I could no longer stand the spectacle. "Is this the pyramid sales strategy?"

"What's pyramid sales?" Gao Feng raised his head. When you are lying flat, you shouldn't raise your head.

Liuhe tried to make peace: "Hey now."

Bushy Beard took out an improbably small comb from his pocket to brush his long sideburns, explaining: "Pyramid sales is the name given to a geometrical marketing network based on layer-by-layer marketing. Put simply, products are generally sold to customers via department stores, but now they are being retailed directly to the customers. Take this body builder as an example; a Hong Kong factory bought the patent to exclusively manufacture the products and I go there every month to take delivery of the goods. I introduce you, you to buy one and your name and family address will be typed into the factory's electronic marketing network. If you talk another three into buying one each and then those three each talk another two into..."

"*Aiya*, it's the same as establishing an organisation for special agents!"

Where were the genealogical books of Benevolent Lenient Village? The Jias had written theirs on a sheet of oilcloth, but it was still motheaten here and there. Had I seen it at Uncle Six Pounds' home? A-Bing was still in my arms. I thumbed through a Hong Kong magazine. Brow fetched some sweets and offered them to me. I didn't oblige her.

"You can put it like that. Liuhe, buy a piece and you can be my subordinate."

"Be your subordinate? Then what about you?" Liuhe asked.

"I am the director for this city. If you can talk six people into buying, you become the head of a small team and you can take delivery of the goods via me or go to Hong Kong directly. You sell six pieces and get enough commission to buy one unit. If your subordinates grow in number – it doesn't matter if you know them or not – you can get a percentage of the net profit just by sitting on your hands every month."

"Money can be earned in this way?"

Shao was putting on weight, but Brow was not growing

thinner. His destiny ruled over hers. She was so bony, yet her breasts jutted up so high. I was eighty per cent sure she had had an operation. It is said that silicone gel can be injected into them. Would I suffer that pain for Old Ran? Get lost!

After fifteen minutes, the swaying ceased and Gao Feng crawled to his feet. The others asked him how he felt. Gao murmured something quietly and the onlookers gave a muffled '*oh*' in chorus.

Someone blurted out: "Let me have a go!" Gao arched his waist and darted glances at Brow and me. I knew he had a dirty mouth and would frequently let fly some obscene words, whether there were women present or not. I shot him a hateful stare, not because he had spewed obscenities again but because he did it in such a low voice so as to show respect to Brow.

The folk of present-day Benevolent Lenient Village had nothing on their past selves. They were too susceptible to the seductions of the world. Now they had sunk down like this – it must be heavenly retribution.

I observed sourly: "Beard, since Gao Feng regards your place as the foreign concession in Benevolent Lenient Village and he likes the novelty so much – as long as he can stand it and is not afraid that his face might be burning with acne – you can just lend the machine to him."

The others guffawed and so did Bushy Beard, though his mouth was obscured by whiskers. "Soon every household in Benevolent Lenient Village will have a piece of this machinery. The Village Head told me this with his own mouth," Old Shao maintained. "If the Village Committee buys one for each family and they have boarding patients, the machine can be used as medical equipment and the cost will be recouped in six months."

Bushy Beard's eyes glowed with a gloating cunning. Another picture surfaced in my mind: the pyramid selling agent must have talked with the Village Head for half a day in a room wreathed in smoke. He would have promised that, if the Village Committee purchased in bulk, the Village Head's name would be added to the marketing network and he would get a handsome lump sum and, furthermore, could draw a certain percentage of the net profit thereafter. The Village Head would have smiled at that, pushed the window open to let out the smoke and then shouted for his wife to roll long noodles, which would be served with lashings of soup and peppery seasoning. Bushy Beard looked at us. He too must have been reliving that sweet moment of sealing the deal and hoping that we would leap into mid-air in feverish excitement. Nevertheless, nobody, not even Gao Feng or Liuhe, showed the least glimmer of excitement. At that moment, I was so proud of my fellow villagers.

"The old Village Head," Lianben laughed contemptuously. "He is a soft egg and we will overthrow him. Has he sensed that we no longer trust him and so he wants to buy us? And, while buying us, catch the booty from the pyramid sales line. He is a soft egg, but when the time to collect the money comes around, he'll find his balls."

That was news to me!

According to the village rules, every member – be they a man or a woman – could obtain a plot of land on which to build a house, and the rent from a row of public buildings near the sports stadium was divided up equally, with even jobless women who married away in the city getting a share. I was not married and Old Ran's native place was still Benevolent Lenient Village. I should be a Benevolent Lenient Village member pure and simple, but how could I have had no inkling of this big event?

Suspicious about the reliability of the news, I let go of A-Bing, went over and grabbed the wine glass from Lianben's hand. "You must have drunk too much foreign wine. If you are not good with words, don't talk. Has your mouth forgotten that slap?"

The others howled with laughter. Lianben's left cheek was bigger than the right one. A fleshy lump had been growing there since he was young and it gave the impression that an apricot was lodged in his mouth. After the artist and his entire family had been slaughtered, the policemen interrogated every one of us like they were hunting for lice with a fine-toothed comb, asking us to leave samples of our fingerprints and footprints. Fatty had to question Lianben. It would have been OK if he had answered each of Fatty's questions with one sentence but, being a born chatterbox (and an inarticulate chatterbox at that), he dragged on endlessly. Fatty lost his temper and gave him a slap across his face.

"Why beat me?" he whined.

Fatty growled: "Be serious."

"How am I not being serious?"

"Spit out that sweet from your mouth."

Lianben then knew that Fatty was mistaken and opened his mouth for him to take a look at the fleshy lump.

"You didn't know this?" Lianben asked me. "You really didn't know? Ha!" He felt ten feet tall. "Do you know that our village has always resisted plans to urbanise it?"

"I know."

"Taking correspondence courses, being an intellectual, of course you know. But now a Deputy Mayor's son, who does real estate business in the south but is not welcome there, has come back to the Western Capital to make his fortune. He's now hand-in-hand with another real estate company and has shifted his attention to this plot of land of ours. *Ai*, Brow, is it your company he's in cahoots with?"

Brow's face reddened in a flash. "I don't know."

"This time under the banner of the city government, they've added pressure inch-by-inch. They ordered the Agricultural Trade Bureau of the district government to seek out the old Village Head. The old Village Head agreed in principle. After he came back, he was showered with abuse. He said with a weepy face that he was a dung beetle trying to prop up a table but couldn't manage it. *Pooh*, he really *is* a dung beetle and he wants to sell out Benevolent Lenient Village. Being the Village Head but never acting in the villagers' interests; isn't he a vinegar-maker? The very sight of him makes me fume. How can a Village Head have such traits? What an ape – still on course towards evolution."

"Don't go on about looks," I retorted. "You are at most ten years further ahead on that road than him."

Lianben tittered to himself. "So, we are brewing up an election contest, but I won't stand as a candidate. We could knock him down and push Grandpa Cloud Forest up, but Grandpa Cloud Forest will never agree, so we've suggested Chivalry. That son of a bitch Chivalry is full of flaws, but he can hold it together in the face of trouble. The rascal rules. His official post is ready and waiting for him, but he has wandered to goodness-knows-where and his soul is nowhere to be found. His old Daddy says he will come back soon, but whenever he's asked when, he won't say a word."

Lianben's words rang true. It should have been a secret scheme but now, thanks to his long tongue, it had become an overt plot. Shao was still smiling, yet his smile was leaden and Brow had bent her head to stare at me.

"Chivalry?" she said.

"Yeah," I replied.

Chivalry and Shaved Head once went to the city to sell sand with a gunny sack full of snakes to be offloaded at the restaurants. When the sputtering tractor reached East Well Street, the street was packed solid: two bunches of crooks were embroiled in an inter-gang brawl. Shaved Head wanted to take a detour, but Chivalry didn't agree.

Shaved Head insisted: "This comes under the jurisdiction of the police."

Chivalry said: "Then who has jurisdiction over the police?"

Shaved Head's barks failed to make those guys step aside and give way, and he even received a provocative tap on the top of his bald head. Chivalry clambered down with the gunny sack in his hand, groped around inside, took out a big three-foot-long snake, decapitated it with a knife, rammed the headless reptile into his mouth and started to suck its blood, shouting: "Fight! If you want to fight, then let's have a fight to the death."

The audience broke up. The thugs withdrew their punching fists and kicking feet, took a look and loosened their legs to run away and, while hiding behind street corners, shot repeated glances this way from a distance. At the same time, a policeman ran up and reprimanded Chivalry for driving a vehicle as tractors were not allowed to enter the city during the daytime.

Chivalry replied: "We are already here. What should we do?"

The policeman responded: "Pay a fine."

"How much?"

"Two hundred yuan."

Shaved Head was on a knife-edge and emptied all his pockets. "I only have twenty yuan and it's all yours."

The policeman cursed: "Don't play games with me. I may not be able to fix others, but I sure can fix a peasant like you."

Chivalry replied: "The city is yours and we deserve to be fined. But no matter how much that fine might be, you should give us a receipt. We really don't have any money. I'll buy cigarettes for you." He gave the policeman a smile, baring his red lips and white teeth, and the policeman smiled back.

He ran across the road and took out the money in a tobacco kiosk. The stall owner then shouted: "Comrade Policeman, the money's been paid and you can come over here to collect the smokes after you clock-off."

The tractor was let go.

"A twenty-yuan fine was more than enough, but you had to go and buy cigarettes," Shaved Head complained. "A carton of *Hongtashan* costs more than one hundred yuan."

Chivalry snorted and said: "I only bought him a cheap packet of *Hatamen*."

Brought up short, Shaved Head shouted: "You are a crook!"

"A minor crook who came across a big crook," said Chivalry.

Chapter by chapter of Chivalry's anecdotes were relayed around the village, almost all of them becoming notorious records. There was no doubt that he was less popular than the old Village Head. The old Village Head, with his kind and friendly manner, was good at presiding over happy events and burial ceremonies and at resolving disputes between neighbours, mothers-in-law and daughters-in-law, and brothers who needed to divide up the family property. Relying upon his seniority and authority, he resorted to the wise old uncle routine to bluff and apply pressure.

But who was better suited to serving the interests of Benevolent Lenient Village? I couldn't give a reasoned judgement. After leaving Brow's home, I felt sullen.

Gao Feng caught up with me and remarked brazenly: "Plum, have you put your face on today?"

"This young lady never does that," I said coldly.

"So, your face still looks nice and ruddy."

"I am a pock face."

"Plum," Gao stood, frozen to the spot. "I haven't stepped on your toes. We talked with Brow, but weren't we just going along for the ride? She is beautiful, for sure, but how can she hold a candle to you in terms of class? It takes three generations to nurture a noble aristocrat. How can she be compared to you?"

I knew that this flattery was unwarranted. Still, it knocked the stuffing out of me like a rubber ball being pricked by a needle. Looking back over my shoulder, I said: "Am I so important? Then let me ask you: on the matter of the election of the Village Head, you've got down to brass tacks like knights twirling lances on battle horses but why, out of all the fellow villagers, did you only keep me in the dark? You think I am still young? You think I am only a woman?"

"How could that be so? We might leave anyone aside, but dare we not put you on the scales of a weighing balance? We thought you knew, we all thought so, and so we didn't think to tell you. I even put your name forward as a candidate."

"What a fart!" I cursed and raised my head. The sun was still fiery red and a tuft of grass on the wall of Little Wei's nearby courtyard had produced spirited, brilliantly-coloured flowers. I smiled unconsciously. "Look, how I have spoiled myself."

"Plum, you are so beautiful when you smile," Gao repeated.

"The wildflowers have bloomed early this summer."

Gao Feng immediately jumped up to pluck one off. He leapt into mid-air, but just as his hand brushed against it, he started to plunge down. He jumped up again and failed once more. The process was repeated three times, startling a chicken inside the courtyard, which started squawking and beating its wings. As I passed the other end of the lane, I could hear Gao hurling loud abuse at Little Wei.

Chapter Four

The 10th of June had arrived already, but Chivalry still wasn't back. Day and night without interruption, the booming, tumbling sound continued on the low-lying land outside the village. Circles had been brushed on to the dilapidated walls in wild strokes using China ink. Inside each circle was daubed the word "DEMOLISH." The characters were ringed with grubby footprints left behind by people kicking the wall with muddy shoes. You wouldn't have imagined that someone could leave a mark so high!

Migrating households having to look for temporary shelters transported their piles of sofas, quilts and coverlets, bed boards, briquettes, vegetable urns, doors, windows, bamboo curtains and mattresses on the back of trucks, handcarts and tricycles. The mostly rotten purlins and rafters of the razed buildings lay around like small haphazard hills. Some people chose to shit behind them. Out of modesty, when a passerby came along they would hurriedly cover their eyes with a scrap of waste ceiling paper.

Doors and windows were removed and all their glass shattered. Business was in full swing for the old rag-and-bone man. He would kick here and there, driving a stern bargain and angering the seller when the deal fell through. Raising a stone, he dashed the lattice windows into splinters. Felled trees, ripped and broken reed ceiling sheets, cracked flower pots and fish tanks, stiff and dry, warped and tattered leather shoes and grass chair mats all contributed to the omnipresent mess.

When homeless people drew their handcarts past Benevolent Lenient Village, the residents would always accost
them and enquire about where their search for temporary
residences would take them, how many new houses would be
allocated to them after their old buildings had been torn
down and if their courtyards would be included in the
compensation estimates? Square metre for square metre, they
were assured of an equalsized new-build property, but how
much would they have to pay if they wanted it to be larger
than the old one? Would they continue to live on the same
site or would they be forcibly relocated to another place?

Angry shouts and curses rose; someone slapped his buttocks
hard and spat skywards, but the saliva landed on his own
face. An old biddy perched on the sideboard of a handcart,
crying. She bemoaned how she had seen out several generations
living there but was now being uprooted in old age. "Are
they going to turn me into a bird?" If she were assigned to
a seventh-floor apartment, it would mean she would never
be able to come downstairs. She was afraid of becoming
lonely. With her old sisters living apart from her, there
would be nobody for a chinwag.

A fat mouse shot out of a heap of old ceiling matter. It
darted along a rut in the ground and, halting in its tracks
not far away, looked in her direction. The old lady shouted:
"This belongs to my family! Hello, hello!" After catching
sight of the rodent, the kids pounced upon it. They had
already captured a dozen or more, pouring paraffin on them,
setting it alight and letting them run across the ground until
they expired. The mouse turned its head, then scurried
back to the ruins and disappeared. All her life, the old lady
had hated mice with every fibre of her body, but now she
pitied this one, fearful that she might not be able to fall

asleep if there were no vermin raising merry hell above the ceiling, scampering through the nighttime like thieves. Her eyes again shed tears.

Her son, who was pulling a cart, chided her in a harsh voice: "Go on, cry. Cry. You haven't managed to rot away your eyes completely yet." With his atrocious-looking face seeming to become even uglier, he spat out a mouthful of thick phlegm in spite and drew the cart away in a jolting fashion.

In front of Benevolent Lenient Village, there still ran a dirt track which, since it had been chewed up by the rubber wheels of passing vehicles, came to be covered with standing water throughout the year. Flies and mosquitoes gathered on the strips of watermelon rinds there and, as people went by, they heard a loud *buzz*.

On the eastern edge of the low-lying land, a house together with its courtyard survived forlorn. Piss-stained quilt covers and other articles of washing hung all along an iron wire that stretched between the locust tree and the jamb of the courtyard gate. This was confirmation that the family had not departed. At noon, a big white sheet of paper was pasted on the courtyard wall. An identical big white sheet of paper was displayed at the entrance of the lane leading from the low-lying land to Benevolent Lenient Village, and a third sheet put on the wall opposite Shaved Head's grocery store in Benevolent Lenient Village.

Believing at first that another batch of felons charged with capital crimes had been executed (notices of this kind aroused people's interest like no other), the villagers flocked over to see how those put-to-death robbers robbed and how those put-to-death rapists raped. They would then gouge out a thick, bright red tick after the name of the chief judge on the notice. It was said that keeping such a tick could ward off evil, though nobody was actually sure where this superstition came from.

This time there was no tick on the big white sheet of paper. Instead, there was this: "Chen XX, who refused to quit his old habitation, is henceforth served notice to move house within a specified time limit, otherwise the security bureau and the police will resort to applying force and demolish the building." The notice was served by means of three official posters, one of which was stuck up at the entrance of Benevolent Lenient Village. That implied that the pressure was genuine and gave a serious warning to the villagers.

On account of this duress, the pitiable old Village Head had been hospitalised. The prestige he accumulated for himself over a dozen or more years had come crashing down within a few days. When his wife – a bald woman – ventured out, she no longer affixed her hairpiece. She broadcast her husband's disease to everyone she ran into in the village: "Night after night he's unable to fall asleep. At its lowest, his blood pressure is a hundred and one and at its highest it's two hundred. He is a lamp in the wind, flickering and ready to die out at any moment." She complained: "Now, I know that if somebody wants to be an official it's better to be one who's high-up. A petty official is nothing in the eyes of his superiors and nothing in the eyes of the folks underneath him. He is a mouse trapped in the middle of a pair of bellows, being blown at from both sides. You're the one who does good things for the villagers; you're also the one who offends them. They don't know what goes on behind the scenes. They only know you."

There was some sense behind her whinging, but nobody paid any attention, let alone believed that the old Village Head was ill. Every day, eggshells and lamb bones were still being dumped on top of the refuse heap in front of his gate. This indicated the reason why he was hospitalised. The old Village Head's official title was never a grand one, yet he had learned all the customary tricks used by high-ranking officials. When something disadvantageous to their career came up or the political climate temporarily became hard to ascertain, or when it was time to divide up houses or confer academic titles, they would be in hospital. Those high-ranking officials could still live a cosy life on the special wards. They could watch TV, soak in warm springs and play bagatelle. The old Village Head was only allowed to stay in a narrow, musty sickroom at the district health centre. He had lost all his gilding. If he could step forward at this critical time, the post of Village Head might still be his. Besides living a glorious life, he would still be able to glean a monthly subsidy of 300 yuan. But, once he had himself admitted to hospital, the villagers became utterly disappointed. He was not only a soft egg, but also a very cunning old hand.

Still, Chivalry hadn't come back.

Sitting on the grinding stone in front of Shaved Head's small grocery store was Chivalry's grandfather. A sometime executioner who served around the transition between the Qing Dynasty and the Republic of China era, he had grown so old his skin was covered with chicken bumps and his head looked like that of a crane. He could no longer remember what happened just minutes ago, yet still rattled on about his past heroic feats: "That professional 'plucker of flowers' on Yang Street in the east of the city – I lopped his head off. The bandit in Sanyin County, Liu Ba – I beheaded him. I have killed so many people that only a ghost knows the true number. And a few among them were celebrities."

"At a quarter to one, Liu Ba was stripped to the waist and

knelt on the round wooden platform. I walked around him, fixing my eyes on the spot behind his ears, until he become flustered and said: 'You still haven't swished your knife.' I paid no attention to him because I knew I ought to gather my qi.[e] Then I suddenly spat out the cold water I was holding in my mouth. Liu Ba, the lout, gave a shiver and my blade fell. You think my sword went straight down? It doesn't work if you do it that way. An angled swish of the blade – casual-like – then the head is lopped off. After that, it shouldn't roll along the ground; it should still be attached by a flap of skin. We called that the *Gourd being Hung by a Golden String*. Bubbles then frothed up on the white stump of his bloodless neck, as if a chrysanthemum had broken into bloom. A lump the size of a small fist wriggled within his belly and then moved upwards. Next, *whoosh*, a column of blood spurted out fully twenty feet into the air."

These words of his no longer had the capacity to terrify fellow villagers. What did terrify them was how he would fix his eyes on the spot behind their ears while he was gabbling on and drinking.

When the big white sheet bearing the relocation order was hung on the wall opposite the liquor shop, Shaved Head asked at the counter inside: "Your Honour, did you see the notice?"

The executioner, who was unable to read, answered: "Where's the fun in putting someone to death nowadays? Any fool can fire a gun."

Shaved Head heaved a sigh, making eyes at me and asked again: "When will Chivalry come back?"

The executioner replied: "He's on his way."

The liquor took effect and he became drowsy.

I didn't understand why the villagers had to wait for Chivalry.

Thirty years ago, the executioner, who had been a lifelong bachelor, got up early and went to the alfalfa fields worked by the production brigade with a crate on his back to cadge a little by stealth. A wolf was sitting on the ridge of the field. The executioner went straight to it with his hands balled into fists. The wolf fled. As a man who all through his life had been eager to compete and show off his strength, he wanted to see if the wolf had been scared enough to deposit a pile of loose shit. There was no shit, but a baby was sleeping there between two vegetable plots. It was a baby boy with a small corduroy quilt as his swaddling cloth. This suggested that it must be some city dweller's child. Had he been carried here by the wolf or was he the bastard offspring of an illicit liaison who had been dumped here and then safeguarded by the wolf for a night? The executioner believed the latter explanation and convinced himself that the baby was waiting for him and had been sent to him by the wolf.

So, he brought him back home and raised him on runny porridge. The baby was Chivalry. As he grew, he never set his mind upon books but was as peremptory as a bandit. He was smart. Whatever he learned, he mastered it, whatever he did, he looked the part, and he sighed because there was nothing challenging enough for him in this world.

Still, he could never follow anything through. Generally, when he was only one step away from successfully accomplishing something, he would unexpectedly do something completely different. He had been known to grow vegetables, to raise chickens, to excavate sand from the ground, to run a prefabricated slab factory and had once gone so far as to take up decorative carpentering. Some even gossiped that he had smuggled and peddled cultural relics.

One day, when he dumped rubbish from a window, *thump*, he flung a Han Dynasty earthenware jar asunder, saying: "Who cares? Worthless, showy, something that takes up space." What other earthly pursuits he had dabbled in, I didn't know. But when I helped Old Ran gather the Ming and Qing Dynasty furniture, he chaperoned me to the market and described the raw materials, the craftsmanship and the artistic grades of the old pieces clearly and logically, with as much authority as Old Ran.

We wandered about the market for the whole morning and many girls with their faces painted red and white were attracted to gaze at him.

I pointed out: "Uncle Chivalry (according to the seniority of the people in the village, I should properly call him uncle), these girls are sweet on you. What say you bring one back to be my auntie?"

"Green persimmons!" he replied.

I couldn't understand him and asked: "What?"

"Not ripe yet," he explained, looking cocky and arrogant.

His mouth never expressed any warm feelings towards women and would invariably spew out curses.

I held my tongue and after a while teased him again: "Uncle Chivalry, why don't you get married?"

He answered: "When you are married, your uncle will be married too." After that, feeling a little embarrassed, he added: "You want your uncle to be a spent shell of a man?"

With a smile, I said: "It's written in books that if a man doesn't get married it is not good for his health."

Now he pulled a gangster's face, retorting: "You think your bachelor uncle doesn't know what a woman tastes like?"

Pooh, pooh, I cursed him in my belly for being such a shit.

It was after we had come back from the market that he

said: "Go fetch Uncle's money. Tomorrow I need to go out."

"What money?" I wondered.

"I put 5,000 yuan under the mattress of your bed." I went back home and lifted the mattress to one side. Sure enough, there was 5,000 yuan there. I went out and asked him when he had done that, why I didn't know about it and how he had managed to hide money at my place.

He chuckled. "Putting the cash there secretly was the safest option. If I'd told you about it, would you still have been willing to keep it for me?"

I was in no doubt he would make a fortune through some shady business and then let me harbour the booty without telling me. So, I asked no more and he didn't enlighten me. In my mind, however, I started to be a little on the alert against him.

Since that summer two years ago, Chivalry had no longer been seen in the village. Had he gone out to do business or just gone to idle around? Nobody knew. He was the kind of man whose shadow was even invisible. Notwithstanding, the people in Benevolent Lenient Village, including Grandpa Cloud Forest, were insistent about electing him the new Village Head. For me, this was inconceivable.

I dropped by to see Grandpa Cloud Forest. Pushing open the fencelike gate in the clay brick wall, I felt I was pushing open a portal into history.

The courtyard of the shrine to the Jia clan had been completely dilapidated for a long time. What had the structure of the three former gates been like? How many pillars had there been in the eastern and western corridors? Had the tea pavilion been octagonal or square? Nobody knew.

In the rainy season last year, a row of walls built from carved bricks with a tracery resembling fish scales collapsed.

That made the three lean-tos in which Grandpa Cloud Forest lived appear even lonelier. Only the ornaments on the roof ridge, the eavetiles and a stone pillar inscribed with the image of pomegranate in front of the gate were left to recall the time-honoured status of the building. Right now, there was a clamour inside and strong tobacco smoke floated out of the lattice window. Perhaps a ghost was here for idle talk again. I didn't go forward to shake the knockers, which featured a hornless dragon and a tiger drooped between two rows of large, bronze blister nails. Instead, I stood my ground on the hexagonal brick paving, gazing at the dim expanse of cemetery behind the building.

The most elevated portion of the cemetery was the burial mound of the ancient ancestor of Benevolent Lenient Village, a one-thousand-branch cypress tree at the head of the tomb. Other one-thousand-branch cypresses would stop growing when their branches reached the thickness of a wine cup, but fifteen branches of this one still advanced side by side until they surpassed thirty feet in height, and could offer a roost to many birds every morning and every evening.

The land around the cemetery used to be a most fertile poppy field. Planting poppies was banned after the founding of the New China in 1949. When people died, they were interred one-after-another around the ancient burial mound. Later, the government banned internment in the earth. More than once, the old Village Head took part in negotiations until the government finally agreed to preserve this plot of cemetery as a unique site in the capital city. Nobody knew if our ancestor actually rested in the huge burial mound, but we liked to boast that we were natives descended from a drummer in the army of Zhu Yuanzhang,[f] the founding emperor of the Ming Dynasty. That drummer might not have been a brave soldier though, coming from a peasant family, but he was certainly an outstanding musician, creating music for as long as he lived. Thus, the *Drum Music of the Ming Emperor* was passed down in our village from generation to generation. For these reasons, Benevolent Lenient Village long enjoyed a good reputation and the cemetery was preserved, which in turn added another plus point to the tourist value.

A clay brick perimeter wall was built to encircle the cemetery and cinerary urns could be kept on the rows of tea-table-sized cement shrines. When people were alive, they possessed sunshine and air and could declare that every place was theirs, but after their death, they occupied a site the size of a tea table. Nevertheless, this was the most exclusive privilege to be had anywhere in the provincial capital.

Before he lost his mind, Grandpa Cloud Forest was the poorest of the poor. Disabled from the waist down, he raised a breeding boar to mate with the other villagers' sows when they were in heat. Perhaps that type of business should not be conducted in a shrine in a cemetery though, strangely enough, no one took exception. Feeding one's mouth, that was most people's basic requirement for survival at that time.

A sow with a coat of fine red hair was led there and hitched to the stone column outside the adobe rooms. The person towing the pig entered with the greeting: "Have you eaten?" Grandpa Cloud Forest was not in the room but in the privy to one side. He came out and, while fastening his belt, replied: "Not yet." The person towing the pig then put down a bag of a dozen or so pounds of corn, which was the breeding boar's nutritious reward. Under the watch of Grandpa Cloud Forest, he proceeded to place two yuan on the table and covered it with an inverted bowl.

Grandpa Cloud Forest offered him a seat, asked him things about oil, salt, firewood and rice, and enquired if the old people were fine and if the children were behaving themselves. After smoking a pipe of tobacco, he led the breeding boar out of the inner room on to the earthen ground to do its business.

The male pig was tall, strong, red-eyed and long-snouted, being of a Ukrainian breed. The sight of the sow fired it up and its penis dripped juice even before it had found the right place. The paralysed Grandpa Cloud Forest bounded desperately over to help and his hands became smeared with the juice. While wiping his fingers with a handful of dry dirt which he scooped up from the ground, he looked on and declared: "Done!"

The boar's siring job was, of course, a proper public service, which was not regarded as at all cheap or indecent. Still, I doubt if Grandpa Cloud Forest ever received the additional gifts promised by the owners of the sows or was able to have a taste of the pig's offal sent at the end of the year as a thank-you. He was supposed to be given a head, a tail, intestines, a heart and lungs. On top of that, I never saw him counting the banknotes placed under the bowl in public to check if it was two yuan or only two fifty cent notes. Come what may, he scraped a living with this mite of an income.

Nowadays, Grandpa Cloud Forest no longer kept a breeding boar, living instead off his god-like medical skills. Unbelievable things happened in the world. After a three-month period of madness, Grandpa Cloud Forest suddenly discovered he had magical skills! How many temples and churches have I visited and how many abbots and pastors with faces inscribed with dignity and ancientness have I seen? Without fail, they reminded me of Grandpa Cloud Forest.

The abbots and pastors were awe-inspiring, making people feel they were respectable but inaccessible like the gods and God Almighty, yet Grandpa Cloud Forest was still friendly and grandfatherly. He couldn't walk and he looked like a beggar. You might even have taken him as a lowly, passive scrap of a man, not deserving of your respect; the type you could happily lark about in his presence with a bold tongue.

"Ha, our intellectual is coming! Come and sit beside your grandpa. We should show our respect to the knowledgeable. Who will pour her some water?"

When I pushed the squeaking door open, smoke surged out like a floating cloud as Grandpa Cloud Forest greeted me. I was an intellectual; so what? All who were present smiled at me. My hands and legs were awkward and I froze on the spot. Mindful of how the neckline of my dress plunged too low and afraid that the others might notice this, I tried as hard as possible not to let the upper half of my body sway. I sat down beside Grandpa Cloud Forest, reached out a hand to wipe off a bit of black dust from the tip of his nose and then folded my arms about my chest.

"A black stain?" Grandpa Cloud Forest said, a little annoyed. "You saw my face was not clean, but you didn't tell me and let me make a spectacle of myself."

"You belong to our grandpa's generation and we thought you had put it there on purpose. A prime minister on the stage usually sports a partly-painted face."

The speaker was Fan Jingquan. He was here as well. My face blushed. I regretted not demurring to Grandpa Cloud Forest's words of praise when he said I was an intellectual. "How can my teacher also be here?" I said as a hasty greeting.

"You still regard me as your teacher?" Fan asked. "A timely arrival. I came here to ask Grandpa Cloud Forest if my white hair could be cured. I didn't get a remedy. Rather, I received a hammering from all sides and now my hair has grown whiter still."

"Just air your grievances. Now your student has come and you've got an ally." Laiwang barked uproariously and they loosened their tongues to argue, not caring if I could understand or not. Fan Jingquan stood up from the cattail hassock and sat down on the chair. He again stood up from the chair and again sat back on the cattail hassock. He kept on blah-blahhing until he foamed at the mouth. He couldn't fight back against others' dissent. Some of them said that Chivalry was good, some cursed that Chivalry was bad, and some were indignant about the decaying standards of morality. Fan turned his head, sealed his lips and took out a miniscule pair of scissors from his pocket to manicure his fingernails.

Someone commented: "Mr Fan comes from the city and he can never bring himself to piss into the same potty as us. Stop talking, stop talking! Plum, you came to look for Grandpa Cloud Forest. You wanted to talk about a nice piece of newly-collected Ming or Qing Dynasty furniture?"

"Don't mock me," I replied. "Speaking of *collecting*, I am here to collect Grandpa Cloud Forest."

"Sweet talk. Grandpa Cloud Forest is a genuine antique. He looked like this when we were young, and he still looks the same way now. He is a piece of living furniture in Benevolent Lenient Village."

"What would you know?" I upbraided the young nephew of Uncle Six Pounds. "That last litter of piglets sired by his hog – if they were still alive – would be older than you are now."

The wretch stood up to beat me amid the others' raucous laughter and warned that he would never again be on speaking terms with me. One household in his maternal uncle's village had a Ming Dynasty bed carved with floral designs. Originally, he wanted to put me on the trail of it, but then he decided he would never do that.

"Such a pipsqueak yet with so many wicked wiles," I cursed at him. "Dare I trouble Your Honour again? If I really needed your lead, I wouldn't be able to find even one piece of furniture."

Next, I peeled his paint a little further, explaining that last month the wretch escorted me to his aunt's home to see a Ming Dynasty chair – a nice piece with delicate components and generous curves. Most special of all, on the backrest there were floral designs and a bas-relief showing two hornless dragons hugging a bank of cloud. The only pity was that its left back leg was shorter than the rest. I settled the price and told them I would return to get it three days later. I never expected that when I went to take delivery, the broken back left leg would have been replaced by a new one and that a layer had been planed off the seat. His uncle by marriage said: "Since you offered such a favourable price, how could I give you something so out of shape?" Now, the chair wasn't worth a copper coin.

The wretch was most afraid of being jeered at like this by me and ran towards the door. I reached out to grab him but missed, and there was a loud rapping at the plank window nearby. It was Brow. She shouted: "Sister Plum! Sister Plum!" I pushed open the side door. A dividing wall had been erected to form a small kitchen and Brow was cooking in there.

"I heard you coming, but you didn't come to see me."

Brow stared at me and suddenly reached out to pull down my collar, exposing my heap of jiggling breasts. I swiftly covered up my chest and cursed: "Slut!"

"You are!" Brow ribbed. "Nice skirt. Normally you wrap yourself up and never show any landscape, doing a great injustice to your breasts. If I were you, I would dress sexy, but how disappointing it is that mine are too small." She bent sideways for me to touch. I soon figured out she was wearing two bras.

"Only this big." She was on her high horse again. "It's already annoying enough. Whenever I go out, I am tailed. If I am reincarnated in my next life, I would never choose to be a woman again."

"Don't show off. You want to give that Shao guy a reason to be envious?"

"Music to his ears. Every day after I come back from the street, he asks: 'Did anyone make a pass at you today?' A man likes it when others pay attention to his wife, but if someone really does darken your door and you strike up a conversation with a stranger, he becomes a boiling pot of envy. Is Old Ran the same?"

"What have I got to make him envious over?" Unwilling to continue with the topic, I lifted the lid off the wok. "What nice stuff are you cooking for Grandpa Cloud Forest?"

"The visitors only chinwag and Grandpa Cloud Forest hasn't had his noon-time meal yet. I said I would go buy some meat to make dumplings. He didn't let me. He insisted that there was leftover rice in the wok and asked me to warm it up."

In the wok were noodles cooked in porridge, mixed with beans and cabbage leaves. Grandpa Cloud Forest's meals were always simple like this. I removed the cover from the squat storage bin. There were numerous bags inside, holding rice, noodles, all kinds of beans and cracked corn. He had no fridge, and salt, pepper and white vinegar were his only condiments.

The shrine was comprised of three rooms. At the eastern

and western ends, dividing walls had been put up to make a bedroom and a kitchen. What was that drawn on one side of the gable of the bedroom? I normally paid no attention. The kitchen might be full of fire and smoke, but the painting on the gable could still be faintly discerned; a warrior sporting a lotus helmet with upside-down tassels, a suit of chain-mail secured at the waist by a phoenix ribbon and a pair of tiger-headed leopard skin boots. The man gripped a single-pointed, eighty-foot lance in his hand.

The native clan of Benevolent Lenient Village had the surname Jia and the Wei clan was said to have only married into the family. Despite this imbalanced relationship, they worshipped the same ancestor. Could it be that the drawing in the shrine depicted this ancestor? He was a man who originally lived to the south of the Yangtze River, a peasant and drummer. Here, though, he looked so valiant and fierce. This was perhaps to highlight his martial skills. What if he were a man of letters? Should he wear a prime minister's hat with two as-you-wish wings, a robe with official insignia cinched by a jade belt and have a five-lock beard? Maybe the painting on the wall of the bedroom looked like this. But what would a picture of my great-grandfather look like?

The people on the other side of the wooden door resumed their conversation. Benevolent Lenient Village folks were usually taciturn, but now they were eloquent in their arguments.

"Isn't what you have said just the tunnel vision of the frog at the bottom of the well?"

"We admit that we are frogs crouching at the bottom of a well, but we love the bottom of the well! Is the sky wide enough? Yeah. But when a bird lands, it perches only on a small twig. How much of a big city can we occupy? Man has only one life, grass has only one autumn. Why, of all people, must we be the only ones who can't lead easy lives?"

"Of course this is not suitable," said Fan. "You can't adapt to it and nor can I. People nowadays have trouble adapting and so did people in ancient times. After the Ming Dynasty ended and the Qing army entered the Pass,^g many committed suicide. Now when talking about history, we wax lyrical about the prosperity and social stability of the Qin Dynasty, the Han Dynasty, the Tang Dynasty, the Ming and the Qing, but nobody sets much store by the chaotic times in between these few periods of great governance. In fact, those chaotic times made a greater contribution. Were it not for the Yellow Emperor and Laozi,^h how could there have been the Han Dynasty? Were it not for the Wei, the Jin, and the Southern and Northern Dynasties, how could there have been the Tang? Were it not for the Jin, how could there be the Ming and the Qing Dynasties? During these few chaotic eras, nations merged, territories were expanded, foreign cultures communicated with us, civil order replaced discord, and each time we advanced by one important step. In the future, will there be new great periods? And when will they come? In my opinion, maybe soon. We might already be standing on the tipping point."

"We don't get it, sir. What are these great periods? What's this tipping point? When we count history, is one hundred years said to be one age? What should we do now? You are a city-slicker; the well-fed don't know how the starving suffer."

"Then I suffer no pain? Although I live in the city, my home village is in the countryside and I grew up there. What is more, my home village is far more poverty-stricken than this place of yours and the life there is much harder. Although I've lived in the city for so many years, in my dreams I am always in my village. How can I have no pain? Society is so insecure, wages are so low and prices are so high. Publishing houses want books that can make money for them and my novels can't find their way into print. I'm already advanced in years, but I still can't find a wife. Even if I could find one, what will happen if I have a baby daughter? The past three generations of my family have each only yielded one son and heir. We can't leap over natural laws and the development of those natural laws can't be denied despite the pain they bring. The problem at present is that we rush everything and, hence, there are side-effects. It is like taking herbs. People living deep in the mountains and the forests will react differently to the same herb than city dwellers. City dwellers are drug resistant; you catch a cold, you should take *Pioneer* antibiotics. But if a mountain guy catches a cold and you give him *Pioneer* antibiotics, he will get other ailments."

"Yeah, we have been plied with *Pioneer* antibiotics!"

"Take none of these medicines; eat your food instead." I pushed the door open with the leftover rice and said: "You are no match for Mr Fan? Though he muffles half his mouth with his hand, all the Benevolent Lenient Village folks together are no match for him. Mr Fan also writes novels. Later on, ask him to read for you."

Fan Jingquan rejoindered: "Yeah, if you launch a joint attack against me again, I shall read my novels and you will all be made to feel drowsy."

"Liuhe! Liuhe!" Brow, sitting on the lower side of Fan's chair, shouted loudly after sputtering a laugh towards him.

Liuhe, his mouth resting on the edge of Grandpa Cloud Forest's rice bowl, had sucked two mouthfuls with a *slurp, slurp*. Brow complained: "There is only a little rice leftover. You're gorging on it and leaving Grandpa Cloud Forest to starve." With a smile, he said that Grandpa Cloud Forest's rice was tasty.

"Then I shall feed my own face," declared Grandpa Cloud Forest, "and won't offer any to you."

The others laughed, saying, "You can't eat by proxy", while watching him eating a bowlful. When Brow stood up to fill a second bowl for him, Liuhe's youngest daughter pushed open the door, tottered in and called out for Grandpa. Grandpa Cloud Forest asked: "What's going on?" The girl answered: "A weirdo is hanging around on the patch of dirt outside. He is sitting on a branch of the walnut tree and wearing a straw hat. He asked if you live here and wanted to ask something of you." Who was this guy? Was he one of those thugs and pricks from the capital city who, having heard that Grandpa Cloud Forest was a miracle herbalist, had come to extort money?

Several guys groped for sticks from behind the door and wanted to run out and tan his hide. Grandpa Cloud Forest raked rice into his grunting mouth with his head lowered and then smacked his lips loudly. He ate in an undignified way and lip-smacking was the hallmark of a reprobate. Grandpa smiled and took out a parcel of tea leaves from a basket behind him and handed it to the little girl, saying: "Give this to him and he will come and kowtow to me."

The little girl went out and after a short while, sure enough, footsteps were heard from outside. The door was pushed open and, on the threshold, a man touched his head against the ground in the whitish sunlight. It was Bushy Beard Shao, and he exclaimed: "Grandpa Cloud Forest really is a deity."

In a huff, Brow criticised his bad behaviour and told Grandpa Cloud Forest: "This is the Shao guy I mentioned to you. He claimed he didn't know you, but I never expected he would pull a trick like this on you."

"A son-in-law of our Benevolent Lenient Village. On your feet, on your feet!"

I thought it over for a while and then got it. A "straw" (サ) hat on the head, a "man" (人) in the middle and a "tree" (木) beneath him made the Chinese character for "tea" (茶). Grandpa Cloud Forest had cracked his riddle. That city guy must be a deep man. The others also saw the light and let out whoops. I saw the anger had left Brow's face and she dragged Bushy Beard to his feet with great glee. Stupid woman; if you marry such a man, you probably think he's trying to warm you when he's actually barbecuing you for food.

"Grandpa Cloud Forest, I couldn't find Brow and so guessed she was here. Sure enough she is!" Bushy Beard went on: "I've come to bring football tickets for you. There is a match tonight and I have bought a dozen or more tickets especially. Who wants to go and watch?"

The crowd cheered and many hands reached out to snatch them. Brow grabbed the tickets from Bushy Beard's hand and distributed them one by one. The first one went to me.

She asked: "Which teams are playing?"

Bushy Beard said: "A Beijing side against a local one."

Brow said happily: "Sister Plum, you can carry Grandpa Cloud Forest there on your back so he can join the fun." I brushed her aside.

There was no one in Benevolent Lenient Village who didn't murmur about the goodness of Grandpa Cloud Forest when they chit-chatted, but Grandpa Cloud Forest must have been too kind. They dumped him and dispersed like fleeing birds and beasts as soon as they had the football tickets in their hands. A man can't live without air, but who actually realises how vital the air is?

In order to register my dissatisfaction, I stayed behind and did not go out. Grandpa Cloud Forest, seemingly more amiable, lowered his head to eat with gusto. The steam from the bowl rose up along his chin and nose and beads of sweat seeped out of his forehead. I didn't say anything and nor did he. Noisy quarrelling came from outside the village.

"Why don't you go?" After finishing one bowl, he looked at me with a smile.

"I won't," I said. "If you want to go, I shall carry you there on my back."

"How can a youngster not like football? Anyway, that place doesn't suit me."

"It's too rowdy there."

Grandpa Cloud Forest chuckled. Everyone was made of glass in his eyes, so he naturally saw through my pettiness, though he didn't reveal my secret and, with a stiff face, I held my tongue as well. Grandpa Cloud Forest raised the bowl and started to lick. Nobody else in Benevolent Lenient Village had inherited this horrible habit of licking the bowl, and his long tongue embarrassed me.

I grabbed the bowl from his hand and wanted to wash it. But he refused resolutely and said: "If you really don't want to go, you can push me to Aunt Five Springs' home instead for some idle chatter, OK?"

We all knew that Grandpa Cloud Forest often went to Grandma Five Springs' place to chit-chat. Grandpa Five Springs was hale and hearty, but Grandma Five Springs had been a sickly pot of herbs throughout her life and, two years ago, had lost the sight in both eyes. Grandpa Five Springs looked after his old mate, but, impatient as he was, he couldn't bring himself to stay at home for long. What's more, the old couple didn't have much to talk about and he often traipsed out on to the street to watch the young men play billiards and gamble.

After a meal, Grandma Five Springs talked with her old man. Even though she couldn't see, she had too much to say, mumbling incessantly. After quite some time, finding that the old man didn't respond, she poked at Grandpa Five Springs, who should have been sitting on the other side of the *kang*, with her walking stick. The stick hit nothing but air. She then realised that Grandpa Five Springs had left long before.

Grandpa Cloud Forest would go and keep the blind old lady company and banter with her whenever he was free. Two people, with only one pair of eyes but four sharp ears; when a fly was circling around they could work out where it was heading.

Tonight, Grandpa Five Springs must have gone to the football stadium. Of course, he wouldn't buy a ticket or enter the place. Instead, he would stand by the peanut and rice wine vendors, amusing himself by people-watching.

I pushed the wheelchair along and took Grandpa Cloud Forest to Grandma Five Springs' home. It was almost dark. As expected, Grandpa Five Springs wasn't home and Grandma Five Springs was still sitting on the laundry stone outside the gate. To her, there was no distinction between daytime and night. Barely had we come around the pear tree in front of her gate, when she shouted out Grandpa Cloud Forest's name.

Chapter Five

The Jia clan inhabited a compound in the west of Benevolent Lenient Village, which was divided into front, middle and back courtyards. The buildings were dilapidated, but the eaves were all made of bricks and wood. Stone lions crouched in front of the gates. Rather than looking stately they gawped at each other in a coy manner. Screening walls rose up behind the gates, and these were carved with hornless dragons, tigers sejant, satin and silk decorations, floating clouds, red bats and lapidary plum blossoms.

Two families who shared the surname Li lived along the small lane in the front courtyard, and parallel to the middle courtyard were another two Li families. The back courtyard had two gates and the buildings inside were arranged on a north-to-south axis, though the main courtyard gate faced to the west. Two brothers used to live here. Owing to the sisters-in-law not being on good terms, when the second son moved house, he deliberately did not sell his old residence to his elder brother but to a guy named Liu.

This Liu chap was rude and unreasonable and, during the course of his life, he pissed on half of his fellow villagers. After his death, he gained a posthumous son named A-Shun who, by contrast, had diligent legs and a sweet mouth like a kitten or a puppy. Outside the gates and across a small patch of earth lay a gentle slope; on top of the gentle slope sat Liuhe's home. Liuhe's father was a mason, who had passed his skills down to him. The son could build houses, renovate kitchen stoves, erect walls and construct *kangs*.

Living in the north and counting from the east to the west were families with miscellaneous surnames like Wu, Zhao, Qian, Nan, and Ran – all of them newcomers.

Back when they built houses communally, the four main rooms going from east to the west formed a courtyard with the corridor and lean-tos, and the latrines all stood in the south-western corner. In the east, a medicinal tree with a huge canopy grew and flocks of birds would vanish into oblivion after being sucked into it. Since Grandpa Cloud Forest had started to practise medicine, the tree came to be regarded as a feng-shui landmark by the villagers.[i] Fan Jingquan once carved a poem in its trunk, a line of which read: "The tree is a refuge and the birds know already."

On the lower side of the village, there used to be a threshing ground together with seven indigo grinding stones and a row of posts carved with ugly-faced human figures, which were used for hitching-up donkeys and cattle. Following the disappearance of the wheat fields, houses had been built on the threshing ground. These were occupied by a family named Wei. To the north of the threshing ground stood Grandpa Cloud Forest's shrine house and the cemetery. Adjacent to the western wall of the cemetery lived the Wei clan, whose houses followed the lie of the land, with some gates facing east and some south. This had the effect that the lanes zigzagged. It was said that the Jia and Wei clans used to be kindred, but several generations back they became estranged. Despite the problem not being so heinous, the Jias nevertheless still looked down on the Weis.

The old Village Head lived in the middle courtyard of the Jia clan. Old Ran was born in the front courtyard, though a distant relative belonging to the Ran family adopted him at an early age and, later on, changed his surname. Chivalry hailed from the Wei family, but life didn't prosper in the Wei household and he stood high on the ladder of seniority (it was foretold that with the arrival of his generation their family line would terminate abruptly).

The village originally resembled an L-shaped walking stick. In recent years, the children of many households grew up, extended families were subdivided into smaller units and building plots were developed in the south and north, transforming the village into something like a rectangle.

A high-rise soared over the eastern wall of the cemetery. The sports stadium nestled in front of the high-rise, which now provided accommodation for the management of the stadium. The building was probably unique in the capital city because it possessed a double wall. At first, business was slack and one customer even committed suicide by jumping to his death. A feng-shui master deduced that it was haunted by ghosts because it stood next to the cemetery. So, another wall was added with windows that were narrow at one end and thick at the other so they looked like standing coffins. The idea was to suppress evil with evil. Business then started to pick up.

After delivering Grandpa Cloud Forest to Grandma Five Springs' home, I sauntered listlessly in a circle around Benevolent Lenient Village. In my mind, I laughed at myself. Tonight, almost all the households had locked their gates and gone to the football stadium. Why should I idle around like a Nocturnal Patron God?[j]

Should I hate the fact that, since April, a weekly football match had been held in the stadium? Should I hate how fellow Benevolent Lenient villagers jumped on the bandwagon even though they knew nothing about football? Should I hate it that the pyramid sales agent Shao tickled them where they itched by sending them tickets? When I went past the entrance of the T-shaped lane outside the back courtyard of the Jia clan, somebody's cat screeched sadly and the next moment a stranger descended with stomping footsteps. He stamped his foot to frighten the cat and the feline fled for its life. He gave chase and then froze on the spot, casting his long shadow behind him. It was the old executioner.

There were three lonesome souls in the empty alleyway: me, the cat and the odd-tempered old man. Unwilling to meet him, I hid myself in the darkness and gazed at him walking away with stomping footsteps. I don't know why, but my thoughts turned to Chivalry, our future Village Head. Could he lead the village and save its land from being gobbled up? Even if we could resist the encroachment of the city, could we resist the temptations presented to us by the city?

I returned to my own home. The patients were not in. I turned on the light to appreciate those pieces of old Ming and Qing Dynasty furniture, doing my utmost to keep myself calm despite the noisy bawling in the distance.

To be honest, back when Old Ran started to collect furniture, I followed suit simply out of love. But, once the ball was rolling, I realised I had a natural instinct for it. Tonight, beneath the light of an electric bulb, I studied a chair. Fashioned out of scented rosewood, its soft curves integrated with its rectangular form. The main frame and skeleton were thin in the extreme, leaving room for many, many attractive large and small pierced holes.

Benevolent Lenient Village had seen many such chairs in the past. Now, most households owned newly-purchased sofas or were enthusiastically cobbling together settees in their courtyards, depositing their old furniture in their utility rooms. Because they had been rendered obsolete, these objects were now valued again purely on their unique aesthetic. Can you imagine what the sinuous backrest, the upturned headrest, the armrests, the goose necks, the three arching decorative battens and the horizontal arching linking battens look like? And how people's bodies felt when the folk from two generations ago sat on them!

Now, the chair was unoccupied. Still, it must have retained the slightest semblance of the humans who had gone before – nature and soul. The portal to days past waxed slowly and, when the gate closed gently, those waves of clamour from the football stadium were shut outside.

At this juncture, the image of a man surfaced quietly in my mind: he had spindly limbs, a pale, unhealthy pudding face and a straggly beard. What was the bond that linked us? Why didn't I find out in the past that he had so many flaws? How could a man's face be edgeless and cornerless like this? Why did he always use a pair of tiny tweezers to pluck out his scraggly beard hair-by-hair?

I sat on the Ming Dynasty chair, entrusting the lower half of my body to it. Then, lying face-up on the floral Ming Dynasty bed, I entrusted my whole body to it. And yet, still feeling turbulent, I turned around and dealt the chair and bed some hefty punches and kicks before going out.

To begin with, I wanted to go to the hustling place outside the stadium to keep my eyes occupied and give my brain a rest like Grandpa Five Springs did. Barely had I bought a skewer of sugar-coated hawthorn berries from a vendor's stall, when I glimpsed Gao Feng in his American-soldier boots being pressed down on the ground by a crowd of people. They were scrambling after something. When Gao crawled to his feet, he shouted abuse loudly, proclaiming that they were all mad dogs and wolves. "If you want to buy tickets, do it one at a time. Why do you snatch like this? Great, now five tickets have been ripped to shreds!" He picked up the tatters of paper from the ground, flung them away indignantly, raised his head and, on spotting me, forced out a smile.

"Gone! One hundred yuan is gone like that." Serves you right, I think, looking at him. Gao Feng, have you also learned to peddle tickets? Gao's weepy face again showed a flash of cockiness. "Plum, you have no ticket, either? There were enough tickets for some bastards to rip these into bits, so how could there not be a ticket for you?" He took out another five tickets from his chest and gave one to me.

"I don't watch football."

"How can you not?"

He frogmarched me through the ticket barrier, handed the ticket to the collector and admitted: "Now I've learned a lesson. These four tickets I will sell one by one."

This was the first time I had watched a live football match. Positioning myself in the stand, I came to know what football meant. Thousands of people gathered together, all of them siding with the home team. When there was any sign of attack, they cheered together, and when the visiting team intercepted the ball, they booed. This was accompanied throughout the game by an intermittent chorus of cursing: "Ref, …your mother!" They yelled like mad and made noises all through the night only because they felt too empty, lonely and bored.

I tried my best to search for people from my village and didn't clap eyes on anyone. I imagined they were standing among those whose shouts and cries soared into the sky and shook the earth, or that they were screaming more fiercely than the others.

Standing up, I discovered that in the crowd in front and to my left were Brow, Old Shao and three other fellow villagers whooping in hoarse voices. After that, they started to argue about how many players from each team were on the pitch. One insisted *ten* and another one claimed *eleven*. Neither could prevail and they had a wager, asking Brow to count. Each time Brow totted up she got different totals. One of them smote his chest. "Ten! Definitely ten! You lose. You should take out ten yuan." An old man nearby looked back over his shoulder and upbraided him: "Young man, you definitely lose."

Unwilling to see and be seen by them, I crouched down and went to stand in another place, laughing at Brow and her gang secretly as well as the other football maniacs.

A football stadium might as well be one huge public lavatory. Anyone, whether they knew about football or not, could come here to empty their bowels.

But then, I thought, a man probably lives his life seeking after sound. When we are newly come into this world, we bawl to announce our arrival. Barely have our mothers left us alone in the cradle when we start to cry so that there is sound around us and we are not lonely. Tonight, Grandpa Cloud Forest had gone to keep Grandma Five Springs company. How the blind old lady was bound to prattle on. Brow and the sales agent were in the stadium. Was A-Bing barking at home? The mice on the crossbeam of my home must have been grinding their teeth.

In the second half of the game, the home team found themselves on the offensive, their attack advancing like the waves of an incoming tide. However, they couldn't manage to score a goal. Their opponents were the first to score when they turned from defence to attack. The goal should have been beyond dispute, yet the frantic long-haired defender for the home team pointed angrily at the linesman and then bent down on one knee in a howling rage, pounding the ground with his fists. All who were present chanted in chorus: "Offside! Offside!" The referee paid no heed and scooted back to the centreline with the ball. The game rolled on.

The players on both sides became vindictive; there were frequent fouls and the yellow card ended up being shown three times. I joined thousands of spectators to chorus: "Goal! Go-a-l!"

Finally, number nine penetrated through three lines of defence and everyone in the sitting area stood up, yelling, but no one was able to hear what they were shouting about.

A number of die-hard football fans on the opposite stands, who were leading the chants, had stripped themselves to the waist and were now running, huge flags flapping and their naked bodies gleaming. Nonetheless, when the ball passed to the goal area of the visiting team, it was intercepted and the defender's clearance sent it back to the other half of the pitch. A defender from the home side skidded over when he tried to intercept. As he fell down, he reached out a hand to drag over his opponent but failed, and the player then entered the penalty area.

Another defender sprinted towards the ball from an oblique angle and performed a flying tackle from one metre away. The attacker tumbled down and rolled to and fro on the turf. A penalty! As soon as the referee's whistle sounded, the players on the home side closed in on him. Thousands of spectators cursed together as one: "Ref – … your mother! Ref – …your mother!" The referee attempted to flee from the crowd of players who had closed in on him, but he couldn't. He took out the red card, but his raised hand was pressed down by the players. They then pushed and shoved. Pandemonium erupted on the stands. Some on the eastern flank jumped down and sprinted to the centre of the pitch. Next, virtually all the spectators followed suit and more and more crowded the grass.

I tensed up, but then something even more urgent happened. A man appeared nearby, stripped to his waist. Standing on the iron guard rails of the stands, he waved his white cloth shirt and shrieked. The horizontal iron bar was very narrow, yet he remained steady.

Chivalry! The villagers had been waiting for him for so many days and he turned up in the football stadium. This great wolf of a man; when did he come back? I shouted loudly: "Uncle Chivalry! Uncle Chivalry!" My shout was buried by the deafening chaos and nobody, either on the stands or below, registered my excitement. Immediately, a premonition struck me: Chivalry would jump down.

I hotfooted hurriedly over to him while shouting his name. The tumultuous crowd barred my way; a man with a painted face simpered at me, brandishing his hands and jumping about, seemingly ready to grab at me and hoist me up like a flag. I wrestled my way out after letting fly a curse: "Hooligan!" En route I stepped on the foot of another man. Even when I had covered quite a distance I could still hear the cursing from behind: "The pussy is turned on as well!"

Finally, I reached the right area of the stands. Chivalry had gone down the guard rails and, his hands grasping the metal bars and his body dangling in mid-air, was going to jump. I took hold of his hands from the other side and cried: "Uncle Chivalry! Uncle Chivalry! You're back!"

"Plum?" He turned his head and, taken aback, stared at me, his body contracting further because of his exertions. His spine was arching and his ribs could be clearly counted. "Plum, let's jump down together. It's damn good. Damn good!"

"You can't jump down. If you jump down, you'll do yourself a mischief. Look around, look around."

People on the stands were still flinging themselves down from all sides like dumplings being tipped into a wok. Some charged to the middle of the pitch immediately after landing; some took a nasty fall and were momentarily unable to get up, but still ran on limply after struggling to their feet. The heart of the pitch became a huge whirlpool in the middle of a river with the referee caught up within it. The players on the visiting team were also caught up separately in a small eddy. Even the players from the home team were surrounded by spectators. You didn't know if they were being rebuked or assaulted or worshipped. Anyhow, people were squeezing, hands clawed the air frantically, the kits of the referee and players were being ripped and a football boot flew past, tracing an arc in the sky.

The loudspeaker again and again ordered the fans to not invade the pitch. Security officers burst out from two tunnels and three video cameras were targeted at the crowd to capture them on film. One man, after relieving a player of his shirt, hurled off his own, put on the new garment and congratulated himself in front of a video camera. Suddenly, someone screamed: "They will finger you because of the tape." The man immediately fled and the crowd stampeded and scattered as if an ants' nest had suddenly been struck by a burning briquette.

Numerous folk crawled upwards along the fencelike gates of the tunnels in the four corners of the stadium. Some successful climbers lobbed plastic water bottles down out of spite; some plummeted down from the guard rails; some, their hands clutching the edges of the cement piers below the guard rails, were hanging in mid-air and writhing like snakes.

I hauled Chivalry up by grabbing his hair and dragging him at a run outside without giving him a chance to explain. Meanwhile, I glimpsed that in the western corner of the stadium the police had pinned down one man and were wielding their batons to knock down another with a shaved head, who was swinging down below the rails. Without thinking, we bundled ourselves out of an exit and left what was happening inside behind. Matters outside were far messier. Many vehicles had been overturned with shouts and curses and the crowds, which thronged to and fro, also inflicted collateral damage on the snacks stalls; the clanking of metal items colliding against each other, the cracking of chinaware, the crying and the caterwauling all combining into a cacophony.

I gripped Chivalry's hand tight as if leading a red-eyed fighting bull, afraid that he might struggle free. A number of times, the human tide felled us and we kept swinging this way and that. Countless discarded shoes lay on the ground. Suddenly, someone gave Chivalry a resounding slap and a woman cursed him for being an arsehole.

"Who's an arsehole? How have I become an arsehole? If you don't like being squeezed too much, sit on the *kang* in your home and nobody will try to squeeze you."

"Why did you tug my plait?"

"Who tugged your plait?"

Chivalry was thriving on this. "Should I be fond of you? Plum, come and compare yourself with her, compare yourself with this Piggy. How could I be fond of her and tug her plait?"

One man nearby proclaimed: "You've done him wrong. Your plait got snagged up on the pen in my pocket."

The woman turned her head and spotted a pen on the tip of her plait. She apologised to Chivalry.

"Sorry? One slap, one sorry and that's it?"

The woman answered: "Then you should pay back in kind."

"Uncle Chivalry," I cried. "Hurry away, hurry."

Chivalry raised his hand and struck out, but when his hand reached the woman's face, his posture transformed to make it a gentle tap. I dragged him to a tree. He tilted his head and meant to pounce over there again.

"You heard that? She cursed that I'm a peasant."

I was antagonised enough to growl: "You are a peasant! Why did you paw her like that?"

Chivalry wrapped his hands around the tree and chuckled.

Behind a row of overturned vehicles, people whooped in chorus: "Hit! Hit!" Those on the left side then flocked to the right.

"What's going on there?" Chivalry asked.

I squeezed his hand like grim death, sensing that the riot tonight would inevitably develop into a disaster and I couldn't let him get embroiled.

Floundering to the left and right, I finally reached the back gate of the guest house with him in tow, but the gate had been locked from the inside by the timid waitress. I thundered against it; it wouldn't open. Luckily, the third window was still ajar. I jumped up and through it and Chivalry followed. We reached the front courtyard of the guest house and dashed out on to the street.

The sirens of the police cars were wailing. Lines of armed police were marching towards the stadium. Chivalry turned around and ran in that direction as well. I leapt and delivered him a hard slap across his face. "You are mad. Crazy! You must be possessed by a ghost."

I was angry to the point of crying.

"So many people, they don't run away," Chivalry commented. "Why should I?"

I hurled more abuse at him and told him of the villagers' decision. I observed him as he stood there frozen.

"Really?"

"I am lying; I am a pig?"

"Why should they have their sights set on me? Tell me, whose idea is this?"

"Grandpa Cloud Forest's."

"Grandpa Cloud Forest?"

Without warning, Chivalry raised his hands and performed a backward somersault.

"Plum," he said, "the villagers are right and so is Grandpa Cloud Forest."

So, Chivalry did care about the village and about Grandpa Cloud Forest. He was a wanderer by nature, but was still rooted in Benevolent Lenient Village.

"Wild and proud now! Wild and proud!" I blurted out.

"Lend me a ladder and I'll climb up to the sky," was Chivalry's enthusiastic response.

Under the illumination from the street lamp, he glared at me ferociously and his eyes sparkled with a stupid light. I drew up my collar slightly.

"Plum, I should thank you."

"Don't thank me. I did this for Benevolent Lenient Village."

"They all say you look like your grandfather. Really, a chip off the old block."

"You're laughing at me for not being beautiful?"

He let out a laugh, his eyes cooling, and slowly shifted away from me. Then, gazing at the passing police cars and murmuring, he undid the shirt that was tied around his waist and tossed it into the middle of the road. A whistling vehicle promptly ran over it. He picked it up and put it on again.

"What trick are you playing?" I asked.

"It's been run over by a car now. That's like saying that I have died once," he replied. "Now, everything is OK. Ha, Plum, tonight I got two slaps from two women."

Chapter Six

It was by means of an earnest process that the villagers selected their Head. Actually, the election ran simply. The villagers all gathered under the myrrh tree to toss soy beans. In order to make their choice, they threw one bean into a bowl denoting a candidate. These were laid out on the grinding stone on the tree roots. Chivalry received the most soy beans and duly became the newly-elected Village Head. It was not done and dusted, however, until the selection was approved by the Agricultural Trade Bureau of the district government.

The former director of the commune, who used to govern Benevolent Lenient Village and was now head of the Agricultural Trade Bureau, hummed and hawed as he came to seek out Chivalry to share a drink with him.

"That riot," he enquired. "No villager had a hand in it?"

Chivalry answered: "No."

"You're lucky not to have been here when the riot broke out. You should take advantage of the fact that I shall still be in office for another two years. Just get on with it."

The only football riot in history to have broken out in the Western Capital was pacified that very night, and yet the various rumours about it started to infect all the city inhabitants like a plague. None of the Benevolent Lenient Village residents had been arrested by the police. The heel of one of Brow's high-heeled sandals snapped in two leaving her ankle sprained. Uncle Five Springs, of course, didn't participate in the brawl but, even so, he was knocked down by the mob, causing the bone in his left hip to become intermittently numb and painful. Now he was able to stay at home the whole day long and banter with his blind old mate.

The riot prevented the match from lasting the full ninety minutes. The National Football Association announced that the result was void and penalised the Western Capital by revoking its right to serve as the home ground for the local team. This would no doubt bring huge shame and deal a heavy blow to the reputation of the city. The leadership of the muncipal government had turned its wrath on the arrested rioters, declaring that the black sheep would be punished severely.

Some were sentenced to one year's imprisonment, some six months and others were fined heavily. A young man in the Institute of Agricultural Science and Technology was released after ten days in custody because no charges were pressed. Fan Jingquan urged him to appeal.

"When studying humans, we should first take them as animals. Football is a sport that tends to make people crazy. There does not need to have been any prior intention to act as vandals or troublemakers. Who should be held to blame? The organisers for their neglectful attitude and their ineffectual security measures? Since no charges have been pressed, why should you be detained? In accordance with Article XX, Section XX of the law, suspects cannot be held in custody for more than 24 hours. Why has it dragged on for as long as ten days? How can you be compensated for your loss of reputation? Who will shoulder your financial loss?"

Fan proved himself to be eloquent, pouring out words like a river torrent. The young man lodged a complaint and the Court accepted his appeal, but while the Court was in session, the police came over and the young man was detained again.

The disqualification of the Western Capital as a home ground meant that all the inhabitants of the capital city,

Benevolent Lenient Village included, would lose the chance to come together and stir up a din. The capital city instantly grew hollow and dead.

From originally being keen to help, Fan Jingquan found he had done the young man more harm than good and was left uneasy at heart. At the suggestion of Chivalry (who else?), Benevolent Lenient Village decided to set off firecrackers. Two large coils each containing 20,000 bangers spooled down around a couple of thick rafters erected at the entrance to the village. Resembling a pair of long dragons, they burst into life. The popping sound shook the heavens and startled the earth, and smoke and papery chads permeated the air.

Many people were enticed over to join the hubbub, misconstruing it as a celebration to mark the release of arrested football fans. The old Village Head was still in hospital. Hearing the roar of the firecrackers, his wife donned her hairpiece and went out to see what the heck was going on. Finding Fan Jingquan standing among them, she scooted over to the hospital to inform the old Village Head, who in turn reported it to the district government.

"Chivalry has gathered together a mob to vent their dissatisfaction about how the riot was settled," he said.

Before there had been time to sweep away the thick layer of paper fragments, a policeman entered the village. The officer was our acquaintance Fatty. After being told that the firecrackers were set off to celebrate the successful election of a new Village Head, he exclaimed: "This has absolutely nothing to do with the riot." He asked about A-Bing and, hence, was welcomed into Brow's home.

At the sight of Fatty, A-Bing barked loudly and trembled without ceasing. That tool of his dangled down longer and redder between his hind legs. Perhaps poor A-Bing might never be able to shake off the shadow of the slaughter. He could no longer remember that this stout chap was the one who saved his life, but felt petrified at the sight of a police uniform as if out of conditioned reflex.

"How come his whip is exposed? Look, look at his whip," Fatty blustered.

Her face now scarlet, Brow kicked A-Bing's posterior.

One folk saying advises that a man shouldn't raise a cat and a woman shouldn't keep a dog, as a dog-keeping woman might be lured into licentiousness. Great must Brow's shame have been over raising A-Bing, whose exposed whip behaved so inelegantly in public. When she kicked him with her red leather shoe, A-Bing had no idea what her intention might be. He reared up on his hind legs to the height of half a man and embraced her leg with his forepaws. He fawned and hankered after protection. Several others tittered. Brow shoved the dog aside and caught hold of his leg to fling him out of the door.

The pretentious Brow manhandled A-Bing in this way. To me it was intolerable. I went outdoors to gather him up in my arms. A-Bing's left hind leg had been wounded. Time after time he wanted to struggle to his feet but failed, his woeful, puzzled eyes still fixed on Brow. Next, tears plopped down. I had never seen a dog weeping before. A-Bing's tears were greyish, murky and thick. They slid down slowly from his long face like wriggling earthworms.

I asked A-Shun to carry A-Bing out to the village lane, but A-Shun took him to Grandpa Cloud Forest instead. Despite being moved by regret at her own actions and wanting to have A-Bing back again, the memory of that incident caused the dog to shiver at the very sight of Brow and so he became

Grandpa Cloud Forest's constant companion.

Once more, Fatty yelped: "That dog!" He then sat down on Brow's sofa to drink coffee and started to relate the horror of the football riot: "Out on the pitch, the referee's head was cracked open and one of his left ribs was broken. Thirteen players were stripped of their clothes and the platinum necklaces from around their necks were nicked as well. Two baskets of missing shoes were gathered, together with six watches and twenty-three pairs of glasses. But it was worse outside the stadium. Three cars were overturned, one minibus was torched, and one small tea shop and a fashion boutique were trashed and looted."

"How many were put behind bars?" Chivalry asked. "Is it possible that, because the police couldn't get the situation under control, they sent out provocateurs to smash the vehicles to create a nasty incident so that they could arrest people?"

"How could your brain swirl like this?" was Fatty's reply.

The officer's face was a picture of solemnity and the atmosphere in the room grew serious. I shot a glare at Chivalry. Chivalry didn't look at me but snapped a small twig from a pot-plant to pick his ears with and hawked out two dry coughs.

"So many shoes were collected? The heel from one of Brow's shoes must have been there as well," I commented.

"Really?" Fatty enquired in a concerned voice. "You haven't run into any football hooligans have you? One woman was boxed in and her face and body were fondled and groped by god knows how many hands. Her clothes were ripped apart strip by strip and her breasts were pawed swollen. Her nipples were even ripped off. Later, she squatted down with her hands protecting her bosom. As if that were not enough, she received lacerations to the area between her vagina and anus. She is still being treated in hospital now."

Fatty's words sent a chill down everyone's spine. Brow even performed a kneejerk gesture. She pressed her right index finger down on the back of her left hand; the back of her hands were fleshy and she pressed once and then again. Pressing hundreds and thousands of times like this, her bones might even get pressed out. Her face was deathly pale.

There were so many people. When the riot started, a huge qi force field must have been formed and taken hold of anybody who was present. It was said that the armed police had not yet arrived when the cars outside the stadium were being overturned. Those few security policemen who were on the scene hastily whipped off their caps and overcoats, so why hadn't this woman avoided the mob earlier?

"She is not beautiful," Fatty emphasised. "Only her clothing was a little too thin and her make-up too heavy. A hooligan went forward to insult her and hundreds and thousands followed. Serves her right. She must have been a whore in her previous life, or a traitor, or Qin Hui's wife."[k]

Ought a beautiful woman to be insulted? And if she isn't beautiful and is insulted does that mean that she was a whore in her previous life? That arsehole Fatty! After finishing taking care of his ears, Chivalry fumbled in his pocket for a cigarette. Instead, he fished out a firecracker, which he wanted to light and fling out of the room in order to listen to the popping sound.

I reached out a hand, nipped off the fuse and murmured in a low voice: "You want to create another cock-up?"

"Are we going to stay here and keep him company for the whole afternoon?" he asked.

"He is a policeman. Be patient."

"Let's have a knees-up at my home tonight. You can come."

"What for? Is it that we are welcoming you back or that you want to treat us?"

"Go drink the wind and shit farts! What should the village do in the future? We should have a plan."

"A new broom sweeps clean. That's all up to you. You should go to the district government and find out how those higher up intend to deal with the village."

Chivalry nodded his head and began to stand up. I tugged the front of his shirt and asked him to sit tight for a moment. He let out a chuckle.

His laughter hadn't aroused Brow's attention. She still asked Fatty: "Those criminals – you've winkled them out or not?"

"Where should we look?" Fatty asked in reply.

"Have a look and see if I am one of them," Chivalry joked.

The others hooted with laughter. Gao Feng, pointing at Laiwang, declared: "I think you are."

Laiwang also piped up: "*Aiya*, Gao Feng is the one who looks most like a criminal. He hasn't gotten married, much less seen a woman."

They then ribbed each other, you pointing at me and saying that I was a criminal and I pointing at you and saying that you were a criminal. Who were the criminals? No one in this world is born a criminal, but everyone is a criminal. For a dozen or more years, the whole society had been denouncing the Cultural Revolution, yet who among those over the age of forty didn't participate in it and who hadn't felt sincerely excited when fighting in that unprecedented political movement?

As to this football match, I was there watching it. All who were present here now were there as well. There were too many people there. If there hadn't been so many people, even if the woman were naked, and even if the guy in front of her were a "flower-plucker," he wouldn't dare behave like a hooligan in public.

Who were the criminals? The referee was one of them, the players were criminals, all the spectators, us included, were criminals, and the lady was a criminal herself.

Fatty and the roomful of people sighed over the woman's ordeal while repeatedly reliving the scene of the victim being insulted and the state she was in when Fatty saw her in the hospital. They had turned her into something choice and rare. With the aid of their imagination, it seemed as though they were peeping through a crack in the door at a woman who was taking a bath, or peeking over the wall at a woman doing her business in the latrine, or watching a porno video to add some mustard to their boring afternoon.

Did Fatty come here to talk about this? It dawned on me all of a sudden that those who were here now were the true criminals, committing the crime for a second time. Those god knows how many hands that pawed off the woman's nipples and then reached out to her vagina and anus from behind were actually *their* hands.

"Is she married?" Their enthusiasm hadn't subsided.

"There was a man in the ward, a pretty lad or so it seemed. When he saw us, he loped away, with a hangdog expression."

"He must want to dump his wife," Laiwang sneered. "A woman's clothes should be taken off by her husband and no one else. How can that man now hold his head high before others? I daresay they will get divorced as soon as the woman is discharged from hospital." Laiwang suffered from psoriasis. He scratched his chest and then flicked out the silvery flakes accrued beneath his fingernails. Even the air became tinged with his noxious odour.

"Her torn pisshole and arsehole might be repaired but her

nipples can't be sewn back on. How would her baby suck milk after she gives birth?"

"Attach rubber ones."

I stood up. A sparrow landed below the grape trellis in the courtyard and then another one followed. Chivalry catcalled from behind me: "Look at this! Look at this!"

After having taunted Fatty, Chivalry remained silent and his horseplay struck me as most satisfying. But what had he taken out to show to the others? Immediately I heard a chorus of surprised shouts: "One male hand and one female hand!"

I did a double-take. The birds outside were still pecking at the food – *pat pat*. Chivalry reached out his long hands there and then. Sure enough, they were not of the same size, thickness and complexion – one was dark and the other pale. I had never paid much attention to his hands. Back when he wanted to jump down on to the football pitch, I grabbed one of his hands, but I didn't notice how it was different from the other. A man should have a man's hands, but his hands were so weird.

"Transplanted," explained Chivalry. "It is very tricky to transplant a hand and yet the doctors can't sew back on a nipple?"

Chivalry retrieved his mitt and the topic of their talk shifted from the woman's nipples to his hands, so Fatty no longer hogged the spotlight. They all asked Chivalry what went wrong.

Two years ago, when he was in the village, his hands were still fine. What had happened to him while he was away during the past year and a half? How had his left hand been severed? Where did he have the operation to give him the new one?

Chivalry only smiled without answering. He was always mysterious. Once again, he reached out his hands and pinched together the thumb and the index finger of his woman's left hand to form the orchid-shaped pose from the opera stage.

Fatty attempted to probe: "Does the transplanted hand function properly?"

"Of course. I can eat, write and work. How can it not function properly, except…" He bit his tongue.

"Except you can't have a slash properly. If you try, the hand will grip it and never let it go."

Laiwang's words humoured them into a belly laugh. Brow and I headed to the courtyard after letting out a curse. Brow couldn't help tittering.

I overheard Fatty say: "The lines of the hand are fine, the solar area protrudes out high and there is a Venus zone. This came from a neurotic woman, perhaps a would-be scholar." His attempt at palmistry was clearly bullshit.

Brow extended her own hands to study them. Pressing together my lips, I dragged her under the grape trellis and the two sparrows took wing. Men are ugly animals, so just let them chew their tongues. I was going to talk to her about A-Bing. But she still couldn't get off the topic of men and mused: "So peculiar. How can Uncle Chivalry have a hand like that?" Then she asked stealthily: "How is Old Ran?"

"His same old self."

"Have you done it with him yet?"

Brow must have been thinking about herself when she heard the story about Chivalry's hands. She was just feigning an interest in me. Since she had been courting Old Shao, Shao had made a hussy out of her.

I replied: "How can I run like you?"

"You are not the forthcoming type for sure. A woman marries a man for good food, nice clothing and great fun.

Why do men all like the Concubine Yang[l] but not Wu Zetian?[m] Because Yang possessed feminine charms."

I brushed her aside.

Brow again smiled at me: "You should help me for once."

"Help you with what?"

"Accompany me to the hospital tomorrow," she beseeched in a low voice. "I no longer dare put it off. I'm scared."

I twigged what the matter was and eyed her in surprise.

Brow was no longer the Brow of days past. What about me? What was I?

Chapter Seven

Chivalry returned home with a transplanted woman's hand as well as a cow's skull and a stone Buddha. The facial bone of the cow head had already been fractured and its two obliquely upturned horns were about one foot long, making the artefact look majestic. The stone Buddha, on the other hand, consisted of a round, flat, thin, white piece of rock incised smoothly with a plump handsome idol of the bodhisattva. The skull belonged to a yak from the snow-capped mountains, a scene which we are all familiar with from the TV. Picture this: stones piled up into a lofty altar and the nomadic people offering sacrifices to Heaven, to Earth and to their ancestors. Sitting atop the sacrificial altar was this grand object. As to the stone Buddha, Chivalry pulled out a copy of an explanatory document, which read:

In the middle of the ninth century, the last bTsan-po emperor of the Tibetan Tubo Kingdom, Glang dar ma (reigned 838–42), was assassinated. Clashes broke out between his two sons, mang' bdag vod-srung and mang' bdag yum-brtan, both finally meeting on the battlefield because both wanted to succeed to the throne.

Then a major peasant uprising occurred. In 922, mang' bdag vod-srung's son, Huakaozan, was slain by the rebels. One of Huakaozan's two sons remained in Yü-Zang and the other one, called Jidainimagong, fled westwards to Burang Zong in the Ali area. Nimagong married there and had three sons. The three sons fought more intently for mastery. One went to Ladakh and established the Ladakh Kingdom, another one continued to consolidate his power-base at Burang Zong near Gangdisê, and the third son, Daizougong, went to the Kugê area in Xangxung to establish the Kugê Kingdom. The Kugê Kingdom stood for more than seven hundred years from its establishment in the tenth century to its collapse in the seventeenth. This stone Buddha was originally embedded in the exterior wall of the imperial palace and inscribed by the Buddhist disciples who were fulfilling their vow to return to that place.

It was not until that point that I knew that Chivalry had spent the past year or two in Tibet.

Why did Chivalry go to Tibet? And what did he do there? Chivalry had buttoned his lips and never spoken about it. The villagers now gossiped incessantly like twittering birds. Perhaps none of them, with the exception of the old Village Head's wife, intended any harm. Nevertheless, they liked passing comments and they were all garrulous men and women who cared more about other folks' business than their own.

The village had a public latrine with four dozen squatting holes. It was built to gather fertilizer during the era of the "in agriculture we learn from Dazhai" campaign. Back then, the collective reserve of manure was frequently raided by individuals. Now the cesspool overflowed with shit and piss, maggots crawled everywhere and flies buzzed blindly. Many people, however, came here to relieve themselves more willingly than ever before and to discuss all kinds of affairs while they were at it. Now, it was time to chew over Chivalry's problem.

Segregated by a dividing wall, the men and women squatted in their respective zones, complaining that their legs ached and proposing that the Village Committee should contribute to upgrading to pedestal pans. All the while, they chattered about distant Tibet, saying: "Chivalry must have gone there to peddle cultural objects and his hand was hacked off in the smuggling operation. Only in that place, where the medical conditions are inferior to those in the heartland, would it be possible for a woman's hand to be transplanted on to his body."

The idle gossip most probably wouldn't reach Chivalry's ears. These long-tongued women and men could argue that white is black when the people concerned were not present but, to their faces, they put on a show of profound modesty and warm-heartedness.

Whenever they encountered Chivalry, they liked to shake hands with him so as to inspect the female hand. Next, a rumour swirled around that when a woman shook hands with him, the hand was lifeless, but when it happened to be a man, the grip grew extremely tight and the little finger even gave the man's palm a tickle. In Chivalry's company, I felt embarrassed about asking too much.

He sent the stone Buddha to Grandpa Cloud Forest, though it was me who decided to place it on the table where Grandpa Cloud Forest took the patients' pulses.

"Uncle Chivalry, the stone Buddha came from the historical ruins of the Kingdom of Kugê. How did you manage to lay your hands on it?" I wanted to know.

"The Kingdom of Kugê came to an end 300 years ago. Some say it was because of the drying out of the rivers and some say it was because of wars. Anyhow, the Kingdom of Kugê ended mysteriously. These stone Buddhas were scattered around the imperial palace and an old Tibetan man was taking care of them. To obtain a stone Buddha, you should go up the mountain with hard liquor and ply him with it. I brought three pieces down with me. By the time I reached the foot of the mountain, the old man had sobered up and retrieved two of them."

After fixing the stone Buddha in its place, Chivalry proposed that we should decorate Grandpa Cloud Forest's rooms. Grandpa Cloud Forest disagreed, maintaining that there was no need. No matter how run-down a place might be, what's the difference between it and a palace when you're fast asleep? "Good point there," Chivalry answered. "But if you knead clay into an idol and leave it in a temple, it becomes a god and is no longer a clay idol. An idol should be painted with a coating of gold leaf every year." Grandpa Cloud Forest only grinned without yielding.

Chivalry then said to me: "If the soft way hasn't worked, let's resort to the hard way. You should cook up an excuse to trick him out of the house and I will decorate the rooms then."

"If he's not willing, let's leave it at that."

One finger of Chivalry's female hand tapped my forehead with a series of tiny clicks. "You are taking correspondence courses. How can you have such a simple brain? Do you think I am in the business of offering alms to the poor? What kind of situation will Benevolent Lenient Village face in the future and what's the policy direction of the Village Committee? As Uncle Cloud Forest is so important for the village, we should join our hearts as one and respect him like a god."

"You mean we should search for a sense of unity? And develop a religious consciousness?"

"I haven't taken correspondence courses and I don't know the jargon."

The plan was carried out covertly. I told a white lie to the effect that Grandpa Five Springs had been bickering with his old mate again and Grandpa Cloud Forest was needed to make peace. I then asked A-Shun to carry Grandpa

Cloud Forest out of the shrine. A-Bing didn't follow them but only paced in circles around me.

After Grandpa Cloud Forest left, we began to mix the brownish red paint in the big aluminium wash basin in front of his gate and then took out all the furnishings piece by piece. These amounted to nothing more than a wooden table, a wooden bed, a roll of bedding and coverlet, a big wooden plank cabinet crammed full of padded cotton clothes for winter, thin summer clothes, sheets and string bags, five ceramic urns filled respectively with rice, noodles, bean noodles, cracked corn, green beans and millet, as well as a china urn of pickled vegetables, a bamboo basket full of medical records, and parcels and bundles of medicinal herbs.

We knew all too well the simplicity of Grandpa Cloud Forest's life. Throughout the winter, he had turnips for almost every meal and would frequently cook an iron wok full of them, simmering them together with rice and steamed buns. In the summertime, a meal of noodles cooked in fermented vegetable soup formed his daily staple. Folks surmised that he wasn't a monk though he lived like one. Still, we had not expected his entire worldly possessions would be as meagre as this.

"Look, is there any money under the mattress?"

"No. But there is a slip of paper, which reads: 'I didn't expect that you would be even poorer than me.' What does this mean? Was it left behind by a thief?"

I carried out a fine purplish china urn, which must be the brightest piece among all the family property. I removed the lid, but it was only an urn of clear, clean water and I know that this was meltwater gathered by Grandpa Cloud Forest in the snowy winter. "Ha, even a president doesn't have celestial water to drink," I observed.

After the adobe rooms had been emptied, Chivalry gave directions to clear away the dust, remove the dividing wall of the bedroom and redeposit the bed at the foot of the wall in the main room. He ordered me to contribute a Ming Dynasty kang table, which was put on the bed. Together, we hauled over a pair of benches capable of seating eight people from the office of the Village Committee. These extended from the bed all the way to the door.

Next, he painted the rectangular lintels and window frames with China ink mixed with clear lacquer, and daubed the four walls with brownish red paint. I had never seen people decorate walls, lintels and window frames in such a colour. Chivalry judged me to be ignorant and added: "The palace of the Kugê Kingdom was painted like this."

I gazed at him. He captivated my gaze and uttered nothing more after breaking into a smile, but his eyes shone brilliantly. What did the imperial palace of the Kingdom of Kugê look like? I had never clapped eyes on it. But the Tibetans paint their four walls brownish red and stain their lintels and window frames black. Had Grandpa Cloud Forest's shrine become the imperial palace in Benevolent Lenient Village?

After everything had been tidied up, Chivalry appeared very happy. Once again, pointing at the walls, he noted that since I knew Fan Jingquan, I should ask him to write some testimonials thanking the miraculous doctor. These could be hung as pennants, framed with glass or placed as tablets. "Do you feel a kind of mystery when you enter this room?" he enquired.

"Yeah. Then even Fatty won't dare to spew bullshit and laugh uncontrollably here."

He knelt down before the stone Buddha and beckoned me to do likewise: "Plum, the statue is very sensitive. Make a wish. Whatever your wish, it will be answered."

"Then your wanderer's heart was moved by conscience. Didn't you return to the village after you stole the stone Buddha?" As sarcastic as my mockery of him was, I still kowtowed, my ten fingernails clasped together, and petitioned in my mind: "May bodhisattva protect our village. We have already elected Chivalry as the Village Head. Let him shake off his former self and truly be a good Village Head."

While making that silent wish, Chivalry murmured in a low voice nearby: "I have walked to the four corners of China, but I still can't shake off my peasant hide. A peasant is a peasant. What place anywhere in the world would offer me shelter like my home village? Even so, the land has been devoured by the city and our village is the only one left. We cannot afford to lose our village. Let all the city residents get hepatitis and all come like pilgrims to Benevolent Lenient Village for treatment. Only in this way can we save our village and our nation. We are the Ming drum people."

I started to giggle so hard that I pitched myself over on the cattail hassock.

"Are we the Ming drum people? Why have I never heard tell of this before? Among all the Chinese peoples, how can there be such a people?"

"Just because you have never heard of it, does it mean there is no such thing?" Chivalry was obviously angry. "Our ancestor was a drummer in the army of the Ming emperor; do you know this? Our earliest ancestors' language must have been different from the local dialect. They got mixed in as time went by, but we still have the *Drum Music of the Ming Emperor*, which was passed down to us. Bear this in mind: we must have a firm belief. If anybody says a bad word about Grandpa Cloud Forest, whether they are in

Benevolent Lenient Village or anywhere else, we don't stand for it. We need to be the same way in this situation."

He was exceedingly earnest and his countenance a little foreboding. "The way you talk really does make you sound like a Village Head," I replied.

Why did he say all these things while I was praying to the stone Buddha? Did the bodhisattva answer my prayers and make him unconsciously choose to shoulder the responsibilities of a Village Head? "*Aiya, aiya,*" I shouted in my mind: "If there really is such a miraculous stone in this world, then that is a great blessing to Benevolent Lenient Village."

Hoping eagerly that everything was true and wishing to further prove it, I requested: "Bodhisattva, can you let A-Bing also come and kneel down here?" After those words had left my mouth, I was overcome with regret. Praying like this was deemed disrespectful to the bodhisattva. A god can only be trusted, but never tested.

What astounded me was that A-Bing, who had been chasing the sparrows outside, slipped in without a sound and sat down beside the cattail hassock before the stone Buddha (although he didn't actually kneel down).

Grandpa Cloud Forest's residence thus underwent a facelift. After he came back home, he only commented, "You've built a temple for me", and moved back in without objection.

It became apparent that a growing number of patients were making a beeline to Benevolent Lenient Village to have their hepatitis treated. Upon arrival, they waited in line on the wooden benches outside the house. Whether they were seeking a diagnosis or wanted a change in their prescription, they pushed the door ajar and entered when it was their turn.

Grandpa Cloud Forest was to be found perched on the *kang* in a baggy, navy blue smock with that small Ming Dynasty table of mine beside him. On both sides of the *kang*, white cloth hangings dangled down from the roof beams and on the two long wooden benches, which extended from the *kang* to the gate, would be myself, A-Shun, Gao Feng and Liuhe. We positioned ourselves opposite each other on the left and right flanks, according to Chivalry's stipulation.

We were Grandpa Cloud Forest's assistants in name only. In fact, Gao Feng and Liuhe had nothing else to do except sit cross-legged and practise *qigong*.[n] This added a kind of awe-inspiring, mysterious frisson. However, after practising medicine for three days like this, Grandpa Cloud Forest became uneasy and drove us away, leaving behind only A-Bing to keep him company.

Since A-Bing decided to follow Grandpa Cloud Forest, the old man applied a poultice to his belly and his exposed whip had retracted visibly. With every passing day, this had the effect of galvanizing his loyalty. He could command the patients to wait in line on the earthen ground by howling. When a patient left after receiving their diagnosis, he would bark *wow!* at the gate, signalling for the next one to go in. If any patient displayed too much curiosity and could not resist peering here and there after entering the room, touching this and moving that, another *wow!* would force him into line.

It was Sunday, and in the evening a film was scheduled to be shown in the village. Screening films was a tradition since the old Village Head held office, and a movie would be projected in the open air every Sunday. Now, every household had a TV and several cinemas stood not so far from the village, yet the tradition continued unabated. In this alone, the characteristics of the village may be discerned. Chivalry set me a task: ask all the people to come and watch the film and insist that Grandpa Cloud Forest be there too. I dropped by at the shrine and saw that Grandpa Cloud Forest was flogging A-Bing like a criminal.

It reminded me of a scene in a play named *Interrogating the Maiden Servant*.° After an "Ah!", old lady Cui called out for the young maiden servant. Next, the pair sang lines in alternation. The vocal work ran smoothly like drifting clouds and flowing water. But when it came to a certain pair of actors – the old man and the hound – both were mouthless gourds.

Grandpa Cloud Forest had positioned himself at the head of the *kang* and A-Bing on the cattail hassock. He was kneeling on his hind legs, his forepaws raised, and had a stinky cowhide shoe placed on his head. On entering the room, I spluttered into laughter and meant to drag A-Bing to his feet.

Grandpa Cloud Forest growled in a huff: "Have I raised this dog to be a thief and turned myself into the head of his gang? Send him back to wherever he came from. If he dares pilfer again, he should get out, out of this village."

Finally, it became clear to me. After A-Bing was taken on as Grandpa Cloud Forest's assistant, whenever a patient brought some sweets and snacks to thank the doctor, Grandpa Cloud Forest would invariably decline. The patient, after going out of the room, would ask A-Bing to grab the gifts back. A-Bing gradually became audacious and started to fetch food and drinks for Grandpa Cloud Forest from who knows where. For example, a parcel of chocolate, a bag of crunchy rice treats, as well as socks and turbans. Today, he grabbed two nearly-new cowhide shoes that belonged to the same feet. In a rage, Grandpa Cloud Forest started to reprimand him. I removed the stinky cowhide shoe from A-Bing's head, only for the dog to reposition it where it had been.

Unable to hold back and wanting to burst into laughter again at this funny spectacle of the man and the dog, I finally forced a long face and said: "OK, maybe A-Bing wants to thank you for curing his exposed whip." A-Bing barked a *wow!* in a very mild voice and darted me a glance at the same time, as if to convey "thank you". Grandpa Cloud Forest was also moved to laughter and admitted: "OK, if Plum hadn't come, you could have expected to be kneeling there until the break of day." A-Bing immediately put down his forepaws and knelt before the bed, his tail wagging, doing his damnedest to flatter.

I told Grandpa Cloud Forest to come and watch the film. He maintained he wouldn't. I explained how Chivalry had asked him along. With his presence, more people would participate and the boisterous atmosphere would make the village look like a village. Grandpa Cloud Forest hung his head, thought for a while and agreed on the condition that he made his way there independently, while I escorted A-Bing to return the cowhide shoes to their owner.

How could A-Bing still be counted as a dog? When he was adopted by Grandpa Cloud Forest, I was afraid that he wouldn't be able to look after him. I had not expected he would train him until he was more intelligent than a man. A-Bing must have been a man in his previous life, or in the eyes of Grandpa Cloud Forest, he had never been a dog to start with.

Clutching the cowhide shoes in my hand, A-Bing led me across the lanes to Little Wei's courtyard. Little Wei wasn't home, but the courtyard gate stood open and a pile of old shoes had been left out to dry on the steps. Barely had I put the cowhide shoes back in place and come out when Little Wei returned with a piss pail. On spying me, he cursed: "Sons of bitches, when you bully me you don't even choose the day according to the calendar."

"What's up?" I was shocked. "Who is bugging you? We are all neighbours. Why should we squabble with each other? Do you want others to laugh at us?"

"Just those pussies and pansies over there in the sports stadium. Those sons of bitches. With their city household registration cards,[P] do they think that makes them gentry?" In a rage, Little Wei plonked the bucket down hard, causing the bottom to unexpectedly come loose. He squatted down to fiddle it back into place and smudged his hands with filth, which he wiped against the adobe wall. "We've slathered shit and piss around their gates to see if they pay attention or not."

"I will go and have a look."

Giving him a pat on the head, I asked A-Bing to go back to the shrine and then walked to the compound at the entrance of the village where the families of the stadium staff lived. The sports stadium and the compound occupied sixty-five *mu*. The prime plot had belonged to Benevolent Lenient Village and was requisitioned in the time of the old Village Head. Requisitioning land was all well and good, but the gate of the compound stood just opposite the entrance to the village and they wanted to build a bike shed at the foot of the left outside wall. The villagers objected. By now, the only thing not to have been taken away from Benevolent Lenient Village was its shape. Everybody, with their mouths agape, wanted to swallow the village.

Unable to find out who the real estate investors that used the government's name were, we took out our wrath on the households living in this compound. For a dozen or so days, a pack of villagers had been voluntarily keeping vigil in front of their gate, screaming abuse and stating that Benevolent Lenient Village would dispute every inch of the land and protect our territory and its skies. They temporarily suspended the construction of the bike shed, but brushed off our protest.

It seemed that, in their eyes, we did not exist. Weaving hither and thither, going in and out, they were preoccupied with their own business. The old gatekeeper also swept the courtyard calmly and then crouched down behind the fence-like iron gate to play Chinese chess with several others.

Their ease and composure irritated us. When I reached that spot, in the dusk, a shiny expanse glistened in front of the compound. I knew the villagers had dumped waste water and mud in the lanes. Those who wanted to go out, however, leapt over the muddy water with their trouser legs hitched high, as if nothing had happened. The villagers had smeared the left pillar outside the gate with shit and piss and were now pouring another bucketful on the one to the right. The foul liquid splashed the gatekeeper, who was sitting inside.

"What's the use of you turning me into a heap of shit?" The gatekeeper finally opened his mouth. "If you are hard enough, come in and pour the shit and piss in front of each door."

"You don't think we dare?" A few of our neighbours wanted to go in with their piss pails.

"Don't walk into his trap," someone warned. "We go in and we've entered their turf. We wouldn't be able to defend ourselves even though right is on our side. Now we are standing on the land that belongs to Benevolent Lenient Village – who wants to risk doing anything to us? Listen, you thieves, if you don't quit building the bike shed, we'll come hurl abuse every day and change this place into a cesspool."

The song that served as the overture to the film drifted over from the village. Many were heading to the T-shaped lane with benches. On discovering that people were squabbling on this side, they thronged over and hooted blindly.

"Hi!" I walked close to the fencelike gate to greet the gatekeeper. "Who is your boss? Who is in charge here? Go ask him to come out. He should give Benevolent Lenient Village an explanation. The problem can't be put off any longer. Before very long all the villagers who want to come and watch the film will join us here. If anything happens, on your head be it."

The old gatekeeper stared at us with an expression of panic. He secured the fencelike gate with a huge lock on the inside, and then trotted to the depth of the courtyard. After a while, a guy in glasses ambled out and we whooshed over to surround him. He immediately removed his glasses, slipped them into his pocket and enquired: "Who is your head? I will only talk with the head."

These guys used to be arrogant. Now, they were afraid of us.

"I'm the boss, speak out," I bellowed.

"You must guarantee that I'll come to no harm," said the man.

"You think peasants are thugs?" I retorted. "The true thugs all live in the city. I shall escort you to see our Village Head. Benevolent Lenient Village has a new Village Head now and is no longer some motley gang."

The man and I approached the open-air cinema, accompanied by the crowd of onlookers. Someone had spirited himself over like the wind to be the first to report the news. Chivalry was already sitting waiting on an old-fashioned wooden armchair.

The man stopped and handed a cigarette to Chivalry, who waved it away, while remaining seated, and asked: "You are from the stadium?"

"My name is Hou and I'm the head of the logistics section of the stadium."

"Oh, a Section Head? I'm the Village Head and I want to see your director. Ask him to come."

The man stood there petrified. It was already dark and we could not tell the colour of his face.

Chivalry directed the projectionist to get ready, but he himself spoke into the microphone: "All fellow villagers, attention please. All fellow villagers, attention please. The director of the stadium has finally promised to negotiate with us about the bike shed dispute.

"The problem of them dumping rubbish at the entrance to our village should be solved at the same time. Our village is not a public loo; we won't allow anyone to dump filth here freely. Our village is not a plate of *tofu* either; it is not here for anyone to grab a piece of. Because of this, I tell you: if they admit their mistakes and stop intruding and harming the interests of the village, none of us, be they men or women, old or young, will go to their compound to pour waste water, dump mud or shout bad words. Whoever violates this shall be responsible for himself. This is all I have to say. Now, let the movie roll."

After these words, he instructed me: "Plum, you're the team leader. Escort the Section Head back and ask their director to come to the office of the Village Committee. I shall be waiting for him there until eight."

Having led the short stack of a director to the office of the Village Committee, I went to watch the film. How Chivalry would negotiate with him, I did not know. When the film had nearly finished, Chivalry sidled up to me with his cloth shirt draped around his shoulders and slapped his belly. He informed me that he had just come back from a restaurant and felt completely bloated.

"You haven't negotiated with the director!" I exclaimed.

"The bike shed will be torn down early tomorrow morning. Dare he go back on his word? He also invited me to the restaurant to dine. The Cantonese restaurant to the south of the stadium is really not bad and one line from the couplet at the gate reads: 'The well-fed sing happily.' Now I really am well-fed and can sing happily."

"That couplet was written by Fan Jingquan."

"Very nice work. Find a time and ask him to write a set for our village."

"That's your job. Fan Jingquan is not the Hou guy. Look, you know how to put on airs tonight. It's lucky that you're only a Village Head."

"A man needs to put on airs sometimes. A pig never grows up without putting on airs. When all is said and done, a Village Head is a government official, Plum."

Chapter Eight

It was the morning of 17th July. As I arose, the air felt sultry like a steamer. Even though I had kept the window open throughout the night, a sour stinky odour still filled the room. The shape of a human body had been left behind on the bamboo sleeping mattress, where it was soaked wet by sweat. Was that another me? I gave it two slaps and this Plum laughed at that other soulless Plum.

Then, I noticed three plump red mosquitoes still crouching in the opened mosquito net. Having sucked my blood to their hearts' content, they could no longer take wing, but I wouldn't swat them with my hands. Instead, slowly crawling close to one of them with a swatter, I made a sudden swish and a streak of dirty blood splashed across the windowpane. Was that the blood of the mosquito or mine? The foul smell was quite obnoxious.

The top of the mosquito net which had been overlaid with newspapers was sagging; another layer of clay from the roofing boards must have fallen down in the night. These 70-year-old houses were as old as Chivalry's grandpa and, moreover, large holes and cracks had appeared in the tile grooves and the eyes of the rafters. Although it wouldn't leak on a rainy day, on a moonlit night round white spots of light could penetrate through.

As I fell asleep, I always sensed they were the old executioner's eyes which focused on the spot behind people's ears. After I set up the mosquito net, the old clay pieces from the roofing boards crumbled down little by little during the night. When I got up in the morning, some landed in my mouth and I felt my teeth being chipped when I shut my gob. The mosquito net had to be positioned there from summer to winter and again from winter to summer to serve as a mudguard.

Tigers and leopards in the Western Capital zoo used to be put in iron cages for the tourists to appreciate. Now it was rumoured that the zoo was due to be converted into a safari park; tigers and leopards could roam freely while tourists appreciated them from cable cars and cages. When that comes to pass, will it be that the people appreciate the tigers and the leopards or vice versa?

I must press on and start reading Book Five of the syllabus for the correspondence course. Barefoot, I hopped over to take a shower under the tap, seeking to rid myself of the coating of sticky, greasy sweat. The mirror got to see everything. Book Five was all Classical Chinese. Did the ancients really speak like that? Last night, I read through *Six Records of a Floating Life*.[q] Yun,[r] the most loveable girl in the world, surely set the mood. Was that mosquito a crane in the eyes of her and her husband? Why should I be arsed with these correspondence courses? Someone who had taken a correspondence course wasn't guaranteed a job after graduation and an academic diploma was of no use in Benevolent Lenient Village. I must have been naive back then, believing that I should uphold the scholarly tradition of my family, believing that I would be a good match for Old Ran, believing that I should be able to have something in common with him. Even if I did become a learned woman, how could I bear to live together with a man devoid of appeal?

Standing before the mirror, I gazed at myself at length. Brow once said: "Sister Plum, get rid of those few black moles and you'd be the most beautiful one of all." I'm not beautiful. I have seven black moles. Looking at me is akin to studying the heavenly constellations. I turned and sat down on the Chinese oak wood pillow-cum-bench to smoke a cigarette. This was a genuine item of Ming-style furniture.

On that day when I escorted Brow to have an abortion, she wept for her father and mother in great agony in the operating room. I sat on a long bench outside pitying her and blaming her; since you chose to do it before you got married, why didn't you take precautions? You insisted that this divorced man was good in every respect, but when, on his account, you were suffering the pain of blood and flesh being wrenched from your body, Shao still had to go scurrying along to do his sales pitch because some company wanted to buy his fitness equipment.

When Brow screamed as if she was being slaughtered, I encouraged her with my hands balled into fists. When her screaming finally let up, the two bottles of yoghurt in my hands were squashed and my legs and feet were dripping all over with pus-like milk. I helped Brow to shamble out and it was not until we reached the street outside the hospital that Shao hurried over. He smiled apologetically at me. I gave him the cold shoulder.

Brow winced. "A bloody lump the size of a fist," she murmured like a spoilt, pampered little girl. Cheap Brow! I looked at the Shao guy. He was a fitness equipment salesman and yet was as sturdy as an ox. He was inflicting damage on her. He didn't say thank you until I reached his home with Brow. But at that moment it was he who whipped out that Chinese oak wood pillow-cum-bench.

Having smoked one cigarette, I still didn't feel clear-minded and so lit another one. I'd been a smoker for five years. Chivalry moaned to me three years ago: "If you go on smoking, you won't find a husband." But I persisted. When I became sweet on Old Ran, I announced that I was a smoker. Old Ran replied: "I don't smoke, but I love watching women smoking." His words told me that he was a wimp and he would end up being a hen-pecked wimp. Anyhow, a woman is a woman. She hopes that her husband will respect her and give her freedom, though she hopes, even more than that, that her husband can keep her under control.

The mice were running amok on the crossbeam again. This rabble of animals must have become accustomed to my early morning smoking and had probably grown addicted to tobacco. It was good that, on this as-dead-as-a-doornail morning, a band of mice were keeping a mature girl company in her boudoir. I smoked and they breathed in what I exhaled.

The traffic on those big streets in the city proper must have been heavy because the rush hour had arrived and the booming noises of people and vehicles, which floated over here like the wind, hammered home the point. These noises didn't belong to Benevolent Lenient Village.

With a kettle in my hand, I scaled a ladder to the platform of the gate awning to water the flowers. Gazing into the distance, I could see that men were still sleeping tight with their heads buried under the sheets on the wooden planks spread out on the sloping roofs of their old houses or in the hammocks hanging between three or four neighbouring elm trees. Last night, these guys played Chinese chess raucously in front of the gate of the stadium compound and outside those work units and departments nearby. Now, they slept like logs.

After raising merry hell before the stadium compound, we came back home victorious, soon realising, however, that as victors we should show the broadmindedness and peace-loving character of Benevolent Lenient Village.

Chivalry called upon those villagers who enjoyed playing chess to establish a better rapport with their neighbours by sharing a game. Now, they were still in a dead slumber. What else could they do? The villagers had lost their land as well as their jobs. Should they go to the South of China to be factory fodder, spiking shoes, fixing umbrellas, making clothes and mending woks like those southerners did in the Western Capital? They were accustomed to noodles and pepper and they didn't eat rice and seafood. What's more they looked down on those piddling little jobs.

There were too many large courtyards in Benevolent Lenient Village and too many unoccupied rooms inside the courtyards, which could be rented out to workers from the factories, mines, enterprises and government units in the vicinity. On top of that, Grandpa Cloud Forest had changed the village into an infirmary so we could live a life of ease and comfort.

"Careful, Lianben! One wrong move and you'll fall down."

"How could that be? I've been sleeping here the whole summer long. Mosquitoes can't dig in their needles and it is well-ventilated. More comfortable than you city guys are."

"What, are there mosquitoes in the city? And you're saying that even with air-conditioning, you need to be afraid of the heat?"

"*Yi*, an emperor looks down on the beggars, but the feeling is mutual. You city guys swarm to work at this time like bees, while we are still sleeping with our cocks directed skywards."

"Nice words, Lianben. Pigs sleep through the day too."

I ducked my head. Fan Jingquan was making his way along the lane, smiling while clutching his arms.

"Mr Fan, it's so early. Why have you come to the village?"

"*Xiah*, early bird Plum! I have a three-day holiday and came to Old Ran's home to write novels yesterday."

"What holy book are you writing that you need to look for so quiet a spot? I was thinking of going to your place to ask you to teach me Classical Chinese."

"I'm sure you're not just coming to me for Classical Chinese."

"I respect you as my teacher. How can you make fun of me?"

"OK, OK. But, mind you, Old Ran's sister-in-law grunts that you haven't been to her home for a long time and now she has a bellyful of gripes."

"Her arm reaches so far and wide. Such a tigress. But I'm not afraid of her."

"If you are not afraid of her, drop by at noon for a chat."

"First things first, let's make one thing clear: I won't listen to you reading your novels."

Looking back over my shoulder, I spotted the patient boarding at my home standing under the gate awning. The woman's husband hadn't arisen yet and she was drenching her face at the water pipe in the courtyard. "Should I ask Grandpa Cloud Forest to change the prescription today?" she asked me. Since her husband was on the mend, her face had brightened up too and her voice had become clear and loud. Yesterday afternoon, she sang several Qinghai flower songs for me. A corner of her upper garment hadn't been hitched down, leaving her cloth belt exposed. This had a lump of stone pinned on it.

"How does Old Xue feel this morning? I didn't hear his usual long sigh." At midnight or early in the morning, the man would heave an "Ah...". Seemingly, there was a stream of foul air in his belly and only this long "Ah..." could relieve the exhaustion from his bones and joints.

"What are you wearing? A piece of jade?"

"Yeah, it's called a Ghost Head. It can drive away evil."

The woman hitched her upper garment back into place and, feeling a little embarrassed, removed the Ghost Head. "Where I come from, the police officers each carry a chunk of this stuff on them. Look, what a nice piece of jade, but the ghost engraved on it is ugly. A ghost is the same as a man: the more handsome he is the more devilish and sinister he looks. But ugliness can ward off evil. An ugly man is also a blessed man."

"Then I am blessed?" I inspected the Ghost Head. The lump of rock appeared darkish green while the protruding cheekbones of the ghost were black like China ink. Grandpa Cloud Forest was ugly and so was Chivalry. That might prove a source of blessings for Benevolent Lenient Village. But Brow found the rich guy Old Shao because she was beautiful and A-Bing had a narrow escape for the same reason.

The patient in the lean-to started to cough so violently it was as if he were losing his breath and preparing to leave this world. The ruddy-cheeked Qinghai woman and I stopped talking and waited for the man to regain his breath. *Kakaka... pooh!* A mouthful of phlegm flew out of the small window. The man was a good sort, except that he wiped nasal mucus and spat phlegm everywhere. His woman, feeling it was an eyesore, blamed him many a time, though he invariably slid back into the bad habit. Reaching his head out of the window and catching sight of me, he uttered in embarrassment: "I can never follow the rules of you city guys."

"This is not the city," I asserted.

The man flashed me a smile and instructed: "Xiu, Xiu, shovel the phlegm off."

The woman did as she was told and, trying to conceal their awkwardness, enquired: "Will Grandpa Cloud Forest issue a fresh prescription today?"

I led them to the shrine. The man refused to allow anyone else to give him a hand and walked unaided, flailing to the left and to the right and floating in his floppy clothing like a man made of paper.

The residents of the village had almost got up. As per usual, some were going to slop out their chamber pots, some were sweeping courtyards, some were standing under the honey-locust trees in front of their gates rinsing their foamy mouths and the lion's share were sitting in a semi-wakeful trance on their thresholds, their eyelids glued together by sleep, their legs and heads under the onslaught of mosquitoes. As they raised their hands to swat them, they observed: "Another bright red day."

Those who were wandering about the lanes were mostly the patients who boarded in the local households. When the patients scattered into different places, we didn't think much of it. But if you came to Benevolent Lenient Village in the morning, you would be taken aback and wonder: what's wrong with the human race? Are they all disease-stricken? Have they all contracted hepatitis? So many victims have gathered together here. Is it because fellow sufferers want to commiserate with one another? Or it is because, it is only when they suffer from a disease that they learn how to cherish these adobe lanes and villages and cherish these dustless, noiseless mornings? Whoever they bumped into, they would force out a smile and pause to give way, being as modest and as self-disciplined as a gentleman.

At this moment, I saw A-Bing paddle up from the small lane and cock up his hind leg to take a leak at the foot of a wall. "A-Bing, A-Bing!" At the sight of me, A-Bing retrieved his leg and started to trot over before going back to scratch some dirt with a hind paw to cover over the piss-stained ground. He then resumed his trotting. The ruddy-cheeked woman swiftly stepped aside to let him by.

"Don't be so polite," I maintained. "A-Bing, are you here to collect us?" A-Bing wagged his tail and barked *wow!* I beamed and asked the patient to follow the dog to where he was going. Sure enough, A-Bing turned his head and walked away.

"The dog is intelligent," deduced the woman. "When I lived in my home village, my aunt lived in the city. Many cats and dogs were raised there. They were waited on more carefully than the people were. But the cats no longer caught mice and dogs no longer bit thieves. Should they still be classed as cats and dogs? Dogs in this city of yours are still dogs."

I reminded her: "Our place doesn't belong to the city. You two always talk in this way. Does a city have adobe lanes like this? Had you come to Benevolent Lenient Village in the past, you would know that trees used to stand everywhere here. Beyond the trees lay alfalfa plots. You should have seen the fragrant dishes we cooked from alfalfa.

"When I was young, our village was haunted by wolves. A huge white circle was drawn on this wall with lime and the sight of it at night was enough to scare away the predators. In the busy scorching days during May and June, Indian cuckoos would mimic the sound of ripening and reaping through the nights. You always say our place is part of the city. Is it because it doesn't look like the countryside and it doesn't look like the city either? We are now at the point of getting jumbled up."

The woman looked at me in surprise, somehow resembling a little girl. I suppressed my excitable thoughts, grinned at her and reached out a hand to wipe clean the sleep from the corners of her eyes. She, blushing immediately, took out a small round mirror from her chest and peered into it.

At this second, a fly darted at me head-on as it zoomed towards the public lavatory. Bored to death, I asked: "Say, how old do you think it is?"

The woman answered: "I don't know."

"A living cultural object, descended from the Ming Dynasty." After having said that and feeling regretful, I fobbed her off with nonsensical questions and queried her about the customs and traditions in Qinghai. As a landlocked region, why was it called Qinghai, meaning "black sea" in Chinese? She replied that it was maybe because there were salt lakes there.

Qinghai natives liked saying the word *hai* and anything big was referred to as *hai*. For example, a big bowl was a *hai wan* and whoever was judged to be strong was very *hai*. I asked her if the cities in Qinghai had villages in their urban areas like Benevolent Lenient Village. She stated that they didn't. The suburbs were the suburbs and they had all become rich now, but many fugitive whores boarded there. When the long-distance truck drivers came at night, you could hear them say: "Twenty yuan. We're downstairs with boiling water." Their words gave you goose bumps.

There was the sound of arguing from the courtyard on the left side of the lane. The words were indistinguishable, but the voices were shrilly audible and next – *clatter, clatter* – a pinkish stiletto was flung over a wall, causing the heel to snap. That shoe belonged to Brow. She alone in the village wore such garish high-heeled shoes. I asked the

Qinghai woman to stay put and walked around the wall to push the gate of Brow's courtyard.

Brow, her face painted heavily with rouge and powder even though her hair had not yet been combed, was standing on this side of the party wall and cursing: "None of your family was in yesterday, so why couldn't I go to get registered? If all your family die, will the patients have nowhere to lodge while they receive their treatments?"

The woman on the other side of the squat wall, being small in stature, was standing on an upside-down crate slapping her fat buttocks. "You scramble for men and for patients as well?" She tossed away the other pinkish stiletto that had been left out to dry on the squat wall.

Brow shrieked: "Just carry on. Come burn down my house!"

"Whoever puts her shoes on my wall, I will throw away the broken shoes."[5]

Brow was angry and about to pounce. I dived over, pushed Brow to one side and said that neither of them ought to be so foul-mouthed. Were they acting in this way early in the morning because they thought it would bring auspiciousness or because it sounded good? The sight of me sent Brow into tears and words failed her.

"Plum is your friend," the woman leered. "Now the puppy can use its master to scare its enemies. You pretend to be wronged. Plum, each family has two registration numbers every month and she has already had two patients boarding at her home. It serves her right that her patients did not have a serious disease and left after ten days. She tried to register the two numbers allocated to my family. In the clear light of day, she lives in this village and so do I. What right does she have to pull the food out of my mouth? What right do you have? Is it because of your water snake waist? Your long legs? Go snare those wild men. What food can't you eat?"

I lost my temper too, yelling: "Your words are ugly, aren't they? One more cuss and I will tell Grandpa Cloud Forest. What is more, I'll ask the Village Head to come. Your family will never have another chance to be given registration numbers."

Deflated, the woman rattled on: "Plum, you take it on yourself to uphold justice. Me losing my patients for a month over nothing! I have three school age children and my mother is a cripple. Should I let my family drink wind and shit farts?"

I interjected with: "Next month, you can have Brow's registration numbers. This is my last word. Is that OK?"

"You said it. Your words are water that has been poured out – impossible to take back."

"She cursed me and that's it?" Brow wailed. "Her mouth is as filthy as an arsehole. How can she drench me in shit, just as she sees fit to."

The woman cockily strutted to her main room while saying: "I can't swear at a good guy, but can't I lay into a bad one? *Pooh, pooh, pooh!*" She went inside and shut the gate.

I hauled Brow to her room. "Why nick her registration numbers? Short of money?"

"My lean-tos are empty and when there are patients boarding there, they can also take care of my house."

Upon entering, I found the pot-bellied salesman Shao splayed at the head of the bed chain-smoking. On catching sight of me, the Shao guy kicked his dirty tissues under the bed and pronounced: "I asked Brow not to live here, but she's dug her heels in. Living in a flat in the city, no one minds about other people's business. How carefree your mind can be then." I brushed him aside.

Chapter Nine

Chivalry ran into me in the lane with the question: "Have you eaten?"

"Since you're the Village Head now can't you act a little more civilised?" I responded. "What era are we living in now? You still go around greeting people in the old-fashioned way. If the villagers still greet each other by asking 'Have you eaten?' it implies you are not a qualified Village Head and can't even assure people of a hand-to-mouth existence." On hearing this, Chivalry pressed his palms together and declared: "Nice words, nice words. Plum, what are you busy doing today?"

"True enough," I commented with a smile. "Reading."

"Reading?"

"Reading is our family tradition!"

"Yi, you sound like the offspring of a great West Guan-zhong scholar. So highfalutin."

My face reddened at his words. "That's a line from Du Fu."t

"You might be classed as an intellectual too. As far as I see it, out of all the women in the village you are the only one who's well-cultivated. Different families nurture different kinds of people. The Village Head in me wants to find an important role for you. You can be a team leader."

"A team leader?" I said with a laugh. "Who can select me as team leader?"

"I'm the Village Head and I can appoint whoever I want. That's the deal."

I tried to stall him, saying it was too easy to be an official.

"I'm serious," he persisted. "Come to the office of the Village Committee tonight with a bottle of the hard stuff."

"*Xiah*, are you asking me to offer up a tribute? If you want me to give bribes, you should allow me to do it off my own bat. If you ask for bribes like this, I can't stomach it."

"The Village Committee will hold a meeting tonight. You bring the liquor. We'll discuss village business while drinking and I'll take the opportunity to announce you as the new team leader. It should make everyone happy."

I walked past him, smirking. He accosted me and asked in a low voice: "No longer hot on Old Ran?"

"Who is gossiping about me now?"

"It's said that a woman will make herself up for her beloved, but you haven't changed at all."

"What should I do to make people think I've changed?"

"Wear pretty clothes and slap on some make-up. A woman is a true woman when she seems the total opposite of a man."

"Do you want to make me a team leader or the public relations beauty queen?"

"You represent Benevolent Lenient Village whenever you go out and about. Our village should be able to boast some beauties."

"We're fighting against the city slickers. How could we follow their dress style?"

"Should I always dress like Chen Yonggui,[u] the farmer-premier from the old days? Should women have bound feet and put on old-fashioned padded cotton coats with buttons down the front when they go to take on the city?"

"OK, I shall find time to buy a few fashionable outfits. You shouldn't say that I am too gaudy."

"You should go downtown today."

"I ought to go to Old Ran's home first. Fan Jingquan is

there and I need to ask for his help with my correspondence courses."

"To Old Ran's home?" Chivalry's face suddenly darkened and he squatted on his haunches to write a word for me. It was a 田 (*tian*, "field").

"Do you recognise this?" he probed.

I nodded my head. "Yeah."

He used his hand to cover the upper half of the character and then the lower half, next the left half and then the right half, then asked: "Do you still know it?"

"You cover its upper half, it makes a *ri* ("fuck"), cover the lower half, also a *ri*, cover the left half, still a *ri*, and cover the right half, a *ri* again. What do you want to say?"

Chivalry knocked at my temple with a finger and pointed out that people of one family think in the same way. Still feeling in the dark, as if I were struggling to reach up and touch the head of a 12-foot-high statue of Vajrapani, I demanded to know what he was driving at.

"Go and tell your Old Ran. If I was not the Village Head, I wouldn't care about anything. But now I am the Village Head, whenever anybody raises his tail I know already what type of fart he is going to release. If Old Ran still refuses to remove the foundations of those rooms, he may as well be a tiger for all I care. In that case, I'd become the tiger-killer Wu Song."[v]

I didn't know what had happened at Old Ran's home to make Chivalry so angry. But Old Ran's sister-in-law, a cunning and wicked Sichuan woman, had more than once taught me a lesson.

When I reached the gate of his courtyard, nobody knew how but that arm-thick persimmon tree in front of the left gatepost had withered to become stiff and leafless. The courtyard wall near the lane had half tumbled down and somebody had cobbled together a makeshift fence out of a few sundry purlins with disorderly cotton wadding and tattered shoes piled on top. The two panels of the gate didn't meet in the middle and when I pushed them open, no sound was produced.

Where had they gone? Old Ran's sister-in-law wasn't in. An unfinished rope hung down from the bolt in the main room. Fan Jingquan was sitting behind the sash window of the lean-to writing. Barely had I gotten ready to creep over there to give him a start, when a brood of chickens began to cluck in the courtyard. Fan raised his head and spied me. He came out and stood on the steps smirking.

"The guys in the village are restless like headless flies, but you are still at leisure," I noted.

"It won't bore me to death. Three pages finished and three pages ripped out. My brain has become like a pig's! I was thinking just now that if you didn't come, I'd need to go to a song and dance hall in the city to find an escort."

"*Xiah*, how could my teacher have morals like that?"

"What's wrong? It would just be to help drive away my loneliness. Society has progressed. Sex now has nothing to do with morality."

"Well done. But why is your hair already white when you still haven't found a wife? I don't know what is on the minds of you men. What's the fun of going after escorts if there is no emotional dimension to it?"

"You've never had that experience and you don't know the feeling. Last year when I went to a song and dance hall for the first time, a friend found me a working girl there. Just as I was pondering how to strike up a conversation and how to create a warm feeling, she said: 'Will you do it or not? If not, I shall leave. There are plenty of others waiting outside.' You see, Ran and I…"

"Don't drag him into this."

"Ran had never been to a song and dance hall before that. Shouldn't we talk about Ran in Ran's home?"

"If I don't allow it, you should stop."

I took out the correspondence course book and tossed it on the desk, requesting that he teach me Classical Chinese. Fan Jingquan surveyed me and packed away his playfulness. We two became student and teacher. Even so, he wouldn't let it lie, and, after tutoring me for a while, started to grumble: "This teacher of yours has become a slave." After a while longer, he groused: "When giving lectures to a student, even Confucius would ask for three strings of salted meat."

"Let Old Ran's sister-in-law cook something nice for you."

"Don't you call Ran's sister-in-law your sister-in-law?"

"Did Confucius give lectures in such a distracted way?"

As he continued to explicate the text, a slapping sound could be heard from the courtyard. Next came the deafening shout of Old Ran's sister-in-law: "Mr Fan, come out and help catch the yellow hen."

I went out. A woman in a sloppy, colourful blouse was leaning against the door frame of the courtyard, clapping a shoe against her shin to get rid of the sand and dirt inside. Her face was drenched in sweat. I chased the yellow hen around the yard, caught hold of the fowl and handed it to her. She shoved a finger into the bird's anus, poked around and confirmed: "Mr Fan, the yellow one is with egg today. Once she's laid, I'll make pancakes for lunch. Plum, when did you get here?"

"Just now." Since her response was indifferent, my reply was deliberately cold. "To ask my Teacher to tutor me."

"Plum is busy now making her way, running here and there behind the Village Head. She seldom comes to eat my sticky cornmeal jelly."

She placed the hen on the nest, employed a bamboo basket to cage it in and fixed me with a gaping mouth. A coating of fine hair was visible growing on her upper lip.

"You don't wear the leather shoes my brother bought for you?"

"The shoes are too small; they pinch my feet."

"The more you run, the roomier your shoes will become."

Fan Jingquan stepped outside, halted under the apricot tree and beamed at us, doing nothing more than smile.

"Plum, I have been here for just two days yet your sister-in-law has mentioned your name seven or eight times."

"I'm cheap. Ran lives apart from us, but I always worry about him. A man shouldn't read too many books. The more you read, the more mule-headed you will become. Originally, he only loved collecting old furniture. But now, the more he collects, the less he leaves behind at home."

"He stores his collection at my place. If you want, I can bring them here for you."

"I didn't say that! Not at all. See, Mr Fan, I've fallen foul of people again."

Anger choked me, making me unwilling to let Fan Jingquan see my face, so I paced to the latrine in the rear left corner of the courtyard. Formerly a brushwood and hay shed combined, a plot planted with coriander and garlic shoots had once stood in front of the latrine. Now, all that had been turfed out to make space for the three lean-tos. The wooden pegs which marked where the foundations should have been were plucked out, leaving behind a half tumbled down brick wall.

Out of the blue, I recalled Chivalry's words and, standing in the latrine, enquired: "You want to build lean-tos?"

The woman immediately ran over and, halting outside the latrine, answered: "Sure, I want to build three lean-tos."

"Your house is already spacious. What do you lack? We farmers only know when we have money we should build houses."

"Even though you're taking correspondence courses, you still manage to be so short-sighted? When the low-lying land to the west of our village started to be renewed, some people were far-sighted and some were short-sighted. Although their old courtyards are all the same size, the new houses given to them as compensation vary. You still don't understand?"

"I don't. Before I came here, the Village Head held a meeting to discuss the problem of houses being built willy-nilly. Clean up the mess early, so that more humiliating things don't crop up later on."

A Chinese toon tree grew by the latrine, its trunk caked in a layer of dried yellow shit by people wiping their arses against it. Feeling disgusted, I strode out to the standpipe to wash my hands. Following me, the woman asked: "You knew Chivalry's been around to browbeat me?"

"Yeah."

"You knew this and you didn't take my side? Mr Fan, give us your comments. Houses are not allowed to be built willy-nilly in the city. Should it be the same in the countryside? Can't I build my own rooms in my own courtyard? That bastard Chivalry will die without any kids, he will never find a wife as long as he lives. He doesn't go around building houses and he doesn't allow others to do so. Who are the rooms being built for? Aren't they for you Plum and that brother of mine?"

"I don't care!" I replied, recalling the 田 (*tian*, "field") character written out by Chivalry. "Can't the others see what is in your heart? The folks are protecting the village and so what about you? You are building rooms, waiting for the day when they are to be razed. Each demolished room is compensated for with one new room. That way you can extort more floorspace in compensation. But your haste suggests that you expect the village will be demolished as soon as possible. Don't all people's hearts get led astray?"

"Exactly so. What's the good of preserving this village? Tumbledown houses like this, no heating, no bath water, no sewerage, clay brick walls and clay brick roofs. Are they as comfortable as the foreign-style buildings in the city? Muffle your heart and tell me: which is better, being a peasant or being a city dweller?"

"Though you might live in the city, you're still a peasant."

"Yeah, as long as I'm a city dweller and providing I've got an education, I can look for a job. If you don't think that way, why do you take correspondence courses?"

"I won't carry on with them then." With an angry swish of my arm, I went into the lean-to. "If you have the guts, go look for the Village Head."

The woman remained in the courtyard, apparently stunned. Then suddenly she started to laugh a dry, stiff laugh. Later, she added: "Why should I argue with you? I'm nuts! Do I want to let Ran start on at me again when he comes back? Plum, my guts are bolt straight. Don't be angry with me. I will go to the shop to buy a blouse and, if Ran comes back, don't spill the beans."

She brought a vacuum flask of boiled water to the lean-to and said: "Drink this when you're thirsty." She unwound her turban to pat the dust from her body and feet and went out.

Momentarily unable to regain myself, I put away my correspondence course book. "I won't study this. What's the use?" Fan Jingquan, however, peered at me and gasped: "It's funny, so funny."

"Where's the fun?" I wondered, smiling unconsciously. "Why should I be angry with her? Come, read your novel for my benefit."

"I haven't the barest outline yet," he explained. "I'm only here to conduct research. But now I can really try my hand at writing novels. Benevolent Lenient Village has offered up too much raw material." Later on, when Fan's only novel to be accepted by a publisher was released, I found that one chapter concerned an author talking about literature with a woman who dwelt in a village on the hinterland between the city and the countryside. That was exactly what transpired between me and him that day. The novel proceeded as follows:

We have been talking for a long time. The baking hot sun has tumbled down from the eaves and again slunk down the steps; a cicada in the apricot tree in front of the window is buzzing in a stiff drone.

The woman has been listening to me with her hands resting on her knees. Later, she stretches herself and lies on her side on the quilt on the edge of the bed. "May I lie down and read the raw materials?" she asks.

"Of course," I reply. "You read my book and I will watch you."

She reads for a while – I know she isn't into it – and asks: "Are the characters in your novel all taken from life?"

"They are written according to the stories of real-life people."

"According to? How much so?"

"When I first kick the ball rolling, I will always think of a genuine person, but next the character under my pen is trans-

formed so that sometimes it doesn't bear the least resemblance to its prototype."

"Generally speaking, only the minor characters will be anchored directly in real life."

"So far, which novel of yours do you think is the best?"

"I don't expect this novel will cure me of the belief that there is no need to write another one. Now I still have nothing to my name because I believe my greatest piece is the one I'm working on."

"What makes a good novelist?"

"A writer should first observe society and study the state of society. His observations should be worked into his novel. How many of his observations in the novel will become a part of the history that is taking shape today? That is the value of the novel itself."

"Then how can one be a good novelist?"

"A writer must see through the dramatic events of his time. When he can do or knows what he should do, he should resolutely take a side. That having been said, he should also constantly keep a certain distance from history. If he must share in a disaster of his time, he should simultaneously stay clear of the disaster so that he can study it and give it a form. On the one hand, renounce those who should be renounced and hate evil resolutely as one does one's enemy; on the other hand, eulogise those who should be eulogised."

"Nice words. But I have read your novels – a small part of them, at least. Why is it that they don't arouse people's attention? Most of them haven't been published, have they, and the editorial department rejected them?"

"Because the contemporary world of letters is smug within its own ivory tower, and novels have lost their purpose."

"True enough, but why do you still write? Will you succeed, do you think?"

"In the last instance, my works may bring success or failure, just like my life itself. But I keep on telling myself: if, as a result of my lifelong struggle, I can lighten or lessen all kinds of heavy shackles which people bear, then I'm correct and I can forgive myself."

I wasn't aware of how much time had elapsed but heard Fan Jingquan's stomach rumble several times. Not until now did I catch Old Ran's sister-in-law talking at the top of her voice in the lane. Her neighbour, the never-serious Uncle Six Pounds, who might very well have been roosting in the Chinese wisteria trellis at the head of the courtyard gate pruning, poked fun at her as she paraded a pair of high-heels with her hair up in a bun. "Are you an eighteen-year-old girl?" She cursed back: "Do you stand so high up there so that you can sneer down at women. Be careful, your daughter-in-law might gouge out that sack of yours." She entered the courtyard through the gate and called out softly: "Ran, Ran."

Fan Jingquan stuck his head out of the window and said he hadn't seen Old Ran come back.

"Who are you talking to so loudly?"

"Plum."

"Plum hasn't left yet! Fine. Plum, see what shoes your sister-in-law has on? How is it that Shanghai people's feet aren't able to grow? Their shoes are so narrow."

I deliberately didn't go out. The woman removed her shoes, changed into slippers and, as she scuttled to the kitchen, shouted: "It's too late, too late. I should make pancakes and then cook sticky cornmeal jelly."

By the time Old Ran came back, the food was done to a turn. On seeing me in the lean-to, he exclaimed happily:

"You've come. Carry on with your studies. I shall chip in in the kitchen."

A while later, he summoned me to come and collect the dishes. I stepped inside the kitchen, his sister-in-law flounced over to the water pipe to wash her face and he chimed in: "Our sister-in-law said you've been here for hours and hours."

"Yeah."

"Fan came here for the quiet to do some writing. How could you chat and laugh with him for so long?"

"We have common topics to talk about."

"What have you been debating?"

"*The Art of War* by Sunzi."[W]

"*The Art of War*?"

"The ninth article of the book: a quick battle forces a quick decision."

I flung the chopsticks away and left the courtyard in a fit of pique. No matter how he pleaded, I gave him the cold shoulder.

Chapter Ten

Crouching at the head of the four big lanes in Benevolent Lenient Village were eight bluish-white boulders which, in bygone days, were used to help people mount their steeds. It was said that four stone drums also once stood at the head of the lanes. Nobody was supposed to ride into the village; the procedure was that they should stop before the stone drums and tie their reins to the horse-hitching stakes or the hoops in the wall. When it was time to depart, they unfastened the reins and stepped on to one of the horse-mounting stones to get into the saddle. Now every trace of the practice had vanished, except for those bluish-white stones.

Every day, aged villagers sat there playing sliver cards. Having lived in the village for a lifetime, the matter they talked about most frequently was how the City God Temple Fair was no longer staged in the Western Capital. They also mithered about the razing of the Bodhisattva Temple in the village. The wandering pigs, chickens and cats were all so familiar to them that they could pick out which one belonged to such-and-such family. Whenever a stranger turned up, they would be sure to move forward and ask: "You have come here looking for whom? Are you a relative or kinsman or friend of…?" They would then escort the stranger to that family. Few thieves bothered our village. All these matters, we told others with great gusto. That selling agent Shao and even the fat policeman had to concede that.

Shao once entrusted me to find a few home-helps from the village for his boss friends. It was such a pity that all the girls came back within a month. On the one hand, they were all impatient and couldn't adapt to urban life because they had nobody to talk with; on the other, their employers loathed the fact they were all chatterboxes. They frequently engaged in idle talk with the neighbours, which then stirred things up. After all, a country cousin is a country cousin, and there is no helping them.

Last spring, Lianben's father reached the end of his life's journey. A-Shun's mother went to make the funeral clothes and to deep-fry wheat flour buns as a sacrificial offering. She was the only one who could handle this business. Of all the people in the village, she wanted to pass this skill down to me and asked me to lend a hand. Lianben, however, quarrelled with his brother over the division of the family property and the old Village Head was called in to uphold justice. By noon, everything was settled.

While the brothers treated us to liquor in the courtyard, someone came in and told the old Village Head: "Gao Feng and Third Boy are having a scrap." The old Village Head blustered: "Fellow villagers, fighting over what? Tear them apart."

The man went away, but ran back after a while and reported: "Gao Feng has wounded Third Boy."

"That bandit Gao Feng," the old Village Head replied. "Then get a move on and send him to the hospital."

The man went out and, after another while, ran in again: "Third Boy is unconscious."

The old Village Head asked: "He has lost his life? Then report it to the police station."

He was used to this kind of business and ran the village with a policy of governance without interference. I ran out to take a look. Nobody had lost his life. Third Boy had regained his breath slowly and, his head drenched in blood like a ram after a fight, was already being helped back home by others.

I returned to the lane where I lodged in a huff. The women there were calm, perching on their respective thresholds sorting through vegetables or doing needlework. They passed a few comments about the fight before going on to gossip about how, although a certain family that lived to the east of the village led a good existence, they had only two daughters and no son. Why couldn't they have a son? If they had earned less money, they would have had one because life is never perfect. Then they said that a certain household in the west had too many children because the wife looked like the pit of a date.

Next, another woman observed: "Little Wei's woman has a wasp-sized waist and small buttocks. How can she give birth?"

Another one cut in: "She's not to blame. The problem lies with the man. When the other men take a pee, they must use both hands to hold it. It's said that when Little Wei takes a piss, he only uses two fingers like he's clasping a cigarette."

A third one said: "Then she needs to borrow some seed."

They put aside their work and counted their fingers, saying who was good in that regard, who was not good and who appeared good but in fact was useless. Then they cackled loudly.

This summer, however, Little Wei's woman did give birth to a chubby, fair-skinned baby son. Little Wei laid on a banquet at home for relatives and friends, and people were heard drinking and playing finger-guessing games in his house every day.

When the baby was a month old, on the third day after the football riot, Little Wei went out with the baby to find him a godfather. It was the break of dawn and nobody was around.

According to the local custom, on that day one must step out with the baby and whoever you run into will become the baby's godfather. Throughout his life, the godson should give his godfather gifts at Chinese New Year and on any festival, and the godfather should give his godson three feet of red cloth, a parcel of red sugar, ten red eggs for luck[x] and twenty yuan at the very moment they first ran into him.

Nobody was hanging around on that day. Little Wei went on with the baby in his arms, thinking that if still nobody came out, he would have to accept the deserted grinding stone before him as the baby's godfather. At that very second, A-Bing came padding out of Grandpa Cloud Forest's home. Little Wei deftly carried the baby, knelt down and pressed the baby's forehead on the ground, proclaiming: "My son's godfather is a dog."

He waved his hand and called: "A-Bing."

A-Bing stood motionless and looked his way.

Little Wei called out: "A-Bing, this is your godson." With his eyes rolling, A-Bing leapt on to a short courtyard wall nearby, walked across the tile grooves to bypass Little Wei, jumped down softly and wafted away like a stream of wind. But anyhow, Little Wei announced in the village that the baby's godfather was A-Bing.

Though this godfather didn't give his son any gifts to acknowledge the relationship, the whole family displayed great solicitude to him from then on. One time, someone in the stadium muttered a disrespectful word about Grandpa Cloud Forest and A-Bing. Little Wei and his wife ambushed that guy and gave him some hearty slaps across his face.

Nevertheless, from then on, things became messed up. When Little Wei's woman went out with her baby – who was given the name Puppy Wei – someone would pull her leg and ask the baby to call him "Sire." "Let your Sire hold you."

To begin with their teasing was a joke, and Little Wei's woman didn't feel annoyed but, later on, it became a stream of wind as people implied the kid was not the seed of Little Wei. His sense of disgrace giving way to rage, Little Wei roughed his wife up at home, gripping her hair to pound her head against the edge of the bed and pressing her to admit whose child this was.

Today, unable to suppress her anger as she woke up, the woman set herself upon an earthen mound on the village road and hurled abuse loudly at the bitches who gossiped about her, cursing that they should be slain by the heavens, that they should be struck by thunderbolts, that they should be infected with plague, that they should get kidnapped and be shot with bullets.

The female rumour-mongers in the next lane nestled on their thresholds trading hearsay as usual as they combed their hair.

"Did you hear, last night there was rowing again in Little Wei's house?"

"They have no peace in their lives. The family is crumbling."

"A man is a rake and a woman is a box. No matter how hard Little Wei sweeps in money, how can their family not crumble when his woman spends money like Brow? Yesterday, I went to his house to borrow a sieve and the family was forcing down noodles cooked in cracked corn soup. *Tut-tut*, how can people still eat noodles cooked in cracked corn soup?"

"Only one baby and see what a wretched life they lead. Her body is smudged all over with piss stains and shit marks. Have you ever noticed her feet? A pair of leather shoes, yes, but they mustn't have been cleaned for three months."

While they were chirping gossip with hilarity, they heard Little Wei's wife cursing in the lane and stretched out their heads to take a look. The wasp-waisted woman, facing their direction with one hand in her trouser pocket, was swaying back and forth as she swore and cursed.

Feeling uncomfortable, the two women headed over to challenge her: "Little Wei's woman, who are you swearing at? Who's caught a fever."

Little Wei's wife retorted by spitting out a mouthful of spittle mixed with phlegm – *Puh!* Unfortunately, this also wrenched out a false tooth. She picked it up and there was a whistling sound from her mouth whenever she tried to speak. "A warm stomach isn't afraid of cold water."

The two women swooped in a counter-offensive and cursed back: "I'm afraid of cold water. So, what? You still have the face to come out and shout abuse. Whether it's your husband's seed or not, you clearly know the truth in your mind. Shouting abuse like this, you can fool your man but can you fool others? The eyes of the masses are as bright as the snow."

The three women then began to trade abuse, one spitting on the other, the other paying back in kind; this side humiliating the other party, jabbing a finger at her opponent's face and the other slapping her buttocks, cursing and dragging in each other's parents, chickens and dogs as fodder for insults.

This turned out to be the most disgusting war of words seen in Benevolent Lenient Village so far this year. Not only were the neighbours stirred up to go outside but, worse still, the staff from work units outside the village and even passersby all squeezed into the lane to watch the farce. I was washing the laundry in the courtyard at that time. On hearing the brouhaha, I ran out to make peace.

Women: the more you try to pacify them, the more vixenish they become. Now, all their words were unrepeatable. One cursed: "…your mother!" One scolded: "What have you got between your thighs to… people? Is it your father's head or your mother's head?"

Then, they started butting into each other. Their words were so downright nasty and I felt embarrassed having to pull them apart. I yelped: "You have the guts to ignore me. Then wait for the Village Head to come and sort this out."

But Chivalry was neither in the Village Committee office nor at home.

I wanted to ask Grandpa Cloud Forest to reproach these women, but he couldn't move easily and, moreover, he never desired any part in such things. There was no choice. I had to call on Uncle Six Pounds. A lock hung on his gate. In the courtyard of Old Ran's home next door, a team of masons was busy. After filling the foundations of the lean-tos, they repaired the tumbled-down courtyard wall with bricks.

Old Ran's sister-in-law charged out, shouting shrilly: "Plum, why did you leave without sharing our meal? Have I put your nose out of joint?"

"Fixing the courtyard wall? Aren't you going to build some more lean-tos?"

"Are you and Ran at loggerheads? You should be on good terms with him."

I tilted my head and caught sight of the old Village Head, who was chatting with the masons while smoking his water pipe. I shouted: "Sir, come out, please."

I hadn't seen him since he was discharged from hospital. Despite being a little thin, he looked fine.

"Little Wei's wife is tussling with some others in the western lane. It's gone on for a few hours already. You should get over there and rattle your sword to make them stop."

"Women," the old Village Head answered. "Let them fight. No one will lose their life in a cat fight."

"But this could have bad consequences. If the outsiders see this, what impression of our village will they have?"

"I can rattle my sword, but this will put me in an awkward position. Out of office; out of command. Where is Chivalry?"

"He is not in the village."

"He's the Village Head, but he's not in the village. Where is he then? Loitering about the city again?" Old Ran's sister-in-law jeered. "As soon as he becomes the head, see what a mess the village is in. Brow hasn't got married yet, but she is sleeping with a man. Xingben's wife in the front lane has given birth to one baby and then another one; now she is pregnant again. We fought the stadium guys before and now we fight among ourselves. We asked a cat to pull a cart, and the cat has pulled the cart into a rat hole."

"Hold your tongue," I upbraided her. "If you are so brave, why did you write a letter of apology to him? The paper is still hanging at the gate of the Village Committee office."

"A County Head is not as powerful as the man who is in charge on the ground. We elected a Village Head, but ended up finding the First Emperor of China."[y]

I again beseeched the old Village Head but he remained planted on the spot, grinning.

Old Ran's sister-in-law continued with her derision: "If you want to make the old Village Head go, you should ask Chivalry to come and invite him."

I had nothing more to say and turned to walk away. When I reached the big myrrh tree, I bumped into A-Shun, who was plodding along with his head lowered. I dragged him to a halt. "Being chased by a wolf?" A-Shun reported that the Village Head had instructed him to look for Xingben. I asked him hurriedly where Chivalry was. He stated: "In the office." On dropping by there, I found Chivalry puffing smoke rings one by one with his feet resting on the desk.

"Easy and carefree!" I bellowed in umbrage.

"What's wrong, Plum? Why's your face so grim? Have one for yourself."

I crushed the fag he offered me and growled: "You are the Village Head, so where did you bugger off to? Three women in the western lane have been rowing all morning and the whole world is pressing in to watch the farce. Don't you know?"

"I know."

"If you know, why haven't you done anything?"

"I have team leaders to take care of these things."

I was choked. Chivalry got to his feet. "Old Ran's sister-in-law wants to build houses and I need to settle this. Xingben's wife is expecting her third child. Didn't you report that to me? Little Wei's wife is scrapping with others and you were unable stop them. This Village Head is being turned from boss to servant. It seems that nothing can be done without me present, so what is the use in having you as a team leader?"

"You can't run the village, so you snarl at me."

"I can't run the village? Let me be a mayor and see if I can run a city." His nose was in the air again. "Let them make a scene. How can you solve conflicts without first airing them, and how can you rule smoothly without first facing up to chaos?"

"OK, let's see how you deal with it."

"Now, here are two tasks for you. First, go and tell the two squabbling women – Little Wei's wife is excused this time while we fix these two gossipy women – to come here with crates early tomorrow morning."

"With crates?"

"Yeah. Secondly, go and buy birth control pills and, for the next few months, sprinkle them periodically in the village drinking pool."

On hearing this, I was astounded. "You're playing silly buggers. How many pills should be put in the drinking pool to take effect? Even if it's effective, it's not only the people who drink the water; so do all six kinds of livestock and chickens and pigs. Do you want the pigs to never give birth and the hens to never lay?"

"If this can't be done, think of a way by yourself. Distribute condoms to the young married guys every day, and those who don't have condoms must not have sex. Come what may, nothing will go wrong with family planning for the time being. We must protect the village and the village must behave itself in a proper way. Nobody should screw with our big expectations."

While he was prattling on, Xingben entered. Chivalry's face immediately darkened to the colour of iron and, slapping the desk, he roared: "Where is your woman?"

Xingben was terrified and shrank back, answering: "I don't know. I was playing mahjong at Gao Feng's home from last night up until just now. What's up?"

"I know you were playing mahjong. But do you know your wife is with child again?"

"I know."

"You know, so why not do something about it? With two babies already, you still want a third? You really are bold to turn a blind eye to me. Do you want to flout the national laws?"

"My wife had a coil fitted after our firstborn. Who was to know that the coils supplied by our government wouldn't work? So, we had our second. When the old Village Head was in office, he thought we had removed the coil and asked my wife to go to the hospital to be x-rayed. The x-ray showed that the coil was still there. Now she is pregnant again – this must be the will of the heavens. What can I do?"

Chivalry grunted and broke into a cold smile. "Don't give me that. I'm telling you, today I escorted her to the hospital to be x-rayed again. Where was the coil? It was pinned to your wife's cloth belt! Now go to the hospital at the entrance of the South Gate of the city to collect her."

Xingben stomped out crying: "The abortion is done?"

"Come back," Chivalry shouted at him. "Give me ten yuan. That's my taxi fare for chaperoning her to the hospital."

A ticket was chucked on to the desk. Brought up short, Xingben took out ten yuan, which he passed to Chivalry. He reached the door then scarpered.

Not until now did I know why Chivalry was puffing smoke rings alone at leisure in the office. Scanning his dark face, I wanted to lambast him as a cruel customer, but couldn't. He gave the impression of still being in a towering rage, and was panting heavily. I poured him some water. He mused: "These guys want to make an ass out of me and so I should return their favour in kind. I'm a peasant myself. How can I not know the tricks these people pull?"

Later, the story of Xingben's wife swirled around the village. Squatting in the public lavatory, I heard some men praising Chivalry on the other side. At the same time, of course, they made fun of him saying that, since he had a hand transplanted from a female, he was sure to know about women's affairs.

After Xingben's wife entered the x-ray room, the radio-grapher took one look at the apparatus and went out to inform him: "The coil is there." Chivalry said: "Weird. You go in there and examine her body." The radiographer did as he was told. Sure enough, Xingben's wife had tied the coil to her waist before being x-rayed. The radiographer went out and told him this. Chivalry gave the woman's rearend a kick and cursed: "Go on, pull your tricks! Pull your tricks!"

The woman was so ashamed and started to run away. Chivalry hauled her up in his arms and carried her by force to the operating room to have the termination performed.

In the afternoon, I went to relay the tale to the two gossipy women, while Chivalry chose to go on a binge with friends at his home until they were roaring drunk. Early the next morning, Liuhe asked me to attend a meeting. I asked how many bottles they had finished yesterday. Liuhe tallied up: "Four people, three bottles of hard liquor and ten bottles of beer. Chivalry's eyes were red even at night-time, but he could still climb up on to his hammock in between the trees. It was just that he snored as if bellows were being pumped. It was so loud, no one nearby could drop off. We called out and threw shoes at him. None of that worked. We had to resort to plugging our ears with cotton balls."

I grinned at Liuhe and continued on to the vegetable stall at the entrance to the stadium compound with the intention of buying a small bundle of amaranthus. On my way back to the office, I ran into Virtuous Liu's wife and Bolt Jia's wife. Each had a crate on her back and had changed into their Sunday best and combed their oily hair smooth.

Virtuous's wife asked me: "Plum, why did the Village Head tell us to do this?"

"How could I know?"

"He is sure to ask us who we think actually seeded Little Wei's son," Bolt's wife reasoned. "We have no evidence. When someone steals a man, we can't hide under her bed.

But, in ancient times, if people wanted to find out if a son was legitimate or not, two drops of blood would be dripped into a basin of water to see if they blended together or not. Nowadays, it's said that it can be done in the hospital by testing the blood type."

Virtuous' wife added: "Puppy Wei is a bastard and everyone knows it. Will the Village Head ask us about this? If he wants to ask us about this, why did he tell us to bring crates? Plum, where did you get that amaranthus?"

I said that a seller of wild vegetables had come to the entrance of the stadium compound.

"*Aiya*, I haven't eaten wild vegetables for so long." She shouted at a child loitering by a nearby gate: "Go pass on a message to your uncle Virtuous and ask him to hurry and buy some amaranthus. We'll eat amaranthus dumplings. Ask him to buy a little more and tell him that the Village Head will pop over as well today."

She hadn't expected that Chivalry would already be staring this way from the not so distant door of his office.

"Be true to your word," he called out.

The two women smiled.

"A treat of wild vegetable dumplings is nothing. A new broom should sweep clean. The lane has been covered with standing water all through the year and it's so filthy, but you haven't sent hands to repair it. Look, these new shoes already look like muddy gong mallets."

Chivalry answered: "I asked you to come today for this exact reason. You two go to the sand pit to the south of the village and carry back sand to spread in a neat layer over the lane. If you can't finish the job by noon, carry on with it this afternoon. If you can't finish it today, come back tomorrow. Finish the job early and go back home early.

You can ask Virtuous and Bolt to bring you packed lunches." With these words, he ducked back into the office.

The two women were frozen dumbstruck, and so was I. Virtuous's wife moaned: "*Ai*, isn't this the style of 'the Gang of Four,'[z] sending us to a study session?"

"There's no study here," I replied. "Only punishment."

Virtuous' wife clapped her hands and moaned: "She steals men and I am required to resurface the road."

Bolt's wife muffled her mouth.

The two women darted a glare at the door and windows of the office and stamped hard on a patch of wet land. The tops of their shoes and their trouser legs immediately became sodden with mud.

I entered the office. The other minor bosses and several prestigious elders of the village – twelve in total – were chuckling in low voices. Chivalry volunteered: "After the lane is well-surfaced, let's rename it 'Gossipy Lane.' Our village has a name but the lanes don't. Plum, write the name on a tablet and hang it on the wall."

Three days later, I followed the order to write this out on a tablet, which duly took its place on the wall at the entrance to the lane. After that, all five lanes were resurfaced with sand or had the clay brick walls on both sides whitewashed with lime, and Chivalry christened each one. One of the lanes earned the name 'Boobs-Pawing' after a night when Puppy Egg Two went to the capital city to enjoy lamb kebabs and beer. Maybe his head was swimming already but, at midnight on his way back, he ran into a girl from the stadium compound who happened to be passing through the lane. His libido surging, he gathered her up in his arms and groped her breasts. The girl was scared and screamed. She managed to struggle free, ran back and gathered a bunch of guys to come back to the village and make a scene. Puppy Egg Two, of course, totally lost face. Later, Fan Jingquan was to see the name of the lane and, feeling it inelegant, changed it to 'No Wantonness'.

Naming the lanes was, however, a minor problem. What surprised us was that today Chivalry put forward two great proposals for us to discuss: one was to renovate and put the cemetery in order and the other to establish a large pharmacy.

First, he clearly and logically expounded the significance of renovating the cemetery and of establishing the pharmacy, then he listed the sources of funding and allocation of labour one by one. His blueprints were complete, but he hadn't leaked the tiniest detail to anyone before he laid them out on the table. After he was through, he solicited our comments as he himself perched, rubbing the cracks between his toes. His feet were so foul-smelling I had to shift my chair to the window.

Of the dozen people, eleven mouths wagged to air their opinions. Some were in favour of the plans, some were opposed and some in favour of one part but against another. The room was wreathed in smoke and the attendees found themselves at a stalemate. When the cockerels started to crow at noontime, we still hadn't arrived at a conclusion. Chivalry tidied up the papers, cigarettes, matches and water glasses before him, stood up, spat out a mouthful of phlegm noisily and cursed: "Pricks! The beating of a gong needs one drumstick to set the tune. That's settled."

I could see outside the window that the wives of Virtuous and Bolt were shuttling sand crate by crate and lining the lane with it. When they passed the door of the office, they would swear in a low voice: "My son, the First Emperor." But they still ambled along doing the job.

Chapter Eleven

Chivalry used up some of the savings from the Village Committee and forced the vendors in the row of public buildings at the entrance to the community to hand in three months' rent in advance. He then used the funds to replace the clay brick walls of the cemetery with ones bearing a bamboo joint-shaped tracery. The roofs with their tile-covered tops resembled soaring eagles. All the rows of terraced burial mounds – except for the one belonging to our ancient ancestor – were razed to the ground and transformed into well-apportioned, three-sectioned compounds.

The buildings were now different in shape. Some possessed two roof tiers with five slopes, some had nine, some roofs were shallow-vaulted affairs, while others had a lean-to-like roof, an arch-like roof, a pyramidal roof or a T-shaped roof ridge. They belonged to neither modern styles of architecture nor those of the Republic of China or the Ming or Qing Dynasties.

All the doors and windows were painted jet black and framed with a white circle on the outside. Meanwhile, the rafters, with their red coat of matte, presented an ancient and mysterious air. The designs were drawn entirely from his imagination. Heaven alone knew where he hired the masons from; artisans who were prepared to assemble a miniature version of a certain ancient village or township.

No city walls girdled the buildings in the cemetery and the neighbourhoods spread out like the *Kun* Diagram,[aa] with four entrances ringed by horse roads. A bell tower rose from the front and a drum tower stood at the rear. In the lanes, there were trees – withered-branched specimens or cypress saplings – millstones, well heads and horse-hitching stakes. Studying each of the tripartite compounds carefully, you could see that the gate awnings differed in height and size and the courtyards varied in width and depth. The side rooms each exhibited an exterior frame, supported either by legs that looked like those of a squat table or by railings. Otherwise the rooms reached all the way down to the ground.

Each of the main chambers was separated into three by colourful decorative screens, one portion being dim and the other two bright. A small table was positioned in the centre and a roll of cloth hung on the wall, on to which was written, in vermilion ink, the words *Heaven Earth Ancestors Parents Teacher*. Below the cloth stood the spirit tablet of the departed. On the rear left of the main room were small replicas of the pig pen, chicken coops and rabbit hutches; on the rear right, the brushwood and hay shed and the latrine.

Each household was allotted a patch of wall, whitewashed with lime and inscribed with the words *Govern the Family according to the Rules*. Since the characters that made up the words would be too miniscule and too dense to be read with the naked eye, they had been substituted by rows of black ink dots instead.

The lintel of each household's gate was decorated with an eye-catching black plaque emblazoned with the number of the house in white. These accoutrements appeared complicated, but being fashioned in miniature, not too much time and money had been spent on them.

The cemetery, which used to be a scenic spot in Benevolent Lenient Village, had now become a bona fide tourist site. Every day, villagers dropped by to gaze at the novelty, and people from nearby factories, mines, enterprises and government units also swarmed in to appreciate it. Someone carefully counted the gate numbers of the village to be occupied by the ghosts. The total figure came to 151 – the precise number of all the households in Benevolent Lenient Village. Of course, Chivalry had done that on purpose. Later, if one family lost a member, a china urn filled with cinerary ashes together with a spirit tablet would be deposited there. Each one was able to find his or her lot, since all the fellow villagers still dwelt in one village and their family members still inhabited the same household.

I went to check out my gate number and, finding that one room had been named the 'Collection Room', I couldn't help spluttering into laughter. Then I tried to search for Chivalry's. An extra screening wall had materialised in front of his house. Written on the screening wall were the words 'Village Rules' and dotted densely below was a patch of fly head-sized characters in regular script. A portion of these read:

A village consists of three wards, and a ward of 30 households.

Go out in the daytime in groups of three and five. Close the village gate at midnight even if someone still hasn't come back.

Should one family fall victim to a fire, the other households must each help by donating a bushel of wheat.

Should one man get married or have a new arrival, the whole village must share a hearty drink. Stir up things or exchange blows and they must smirch their foreheads with lighted incense sticks.

Thieves, rapists or adulterers – cut off their fingers and wrench out their tendons.

Should one household harbour fugitives, all the other thirty households are implicated.

Again, that was the handiwork of Chivalry. He didn't know Classical Chinese and cooked up this jingle off his own bat. I examined the frame of his gate again. No words to the effect of "Residence of the Village Head" had been written there. Nevertheless, the fact that the village rules had been inscribed on the screening wall of his home signified how confident he was of still being the Village Head forever (even after his death!).

So many visitors weaved in and out, all of them passing through the front gate. This disturbed the routine of Grandpa Cloud Forest. Therefore, a wall was built behind the shrine, leaving only a small door, which was normally locked. Another gate came to be erected in the north of the cemetery. Chivalry's grandpa, the straight-eyed executioner, stayed there day and night selling admission tickets. "Ha," his hand chopping down (a habitual action throughout his life) while he mused: "For half my lifetime I chopped off folks' heads and now I have become the beast that guards the tombs."

One day, Gao Feng travelled downtown to hawk vegetables. He used to grow his own and, every morning, would go to the wholesale market with Chinese cabbage, cucumbers, green beans and tomatoes to sell in bulk. Now, having no land, he was forced to pop over to the wholesale market to buy produce and then sell it along the streets. He felt he couldn't breathe easily. After coming back home and pondering how he was already twenty-seven or twenty-eight but still a bachelor, he ducked his head and fixed his eyes on the pin-ups hanging at the head of the bed.

His mother came along with a teapot to pour him a drink. He snatched up a tea bowl and knocked it against the spout of the teapot, booming: "What's the use of this? Except for pouring water!" The spout fell off. His mother returned to her bedroom to shed tears and, knowing that her son was in want of a wife, made a beeline for Chivalry to air her grievances. Chivalry came to look for Gao Feng, bringing with him a Tibetan yak's head, a length of white wooden board, a bottle of China ink and a writing brush.

"Really want a wife?" Chivalry probed. "Good-for-nothing; can't find a wife, so you take it out on your mother."

"You haven't got married," Gao Feng replied. "Do you want to turn Benevolent Lenient Village into a bachelors' camp? The village has no land and no factories and your mind is only on rebuilding the tombs. After the cemetery is done, are all of us meant to curl up and die?"

"It's said that you have beady eyes. Too true. No wonder the others didn't elect you the Village Head while I was away. Now, what a situation is our village facing. If you can't take the first step steadily, how can you take the second? What's wrong with renovating the cemetery? Our country has rebuilt the Yellow Emperor's[ab] Mausoleum and folks offer homage there every year.

"Why? After we have finished renovating the cemetery, we will wait and see. If the city and district governments don't interfere, that means they silently agree with us. If that's so, this place will become a honeypot for sightseers with tickets being offloaded by the bundle. That ought to prevent our village from being demolished. In turn, that'll boost our confidence, giving us the nerve to set up a large pharmacy, giving you a job and giving you money to spend. Then will you still be single?" With these words, he slapped Gao Feng on the crotch, scoffing: "You have a limp thing, so what makes you wild and cocky?"

Gao Feng coughed out a laugh and countered: "Don't grab it with that hand of yours."

Scarcely had I stepped through the gate and heard them sharing men's dirty jokes, when I turned around and began walking out.

Chivalry tugged at my sleeve, asking: "Why did you come?"

"Gao Feng's mother said he was flinging around dishes and bowls at home and I've come to have a look," I replied. "Nothing serious."

"Gao Feng is crying out for a wife. Find him one."

"I haven't even found someone for myself, so why should I find someone for him?"

"You're through with Old Ran?" Gao Feng pried.

"Whether we're through or not, I'm in no mad rush."

Chivalry surmised: "If Plum isn't worried, why should we be? Gao Feng, you're better with the writing brush than me. Write a few characters on this piece of board."

Three words, *Why Come Here*, came to be sketched on the wood. That was Chivalry's idea. Why? Why did he bring the yak's head here? Chivalry didn't say anything but marched us over to the cemetery. He hung the yak's head on top of the wooden stake at the entrance to the burial ground and pinned the wooden board beneath it.

Rapping the thick upturned yak horns, he whispered with a smile: "If Gao Feng wasn't pining after a wife, I wouldn't have thought of putting the skull up here. Plum, read these words and tell me: what do they mean?"

The more I read them, the more alternative meanings I sensed they had. Even so, I didn't know which one was accurate. "I won't tell you," was my response.

As expected, the renovation of the cemetery reached its completion without any interference. After the first phase had been satisfactorily accomplished, Chivalry started to make preparations for the pharmacy. The three rooms of the Village

Committee building were selected for conversion. They were already old. The walls, which were once whitewashed with lime, had peeled extensively, giving them a piebald complexion. Reed mattresses formed the ceilings and patches had been stained by leaky rainwater and rat piss, making it as unsightly as if they had been run over with a dirty mop.

However, the four walls were jam-packed with certificates and pennants of merit. The two oldest merit pennants were awarded during the "in agriculture we learn from Dazhai" campaign. One of them was in recognition of being an advanced unit at levelling the land and one for being a role model in sinking wells with machinery.

Later, the farmland was gone and only the well to the south of the village hadn't yet caved in, having run dry long before, it was overlaid with sweetcorn stalks throughout the year. Three years ago, an appalling multiple murder was perpetrated in the Western Capital. Suffice to say, the bodies ended up being dismembered. Three legs, all from different people, were found inside the well. After this, it was filled in and a peach tree was planted in its stead. The peach tree blossomed this year.

The certificates and pennants of merit represented the old Village Head's proudest achievements, his reason for securing consecutive terms of office and his excuse for not stepping down. According to the mother of Shaved Head the grocer, one night after he came back from hospital, the old Village Head cried alone surreptitiously at the gate of the office. I didn't know if he actually cried or not, but the news genuinely saddened me.

Chivalry told me that he had once seen whores in a city in the South of China. Every day, a group of them would sit on the steps below the balustrade of a garden under a flyover, waiting for the rich whoremongers to take them away. One morning when he went past, a lot of prostitutes were crouching there, among them an aged woman whose face was encrusted with heavy powder (not enough to conceal her wrinkles though). In the afternoon when he went past there again after finishing doing his business, the young women had all gone and only the old woman remained on her own.

I wept while listening to his story. It made me think of the old Village Head, even though I was, at the same time, resolutely opposed to him being re-elected. Thus, as we were emptying the three rooms, I suggested that the certificates and pennants of merit should not be destroyed but a small room set aside for their preservation instead. Chivalry agreed. "Yeah. Later when I'm no longer the Village Head, and the great pharmacy is no longer in operation, the plaque of the pharmacy ought not to end up being burned as firewood."

Two big rooms were partitioned off to form the pharmacy and the third one was divided into two, the first half being the office of the Village Committee and the pharmacy, and the second the collection room for the certificates, pennants, gongs, drums, horns, blunderbusses and such like used in ancient rural festivities.

Once the meticulous preparations were completed and the necessary business procedures gone through, we set about purchasing medicinal herbs in bulk. Grandpa Cloud Forest was endowed with miraculous medical skills as well as a unique understanding of herbs. In the past, when he gave a patient a prescription and they took it to the city to buy the drugs, they were rather nonplussed with the pharmacies there. He asked rhetorically whether the identifications of medicinal herbs made by Li Shizhen in his *Compendium of Materia Medica* were accurate or not.[ac] Of course they were accurate. But that wisdom was set down in ancient times and now the climate had changed. Many herbs were no longer gathered in the wilderness but cultivated using fertiliser in a fraction of the natural timeframe, and they were harvested out of season and at the wrong time. This led to great disparities in their pharmaceutical properties compared with the old days. On top of that, people had grown accustomed to taking Western medicine if they got a headache or a fever, despite Western medicine having side-effects.

Taking into account the human body's resistance to drugs, the amount of this or that dose of herbs recommended by the ancients proved no longer amenable for patients in the present day. Accordingly, he emphasised that we must collect herbs in mountainous areas; we should buy capillary wormwood herbs grown by the riverside but not from a gulley or on the tableland; Sichuan chinaberries should be harvested after Frost's Descent[ad] but not before it; and the rhizomes should be bought from Sichuan but not from Yunnan. I had never expected that, after going out to do the purchasing for the first time, Chivalry would invite me to be in charge of the pharmacy. OK, that was fine and my business cards were printed with my new title on them. I headed downtown to visit and take notes at renowned medicinal herbs pharmacies such as the Prosperous Hospitality Hall, the Distinguished Prosperity Hall and the Successful Harvest Hall. From these, I also headhunted three retired pharmacy hands and recruited several helpers for them from within the village.

The pharmacy was presently laid out over the outer court, the inner court, the miscellaneous room and the fine goods room. The division of labour was precise and everyone was allocated their responsibilities. The counters in the outer court ran the business, boasting a First Counter Keeper, a

Second Counter Keeper, a Third Counter Keeper and a Last Counter Keeper. The First and Second Counter Keepers were the senior hands from Prosperous Hospitality Hall, taking charge of identifying raw materials and the liquids and pills. They were familiar with the medicinal properties, effects and usages and, moreover, were able to do the accounts and write prescriptions, and knew how to receive guests.

In the cutting room of the inner court, the first cutter was a master hand from Distinguished Prosperity Hall who specialised in slicing fine herbs. In the darkness, without the assistance of a lamp, he was able to cut American ginseng, pinellia tuber and betel nuts into very thin, tender slices and, what is more, he could mould Chinese patent medicine into pills or grind them into powder. These people had been engaged their entire lives in the medicinal herb business and were highly dedicated to their work.

I never needed to worry. Above all, Benevolent Lenient Village had a god in the shape of Grandpa Cloud Forest and, should anything run awry, I could turn to him. Once open for business, everything in the pharmacy seemed to run smoothly and look the part. Even Uncle Six Pounds heaped praise on me: "Running the pharmacy was pre-destined three hundred years ago and Plum has been waiting for more than twenty years to be the manager."

I asked A-Shun to be an apprentice in the pharmacy. Early every morning, he arrived to do the cleaning, set up the stove to boil water, matched the herbs to the prescriptions and lent a helping hand to the counters and the inner court. He was a smart kid and everyone adored him. Within a matter of days, he was already on intimate terms with the First and Second Counter Keepers and had learned how to ingratiate himself by using self-deprecating humour.

A-Shun said: "Grandpa First Counter Keeper, there is a question I'd like to ask."

First Counter Keeper answered: "Spit it out. There is nothing Grandpa doesn't know."

"There is a bridge, which can bear a maximum load of two hundred pounds. Now, a pig wants to go across, but it weighs 250.[ae] How can the pig make it?"

"Slaughter the animal and then bring it across in joints."

"If the pig is slaughtered, it is no longer a pig but pork."

"Reinforce the bridge."

"Who will do that?"

First Counter Keeper fired the question back: "Then, how?"

A-Shun stuck his head out to ask First Cutter. First Cutter, whose face always looked like a slab of iron, replied: "Any way it pleases."

A-Shun dared ask no more and turned to ask First Counter Keeper: "You get it?"

First Counter Keeper answered: "I don't."

"You want to know the answer or not?"

"Of course."

"Well, right now the pig is racking his brains to work out the answer!"

First Counter Keeper grabbed A-Shun to beat him and the old and the young all laughed themselves down on to the floor.

After that, A-Shun needed to fetch some precious herbs. He went to the inner room to see First Cutter and called out "Grandpa Master Cutter" three times.

First Cutter replied: "I got it."

A-Shun said he needed to get some ginseng, deer antler and Chinese eaglewood incense. Without saying a word, First Cutter removed a ring of keys from his cloth belt, fumbled a key out without looking and shoved it into a keyhole. The lock clicked and it turned out to be the ginseng box. He took out another key, shoved it in and it turned out to be the deer antler box. He produced a third key, shoved that one in and it turned out to be the Chinese eaglewood incense box. A-Shun exclaimed: "Grandpa Master Cutter, you are so skilled."

First Cutter buttoned his lip and sat down to slice up the herbal medicine. In the evening, after closing time, First Cutter, who was an old widower, lodged and slept in the pharmacy instead of going back to his place. A-Shun returned home late to learn how to use the abacus under the light of the electric bulb. He also studied how to read the form of prescription sheets and how to distinguish between the various herbs in the drawers. Abruptly, he raised his head and saw that First Cutter was sitting there like a withered tree trunk.

A-Shun felt spooked. "I thought you were sleeping."

First Cutter admitted: "I can't fall asleep."

A-Shun then lowered his head to pluck the beads of the abacus again.

"When a man gets old, does he dread death, love money and find sleep difficult?"

First Cutter didn't make a sound. Believing that the old man must have been pissed off, A-Shun lifted his head, but it transpired that First Cutter was listening with a tilted head. The old man then asked: "Is someone coming to get some herbs?"

A-Shun replied: "No."

He stepped out, opened the gate and scanned outside. The lane was serene and deep and not a soul was to be seen. He shut the gate and sat down again.

First Cutter persisted: "But there was the sound of footsteps."

A-Shun held his breath to listen again and still nothing stirred, but when he looked back and spied his own shadow on the wall, he was terrified out of his wits. Later, he no longer had the courage to stay at the pharmacy at night.

In the afternoon, I purchased a number of wooden buckets of local honey from the Zhongnan Mountains and helped First Cutter make medicinal pills and powder in the pharmacy. After it had been dark for quite a long time, I became so tired I yawned ceaselessly. First Cutter's eyelids twitched. He pinched a bamboo strip and put it on his eyelid while drilling it into me that pulling one's hair could drive away fatigue.

"The flame above your head is high. The healthier you are, the higher the flame rises. If a man is going to kick the bucket, the fire dies out."

"Grandpa Lu." Lu was the surname of the First Cutter. "A-Shun is as timid as a rabbit. His skin must be like a suit draping around him. One tug and it can be ripped off," I noted.

"Is he a posthumous child? Man is neither afraid of tigers nor leopards, only hairy worms and his own shadow." First Cutter came over all serious. When a man has lost his teeth and his lips have shrunken inwards and become smaller and smaller, his face eventually looks like a baby's bumhole. "I always feel there is something weird about Benevolent Lenient Village: either a treasure trove or a demonic hex is buried underground."

I signalled for the old man not to go on and listened to the crickets chirping at the foot of the walls and outside the door. I stamped my foot. The chirping abated then resumed after a while. First Cutter saw me out of the door and asked me to carry a torch. I declined. Each lane or road of the village, including every small pebble, knew me, though I didn't know them. After going past one lane, I lost my bearings. The residences for the departed in the cemetery each had a name plaque, but the numbers didn't correspond to the proper sequential order. Neighbouring Number 9 was Number 35, and Number 88 stood in the same row as Number 23. What did this mean? Why did Chivalry arrange them like this?

The lane seemed very, very long. Why couldn't I reach its end? I stretched out a hand to grope. It was soft. How could the clay wall be soft? Moss sprouted everywhere yet, in the absence of even a drizzle, how could these walls be carpeted with the stuff? The insides of a snake were just like this – dark, humid and rangy. In a cartoon, when a man is swallowed by a snake, he will pass out of its anus whole except that he has lost his ears and nose.

Everywhere, people caterwauled: "The police are coming! The police are coming!" The crowd stampeded to the left, like rats. History is created by people. People were shouting on the left: "The police! The police!" The crowd then stampeded to the right, patting a glass gate and shouting: "We are from Benevolent Lenient Village!" A pudding face appeared from behind the glass, pressing against the pane like a flattened, air-dried persimmon, but he refused to open the door.

Why couldn't I find the date tree that stood in front of Grandpa Five Springs' home? To start with, I was walking eastwards, then I had the sensation of heading south. *Haul it up, don't allow it to touch the ground and pour some water to stifle it!* Standing there for a while, I believed I was heading west, so I turned around and walked on.

Immediately after turning around the wall of Gao Feng's

courtyard there ought to be a small lane, and walking along the lane for one hundred metres should have brought me to my home in the south-western quarter.

Nonetheless, in an instant I was plunged into utter confusion. Truly. I wasn't heading north, was I? The more I walked that way, the further away from my home I would be. Surely, I had trodden the better half of a circuit around the village. All of a sudden, terror stuck me. Where was my home? Someone was jabbering loudly and as clear as a bell: "One cup for you! One cup for me!"

A triangular patch of white light shone on the road ahead and two door panels were faintly visible within the brightness. Peering through the crack between the panels, I caught sight of the old beast who guarded the tombs. He was still crouched inside drinking. Lifting a cup full of wine, he slurped it down and, lifting another cup, emptied it again.

Instantaneously, my mind cleared: I had wandered into the cemetery. Still panting rapidly, I pushed the gate open and entered. The executioner's face was ruddy tonight, yet his countenance appeared kinder.

"You've come here to join Grandpa in a drink?" the executioner asked.

"I was making up pills and powder in the pharmacy and have just finished my shift."

The executioner passed a pancake over to me. That was his chosen accompaniment to liquor. I declined. A sesame seed tumbled off into a crack in the old table and, when he slapped down hard on the wooden top, it jumped out again. His hand caught it just in the nick of time. He daubed some spittle on his finger as an adhesive for the sesame seed and then popped it into his mouth, declaring: "Why bother? Cloud Forest has his own medicine to cure disease."

He was correct. Besides the medicine bought from the pharmacy, Grandpa Cloud Forest would prescribe certain medicinal catalysts, some powdered and others granular. It was solely because of these accelerants that his remedies were effective. Someone determined that they should study his prescriptions. A common or garden doctor might prescribe the same herb to his patients, but it did not cure liver disease. Grandpa Cloud Forest's prescriptions were magical in their efficacy, though he would never disclose the secret formula behind his catalysts, not even to us.

"That rascal Cloud Forest knows magic," the executioner recalled. "In the 1920s, I once saw a guy by the name of Zhang who knew the ghostly Eight Diagrams.[af] When he walked at night, he recited a magical charm and ghost servants would come to carry the sedan-chair for him, so bystanders saw him walking without touching the ground.

"On top of that, he could suddenly make a jumping fish fall into the courtyard from someone's eaves or cause steamed buns to change into cobbles the moment the steamer lid was lifted off.

"In the first half of his life, Cloud Forest was nothing special to look at. That cripple didn't have two beans to rub together. When he went mad, that was a different story. Without warning, he had so many magic skills. That cripple – *hee hee* – he must have been born at the right time. I know his childhood name was 'Blind Woman'. Fancy that, a man called 'Woman'. And a 'Blind Woman' at that! His father's childhood name was 'Nameless'. His name was 'Nameless'."

I lifted the wine bottle and planted it down before me. Then I arose with the intention of adding some to the executioner's cup. Before I could, the bottle toppled over and shattered. That was deliberate on my part. I knew that as long as there were spirits to be had, the old chap would drink on, talking endlessly.

Grandpa Cloud Forest was the soul of Benevolent Lenient Village and our god. I didn't like to hear him referred to as a mere doctor, or have his disease-curing masterstrokes put down to basic *qigong* or magical skills. Much less did I like to hear the old executioner dredge up the details of his origins like this.

I once discussed Grandpa Cloud Forest with Fan Jingquan. Fan reasoned that great people all look plain or have at some stage suffered an awful disaster. Like dragons, they are substantial enough to block out the sky or else may contract themselves until they can be held in the hand. They are born that way and fuse together man and nature in one. Their wisdom, their kindness, their wonder and charisma make the people who approach them feel that they are a god.

Fan Jingquan used poetic language to rhapsodise Grandpa Cloud Forest. I couldn't. But from the bottom of my heart, I knew what Grandpa Cloud Forest meant to us and how we should respect him.

As I left the cemetery, I repeatedly asked the old executioner not to see me off.

Pulling the two gate panels shut to prevent the sound which resembled a hooting owl from coming out, I trudged around the wall of the shrine to reach home.

The gate and windows of the shrine were black and not a sound was to be heard. The trees on the earthen ground were silent as well. Grandpa Cloud Forest must have fallen asleep, and so had A-Bing. A thought seized me: if this was Japan, wouldn't the one who is sleeping peacefully like a baby here tonight be the Japanese Mikado?

Chapter Twelve

After being in business for a little over a month, the pharmacy had reaped a good harvest that exceeded our expectations. Every family was granted a share of the dividend. I compared notes with Chivalry. We decided that all the villagers should assemble under the myrrh tree and Grandpa Cloud Forest would be invited to dole out the money among the households. The villagers gathered in festive mood. A-Shun's ever-considerate mother simmered two pails of green bean soup at home and carried them over, shouting at us to drink a little to assuage the effects of the heat.

Little Wei's wife and I sat on a grinding stone watching the clamorous scene while she fumbled a roll of banknotes out of and into her bra, all the while gabbling on about how she had her eye on a pair of snug-fitting white sandals in a shop. Uncle Six Pounds, who was standing nearby, darted over without warning to snatch the money.

The woman screeched shrilly: "You dirty old dog!"

Uncle Six Pounds responded: "Look how brazen you are, fingering them out and poking them back in, then fingering them out and poking them back in. You are flaunting your cloth sack-like titties."

"Old goat, you really do come from 'No Wantonness Lane', don't you?"

"Shush! How can you broadcast that we are having it off in a place like this?"

The others brayed with laughter.

After that, Uncle Six Pounds bent over and piped up

again: "Today is a good day, divvying up the money and gilding Chivalry's face to boot. So many people have come. If you don't take the lead in spicing it up with some mustard, when will you find a better occasion in the future?"

The woman asked: "How do we spice it up?"

"Pile a grain sack."

The woman simpered. Also tittering, I stepped down from the grinding stone and walked away. Pile a grain sack was a bawdy game in Benevolent Lenient Village.

Spontaneously, a gang of women would press a clubbable guy down on the ground, undoing his cloth belt and using it to bind his hands behind his back. They crammed his head in his crotch, lifted him up like a sack of grain and deposited him on a grinding stone.

When I was young, the villagers laboured together. While hoeing the wheat fields in June or hammering the wheat stalks on the threshing ground, the women frequently planted Uncle Six Pounds down like a grain sack. Uncle Six Pounds had got used to all kinds of jokes, and was unwilling to toil as well. The "sack" would be made to stand there for half a day, but Uncle Six Pounds enjoyed this and even sang *Zhang Lian Sells the Cloth*[ag] gloatingly with his head in his crotch.

Later, Benevolent Lenient Village had no land, people no longer laboured together and meetings were seldom held. But, whenever someone built a house or secured the cross-beam on the roof, or a baby was one-month old and the parents threw a celebratory feast, Uncle Six Pounds would frequently play the role of the grain sack. I could see how, after some cajoling, Little Wei's wife might conspire with a gang of muttering women to hatch such a scheme.

One said: "Not Chivalry. Such a hard guy, if he cannot put up with this, it isn't any fun."

Another one added: "He hasn't gotten married and his thing shouldn't be exposed in public. If we want to do it, let's do it with an old guy."

They started to whisper conspiratorially to each other again. Then the four of them inched over towards Chivalry, who was sitting behind the long table but, when they brushed past Uncle Six Pounds, they made an impromptu about-turn and threw him off his balance and started to untie his cloth belt. While struggling, Uncle Six Pounds gasped: "Old arms and old legs. *Ai! Ai!*"

The four women howled: "We especially look for you to fix, you old goat."

His hands were tied behind his back, his head crammed into his crotch and, after a roar, he was lifted and deposited on the grinding stone. Uncle Six Pounds continued to chunter at first, but after being slammed down on the stone, he was afraid to flinch. His uncharacteristic response caused the villagers to catcall, and many ran over wielding switches pulled from trees to jab here and there across Uncle Six Pounds' body. All the while, he showered Little Wei's wife with abuse as his head remained pressed into his groin.

When all was said and done, I was a girl and felt ill at ease with this type of spectacle. I went and sat beside Grandpa Cloud Forest, where I was joined soon afterwards by Chivalry, who fetched the old chap's water pipe to puff – *slosh slosh*.

Today, with cockiness inscribed all over his face, he wore an authentic silk jacket with buttons knotted down the front and his beard had been shaved clean, making his facial bones even more prominent. One wave of raucous din and wanton laughter crashed towards us, soon followed by another. He shot a glance in the direction of the grinding stone, broke into a smile and sucked in a mouthful of heady smoke, which he then puffed out towards A-Bing's nose, causing him to choke, yelp and skedaddle. He inclined his head to ask me why there was such a huge pile of rubbish at the southern end of our village. Which family dumped it there? Or was some government unit responsible? There was a row of plastic buckets beside the piss pool in the public lavatory. Was some factory using the urine to refine a sort of precious medicine? And why had nobody said anything to the Village Committee?

"Still talking business?" I replied. "They wanted to dump you as a grain sack just now."

"I'm not used to larking around with these women."

I pursed my lips and carried on: "*Yi*, you're the Village Head and you should pay attention to your personal image. But have you noticed it or not? Just now when the money was being handed out, it was Grandpa Cloud Forest who did the dealing, though they all came to shake hands with you. You are Mei Lanfang now!"ah

"Mei Lanfang? That Beijing opera singer? I don't understand."

"Then you should know Lu Xun.ai Lu Xun said: 'Men love Mei Lanfang because he plays women on the stage and women love Mei Lanfang because he is a man'." With these words, I sensed I had gone a little too far and so hurried to shift the topic to village affairs. "Originally, it was prescribed that each household should take turns to have two numbers registered, yet frequently a certain household tries to poach another's numbers. Because of this, there have been a series of squabbles and disputes. Can we issue them with coupons, which Grandpa Cloud Forest alone will redeem; just like how water coupons were issued in the old city forty years ago?"

I wasn't sure exactly how matters were conducted forty years ago, but according to the recollections of the older generation, back at that time the well-water consumed and used by the whole city was either salty or alkaline and people's teeth became blackish-yellow after drinking it. Only the water lifted from one well inside the Western Gate of the city was sweet and the Water Bureau sold coupons for it. Every day, the water-transporting cart would distribute water at a set time and one bucketful would be exchanged for one coupon.

"Good idea," Chivalry commended. "This manager can be my assistant."

"*Yao*, you have grown proud since you were made Village Head. You have learned from the rich guys in the capital city and want me to be your secretary."

"I daren't ask someone like you to be my secretary. On the first day, you will serve as a secretary should; on the next you will be plotting how to become the Village Head yourself."

"How can you see me like this in your mind?"

"If you weren't a born iron lady, how is it that you can't get on well with Old Ran?"

"Plum and Old Ran are not getting on well?" asked Grandpa Cloud Forest.

I blushed and glared at Chivalry. He said: "I don't want a secretary, but Grandpa Cloud Forest needs one."

"A-Bing is my secretary," Grandpa Cloud Forest explained. "He can find his way to each household and knows everyone in the village. Whoever I ask him to look for, he will bring them to me more diligently and efficiently than any human being would."

Chivalry called for A-Bing. A-Bing leaped up before the table, reaching the height of half a man. His body ended up almost horizontal in the air.

After he had landed with a roll, he sat quietly. I surmised: "Since he's been staying with Grandpa Cloud Forest, A-Bing has learned all kinds of skills. Uncle Chivalry, the way I see it: when you've been Village Head for a few more years, you too will end up with the air of a government official."

Chivalry replied: "As a monk, you should knock the wooden fish and, playing an old male protagonist, you should blow at your false beard. You think I have no masterstrokes? Sometime, I shall show you and your eyes will be opened."

I asked him what masterstrokes he had, but he refused to talk about it.

Two days later, I travelled downtown to the City God Temple. It had been dozens of years since the temple fair was staged and the place had been turned into a small commodities market. I placed an order in a small mahjong workshop to have several hundred glass registration coupons made. Then I returned.

Those two mischievous old boys, the First and Second Counter Keepers, were wrapping up herbs while chanting. Seeing that First Cutter, who was crossing the threshold, had plugged his ears with papery pellets, First Counter Keeper cursed him: "*Neither a singer of ditties nor a drinker of wine, a man's life is worse than a dog's, you'll find.*" First Cutter brushed him aside, dragged me into the collection room and burbled: "It's screwed up."

"What's screwed up?" I asked him.

"Benevolent Lenient Village is on the verge of collapse."

"What's happened?"

"I'm asking you and you don't know either?"

I went out and questioned the First and Second Counter Keepers about this. They didn't know what had happened either. I pressed First Cutter further. He only threw out the injunction "Go out and ask others" and would say no more. I approached the entrance of the lane.

A greatly perturbed Little Wei was searching for me, recounting how, mid-morning, someone from the Agricultural Trade Bureau came after Chivalry. The two of them quarrelled loudly at Chivalry's home. The news got around in a trice and many bent over the wall of his courtyard to eavesdrop. The government guy asked Chivalry to sign an agreement about the reconstruction of Benevolent Lenient Village. Chivalry was resolutely opposed to this. Rapping his finger on the table audibly, he claimed that, according to the proposed general urban plan of the city, no important buildings or main traffic routes were scheduled to be constructed here. It must all be down to some real estate businessmen who wanted to hit the jackpot and had this land in their sights.

Why should Benevolent Lenient Village be demolished? The real estate businessmen were not doing this under the banner of the government and no partnership had been sealed between the government officials and the businessmen. If it formed one aspect of the government's general plans, why couldn't a plot of unspoilt land be preserved as it was? Needless to say, the styles of housing, the lanes and the cemetery of Benevolent Lenient Village could be said to boast their own unique characteristics. Furthermore, it had its own resident healing pedagogue, Cloud Forest, and a peerless medical network.

Parks were being laid out in the city, landscaped with artificial hills and streams. What was wrong with a village being among them? Chivalry started to fling tea cups while he was ranting on. One cup landed at the threshold and the leftover leaves and tea splattered all over the gate. The other cup smashed against the laundry stone in the middle of the courtyard.

That guy stood up and declared: "Chivalry, what are you going to do? You want to beat me?" He went out in a paddy, though on seeing that many people were standing outside, he doubled back again and insisted: "Chivalry, you should be responsible for my safety. I am a man from the government!" Chivalry saw him out of the gate.

A ferocious-looking Lianben pounced with his body bent askew while yelling: "Who will demolish our village? Who?" The man's face turned green in utmost dread. Chivalry called hastily: "Lianben, Lianben, don't do anything foolish." Lianben swung a hand over with vicious force and the man almost retracted his head into his belly out of fear and trembling. However, Lianben was acting the goat. He merely slipped a cigarette behind his adversary's left ear and gave his back a hard slap, growling: "On you go."

"The man left then," Little Wei recalled. "But at noon, Chivalry was pressed to go over by a telephone call from the District Head."

All the villagers were waiting for Chivalry to come back. The annoyance of waiting for someone is enough to kill anybody. Little Wei's wife scuttled over to the entrance to the village three times, shouting that she would reward the Village Head and had cooked marinated lion-head meatballs in brown sauce especially. But Chivalry still didn't return.

That night, before the entrance of the stadium compound, the Benevolent Lenient villagers lost every last round of Chinese chess and hurled abuse at each other's mothers, before putting away the gaming sets and going back home to sleep. At midnight, a tricycle brought the roaring drunk Chivalry to Shaved Head's grocery store.

The next day, I dropped in to see him. His room was packed with people and Chivalry offered me a seat with a grin. His smile came across as downright heinous, however. He had on a small straw hat that did nothing to cover a fist-sized, purplish, congealed blister on the left side of his forehead. One of his eyes was swollen. He informed us that there was still no prospect of a resolution to the problem and that further negotiations were necessary. None of us ought to be susceptible to external influence but should mind their own business. My guess was that he was in a filthy mood and, having left the district government, went to a watering hole to drown his sorrows. Consequently, he got blind drunk, keeled over in the street and was fetched back home by a stranger on his tricycle.

At this time, it dawned on me what drawbacks Chivalry faced in not having a wife. A man might have a round waist and strong arms and look formidable, but in fact he might not be able to stand wear and tear and was more in need of care and concern.

After leaving the building, the folks still lingered outside his courtyard, not wishing to leave. I shared with them what was on my mind. Many started to sigh, complaining and blaming Chivalry for not getting hitched. They reviled the mentally-unsound old executioner, who neither prepared Chivalry a bowlful of warmed-up rice when he arrived back home, nor was capable of mouthing a few soft, sweet words when he had been simmering with rage outside.

Bolt then egged on Little Wei's wife, saying: "Your mouth can normally talk water into oil and you are still young with lively eyebrows and eyes. You claim you are a flower that has been planted into the cowpat of Little Wei. Why don't you develop your natural resources and go to show your concern to the Village Head?" Unable to ward off this praise, Little Wei's wife requested that the others go back home. She tided herself up from head to toe, rinsed her mouth (she had just eaten garlic) and slipped over to Chivalry's home. Nonetheless, after a while she came out, noting that a female was there slumbering in the Village Head's bed. Her head was buried beneath the quilt, but one of her hands was prodded outside. In her view, it was a very tender and fair-skinned hand.

The others laughed at the daft woman. Once again, Chivalry slept at home with his head buried beneath the quilt and didn't go out for half a day. The villagers, worried about Benevolent Lenient Village as well as about Chivalry, were compelled to consult Grandpa Cloud Forest. Coincidentally, he was seeing a patient, whose prescription included female ginseng,[aj] felwort, Chinese foxglove root, Baikal skullcap root, hairy asiabell root, five-leaf chocolate vine, Chinese plantain and ox bezoar. But the stock of five-leaf chocolate vine had been used up and the new herbs were yet to arrive.

The moment I stepped into the shrine, Grandpa Cloud Forest pronounced with a laugh: "Need to swap another kind of herb?" The sage had a premonition about everything. Even so, as such a big event happened to unfold in the village, how come he didn't mention a word about it?

Dragon leaf tea from the Northern Mountain was being brewed in a gurgling white iron pot on the small, charcoal-fuelled clay stove and a bitter smell suffused the room. "Change for 15 grams of Chinese goldthread and 50 grams of white-flowering snake-tongue grass." He poured the tea into a small porcelain cup. The tea was extremely strong and tumbled down like a string. He took a sip and smacked his lips loudly. "You want some? It'll cure your headache."

I didn't want to drink and I didn't want to watch him as he ate and drank like a beggar, so I leaned against the stone railings outside the gate. A car horn was blaring in the lane on the other side of the earthen ground. A-Bing sprang out, then immediately recoiled, his entire body shivering. The car had already stopped on the earthen ground and the fat policeman climbed out.

"*Yao*, it's Fat.... Oh brother!" I kept A-Bing clamped between my legs. "You got the credit for cracking the case, were given the 200,000 yuan reward and used it to buy a private limo."

"Who gave me 200,000 yuan? Will you?" Fatty sported a necktie. He was as wide as he was tall. "Don't get me mad by mentioning the 200,000 yuan shit," he yelled.

"I won't borrow from you. A notice was hung everywhere on the streets, announcing that whoever provided the crucial lead would be given a 200,000-yuan reward. It was you who cracked the case and even the criminal said: 'Now Brother Fatty has hit the jackpot.' Still, you haven't got the money. Even a ghost won't buy your words?"

"The prize money goes to the informant. I am a policeman and solving cases is my job. I only won the first distinction and was rewarded 1,000 yuan," he clarified while entering the room, unbuttoning his upper garment on the way and baring his expansive belly, dripping with sweat.

Grandpa Cloud Forest greeted Fatty and invited him to take a seat. Then he instructed A-Bing to grab the cattail leaf fan from the head of the bed for him. Still trembling, A-Bing refused to budge. "Even now, A-Bing is afraid of you," I shouted, "A-Bing, go to Brow's home and ask her to join us. Tell her that her old flame has come."

Fatty barked: "Nonsense, you want Old Shao to kick my arse, don't you?"

"An old flame doesn't mean there is an illicit relationship between you. A man always thinks of something good when he has immoral ideas in his mind. If you are not here for Brow, tell me what you are here for."

Fatty then smiled and said that he was here to invite Grandpa Cloud Forest to see a patient.

"Maybe you don't know, the woman who was wounded in the riot is the would-be daughter-in-law of a leader of the city government. Even after being discharged from hospital, she refuses to go out and will see nobody. She's prone to fainting fits and her mouth spews out foam – green foam. Weird or what? Those highfalutin doctors in the downtown hospitals have all gone over to have a look, but she's never shown the least sign of recovery. I recommended you and the leader arranged this car to chauffeur you."

Grandpa Cloud Forest was still drinking tea, pouting his lips and smacking especially loudly.

"You must go," Fatty urged. "For one thing, you can save a life, and for another, you can earn me some face. Who knows, if you cure her, the leader, in a moment of great happiness, might grant you a plot somewhere in the capital city to build a hospital specialising in difficult diseases."

"You want to undermine Benevolent Lenient Village?" When a tree is to be transplanted, if you brush it in water and rid the roots of clinging earth and dirt, it may be clean for now but it will never survive in its new place.

"Every patient is equal," I said, "Whoever comes is a patient, and even though she might be a leader's prospective daughter-in-law, she should come here herself to see the doctor. Word has it that the woman is already married. How can she be said to be unmarried?"

"Without a marriage certificate, no matter how long you

have cohabited, you are still unmarried," Fatty replied. "Brow hasn't got married yet, but can you stop her from living together with Old Shao? When you and that research guy get married, don't forget to give me some wedding sweets."

"You know everything, supervising Benevolent Lenient Village in secret."

Fatty slapped his belly. "Don't forget, I am a policeman."

A-Bing ran in from outside and barked wow-wow-wow in front of me.

I looked out and couldn't spy Brow. Then I knew Brow wasn't home. Fatty swore blind: "A-Bing hates me and he hasn't even gone to call Brow."

"Comrade Policeman Wang," Grandpa Cloud Forest, seated on the cattail hassock, opened his mouth. "I can't promise you I can cure this woman, but I should go over and take a look."

"You are a miracle worker and there is nothing that you can't do," Fatty squinted at me. "Can you go there now? I know Your Honour is fond of noodles cooked in fermented vegetable soup. Before I came, I asked his home-help to find some. The leader is also waiting for you at his home."

"Let's put it this way," Grandpa Cloud Forest replied. "The place where I live is under the jurisdiction of the district government. Wherever the District Head asks me to go, I will go. You must know this: a County Head is not as powerful as the man who is in charge on the ground."

I hadn't expected Grandpa Cloud Forest would agree to go and see the patient and, what is more, I couldn't understand him being so considerate towards the District Head. I wanted to say something, but didn't, simply removing a tree leaf that had become stuck in my hair. Chivalry slept in his bed with his head buried under the quilt, a habit which must cause disease.

"What do you think?" Grandpa Cloud Forest enquired. The way Fatty looked revealed that he was obviously unhappy, his face being red here and purplish there. "My face is small and I am not qualified to invite you over there."

"Sorry, Comrade Policeman Wang. Plum, go and buy a pack of cigarettes. They must be 555 brand. Comrade Policeman Wang smokes foreign cigarettes."

Fatty stood up and left. Grandpa climbed down off the cattail hassock and edged towards the door to see him off with the help of a pair of tiny hand-held crutches. His two legs entwined like tree roots, and his crutches pushed against the ground once, allowing his body to swing forward one step.

He said: "You're leaving, Comrade Policeman Wang?"

Fatty answered: "Yeah. As long as a man has money, he will put on airs and graces." He plonked himself back in the car and reversed it out of the lane. Grandpa Cloud Forest then invited me to go to the front of the vehicle to direct him as he backed out. The car drove out of the lane before my gaze and stopped outside Brow's courtyard. Fatty clambered out so he could knock at the gate and returned, mumbling: "Sure enough, Brow isn't home." The car then sped off, its horn tooting.

I didn't head back to the shrine. Grandpa Cloud Forest was a man with no worldly concerns; before these bureaucrats and policemen, he stood as a bank of free-moving cloud or a red-capped wild crane. Unbelievably, he revealed himself to be more humble and useless than usual. I felt bad for him and for Benevolent Lenient Village too.

The next day, the District Head, as expected, sent a car to collect Grandpa Cloud Forest.

In the afternoon, Old Ran's mother celebrated her 73rd birthday – *at 73 and 84, you will go to King Yama without being invited at all* – and every one of their relatives dropped by to congratulate her and eat longevity noodles. Old Ran did not risk coming to the pharmacy to invite me. Instead, he sent his nephews and nieces three or four times, as if the Song Dynasty emperor was pressing the victorious Yue Fei to withdraw by issuing twelve imperial gold tablets in one day. [ak] Feeling a little angry, I purposely did not oblige him. Old Ran then entrusted A-Shun's mother to invite me.

A-Shun's mother persuaded me: "The old lady had been living in Old Ran's elder sister's home for two years and moved back ten days ago, but you didn't go ask after her health. Today is her birthday. If you still don't go, Old Ran will lose face."

I was forced into a compromise, promising: "OK, I will go and that's it."

At the entrance to the lane, I spotted Grandpa Cloud Forest edging forwards with his hands pushing against the ground. A puddle of muddy water had accumulated in front of the grinding stone and he couldn't manage to cross it. A-Bing barked. Nobody else being around, I raced over and hauled him across the puddle on my back.

"Plum, how does this shirt look on me?" Grandpa Cloud Forest intoned happily.

"You bought it?" He was wearing a white satin shirt, which had unfortunately just been stained by the mud as the back became sodden with his sweat.

"The patient boarding at Virtuous's home insisted on sending this to me. I refused and he burst into tears. I thought it might be useful for wrapping my body in after I'm dead. Who was to know that I would get this opportunity to wear it."

"Today you're a guest of honour, invited by the District Head and the Mayor; tomorrow you might be a committee member of the Political Consultative Conference," I sneered at him, immediately regretting having done it. I wanted to say something else, but felt tongue-tied.

"The District Head said the same thing, suggesting he would recommend me," Grandpa Cloud Forest said. "Why should I be a committee member of the Political Consultative Conference? I've no legs to speak of, a mouth fit only for eating and breathing, and everyone is disease-stricken in my eyes. How could I be a committee member of the Political Consultative Conference? *Hee!*" He randomly asked: "Plum, have you ever eaten lobster?"

"No."

"I have. But it doesn't taste good."

I flashed him a smile and asked him back: "Grandpa Cloud Forest, you show off. Your belly is full of delicacies from the land and the sea, but I haven't had anything for a day and Uncle Chivalry hasn't had anything for two days. Where are you going? Has eating too much blocked your guts and you are stretching yourself?"

Grandpa Cloud Forest laughed from his position up on my back and said: "I'm looking for Brow. Plum, put me down. I don't smell good."

A man has an aroma and each one is different. The odour from Grandpa Cloud Forest seemed neither sour nor rank, with a strange hint of turpentine. "Our smells are identical except for an extra dash of lobster," I observed and carried him to Brow's home.

I had to rattle the gate knockers for quite a long while before Brow came out. Apparently, she was sound asleep. Her hair was dishevelled, but she had put her face on and applied too much scarlet red lipstick.

"Preener!" I cursed at her. "You took half a day to open the door. Touching up your make-up."

"I've gotten used to it, or else I feel I don't have a face," Brow replied. "How was I to know that Grandpa Cloud Forest was coming? I might not comb my hair, but I can't show my true face to others."

"Grandpa Cloud Forest is looking for you for some reason or other."

I thought that Grandpa Cloud Forest must be exerting himself mightily to get over here on account of something urgent. Actually, he came here to ask Brow to go to see Fatty, saying: "I might have offended the policeman and I can't walk there to apologise. In Benevolent Lenient Village, only you, Brow, are familiar with the policeman and you must go see him. The sooner the better. If the policeman says anything unpleasant, swallow it and after he is through remember to tell him that, if someone needs to see me, as long as they are recommended by the policeman, they can come at any time and I am at their service, or I will go wherever required."

Finally, he confirmed with Brow: "You got that?"

Brow answered: "Yeah."

Grandpa Cloud Forest heaved a long sigh and said: "Plum, your eyes are not as good as Brow's in buying clothes. Look at her dress. It fits so well and the colour is so fresh and striking."

"You know this?" I remarked and sensed that there was no rhyme or reason behind Grandpa Cloud Forest's behaviour. Why should he live a worthless life? Since he had already pissed on Fatty, why should he call back? What had been wrong with him over the past day or two?

At the precise moment when I felt myself unable to find an outlet for my blind wrath, Old Ran, knowing that I was at Brow's home, ran over post-haste and begged me once again to go to his home, insisting that all his relatives were asking about me. If I didn't put in an appearance, he would lose face. A fire of anger surged in my heart. Previously, I wanted to visit his home after sending Grandpa Cloud Forest back to the shrine and now I didn't want to go at all.

I told Old Ran: "I am a human being, not a piece of something used to gild your face. You don't want to lose face, but have you ever considered if I'm a daughter-in-law of the Ran family, or if I'm willing to be one? Why didn't you tell your family about the conflicts between us? By sending people to press me again and again, aren't you deliberately trying to show how I'm at your beck and call? *Pooh*, I won't go, won't, won't. Any other day I could kow-tow and bow to your mother and take care of her shit and piss, but even if the Queen Mother of the West threw an immortality peach banquet today,[al] I wouldn't go!"

Old Ran stood weeping. His tears drew smoke from my seven orifices. I stormed out of the gate and back home to sleep.

Afterwards, I learnt that Grandpa Cloud Forest had gone to the Ran household to share in the longevity noodles. Chit-chatting with the aunts and aunts-in-law of the Ran family about every last domestic affair, he also explained apologetically how he had sent me downtown to get a batch of herbs from Prosperous Hospitality Hall. He asked after and congratulated the old lady as my proxy. Nevertheless, he ended up drinking too much and barely had he got back to the shrine when he threw up.

Chapter Thirteen

As matters transpired, Chivalry, who had a mint leaf stuck to his forehead and a sash of walnut leaves about his waist, came back from his second visit to the district government a much more spirited man. Flaunting a newly-bought piece of headgear that resembled a top hat woven from bamboo strips and a pair of dark sunglasses, he swaggered into the lane with his hands clasped behind his back. He walked as far as Gao Feng's home whereupon he commanded Gao to summon all the villagers for a meeting.

The meeting was held on the earthen ground beneath the myrrh tree. Chivalry stood atop the grinding stone and proclaimed: "A man should live like a man. Once poured out, water cannot be retrieved and the Yellow River will never run backwards."

He removed his sunglasses and folded them so they hung from the neckline of his T-shirt. In this way, he struck a pose like those actors in the downtown theatres. "The folks of Benevolent Lenient Village are incapable of laying soft eggs. We won't loosen our mouths unless they use pliers to pluck out our teeth." He took off the small bamboo strip hat and put it back on, pressing the brim down so it skirted his brow-line. "Now we are at the primary stage of socialism and the primary stage is like a basket that can hold anything. As long as you can keep up a career, you will find recognition and support." He plucked his sunglasses from his neckline and again took off his bamboo strip hat to give it a flick. "The only fatal option is never doing anything and thereby never achieving anything. No ambition and no resolution spells a bitter fate; if your fate turns out bitter, you shouldn't whinge about the government."

Chivalry had never been so cocksure and had never spoken so vigorously and forcefully. Moreover, he looked as if he were putting on a performance. Brandishing his arms and waving his hands, he incited the masses. Had these been ordinary times, everyone would have been amused and laughed, with someone saying: "Chivalry, you're hyperactive, playing a hero in a drama." However, the villagers, whose hearts had endured several days of torment, now all stood in the seering hot sun with gaping mouths, lapping up Chivalry's words; words which normally did not belong in the mouth of a peasant. Nobody knew why he spoke like this. Nobody knew what concrete matter he was going to address after these remarks. No one said a word. Instead, they stared at him and at each other.

"Look at me. Tell me," he pointed at Bolt's second uncle, "if I'm right or not?"

"You are right!" Bolt's uncle replied.

"Which part is right?" Chivalry jabbed a finger in his direction again. The sun had become murderous and there was no wind; people's foreheads were shiny with profuse sweat. Chivalry was still asking: "Tell me."

"It is right because you said it."

The others howled with laughter. The laughter lasted for a short while and, after that, the silence weighed heavily. Bolt's uncle didn't mean to be sarcastic or witty; he said it in the spirit of peace and his words were right. The others laughed at his answer.

Here was a man with a cerebral problem and everyone knew that, but in the past when advanced individuals were to be selected, he was always a candidate. He learned to read a little in the 1958 Anti-illiteracy Campaign and could work his way through the *Selected Works of Mao Zedong* with difficulty, still studying the four volumes whenever he was free. But he was really old. His biological son taught in another county and his daughter-in-law followed him to be a hired hand in a seamstress's shop. Nobody took care of the home and the son paid a young man to wait on them, his bed set up in their bedroom in case any emergency arose at night.

One day I went to his home. His paralysed bedridden old wife was being fed. He said to me: "Plum, look, why still feed her? Just let her die." I knew he was in the grip of his condition again. He went on: "After she dies, I will get remarried. Someone has found a sixty-year-old woman for me and she will sleep on that bed every day." He pointed at the young man's bed. "I'm a man of the Party and our Party doesn't allow polygamy, but I can't get married if she doesn't turn up her toes." Now the silly old duffer could actually say: "It is right because you said it." This must be a miracle.

But our laughter proved shortlived and we resumed listening to Chivalry with serious faces.

What gladdened me now was that Chivalry's posture and air as the Village Head were sufficiently well-honed that he could perform properly in public, and he already realised that he had established his authority. Folks in Benevolent Lenient Village behaved like this: when someone was to be appointed leader, some would utter good words and some would utter bad, but whenever someone was in office, everyone would swallow orders. Be they old or young, man or woman, now that the fellow was in post, he was their head and brain and they entrusted everything to him.

After this meeting, Fatty jeered at us, cackling, "You are all peasants from head to toe." But is there any place in the world where folks don't act like this? The higher someone has climbed up the bureaucratic ladder, the more likely that is to be the case. When the former Party Secretary of the Western Capital was still in office, wasn't the current Party Secretary only third in command? However, after the former Party Secretary retired and the third biggest boss took his place, didn't the former number two boss need to take notes obediently when the new Party Secretary gave him directions?

One proverb has it that *the commander's tent is made of iron and the officers come and go like water*. What really matters is not the officers involved, but the tent itself.

"I mean," Chivalry continued, "A Village Head is a petty official, so petty that the people pity him. In my eyes though, all the world over, only Village Heads are true public servants. On the other hand, if a Village Head wants to make a fortune, money is up for grabs. I can sign a contract with the district government and the real estate companies to sell the land. The price of one *mu* of land floats between five hundred thousand and two million yuan. With some sly ruses, I can pocket a few hundred thousand or two to three million yuan off the books.

"At Laixiang Village in the eastern suburbs and the Liu Family Fortress and Two Bridges Village in the northern suburbs, their Village Heads all did this. Now, these villages are gone and the villagers have been resettled, but the Village Heads are running companies. They've become moneybags, driving *Hyundai*, drinking *Blue Ribbon* and indulging in monkey business with the younger generation."

"Monkey business with *the younger generation*?" someone whispered.

"The younger generation means seeking out green lovers."

Chivalry was not distracted by this but carried on: "Since I, Chivalry, became the Village Head, I haven't wanted to make a fortune. I've simply wanted to run the village well. I came on the stage when the fate of our village was hanging by a hair and my mission is to save the village from extinction. I have wandered all around the country, but the most beautiful place is still Benevolent Lenient Village and my greatest concern is still Benevolent Lenient Village.

"Our village is safe, our respected ancestors won't reproach us in the Underworld, our offspring will remember us and they will erect pagodas and build temples for us."

Gao Feng sang in a low voice: "I'm a wanderer who has been all over the country."

Many began to chuckle. The song was cooked up by Chivalry after he came back to the village. Now, Gao Feng chanted it casually, and many others picked up the tune, humming while still chuckling. Chivalry also laughed and said: "If you want to sing, do it seriously."

Gao Feng closed his eyes and raised his voice:

I'm a wanderer,
Who has been all over the country.
I'm a bachelor,
Who has dated girls from every province.
When a Beijing girl dates me,
With her political tricks, I don't agree.
When a Guangzhou girl dates me,
With her money-centred talk, my ears don't agree.
When a Shanghai girl dates me,
With her homemade clothes, my body doesn't agree.
When a Xinjiang girl dates me,

With her bad BO, my nose doesn't agree.
When a Jiangsu girl dates me,
With her favourite sweet food, my stomach doesn't agree.
When a Gansu girl dates me,
With her too ruddy face, my eyes don't agree.
When a Sichuan girl dates me…

The song rolled on about the girls of one province after another – humorous, intriguing and roguish. What Chivalry's life over the past two years might have been like surfaced in my mind. The girls from which other provinces had he dated as well? And what kind of girl did he want? When the girls of every province had been declaimed, none found favour owing to this fault or that:

So far, I still don't have a wife-to-be,
The life in my home village most suits me.

All who were present whooped, guffawed and cheered.

"Silence! Silence, all of you," Chivalry clapped his hands and made a stop signal with his hand like a referee in a basketball match. The song ceased. He put on his sunglasses again. "Do you guys know America? Anyone who has ever gone to school has studied history and geography and knows that America was home to the Indians, but after the white Europeans went there, they occupied vast areas of the continent and what happened to the Indians? They ended up being wild outcasts driven deep into the mountains and the forests. No more talk of these long-distant events. Let's say something about what we are familiar with. Now there are a great number of hired hands in the Western Capital and what are they doing? When a high-rise is being built, they transport bricks; when a road is being built, they dig the ditches; they wash bowls in restaurants; they ferry furniture for department stores. Because they come from the countryside and they are peasants, they can't enjoy a citizen's social benefits and they can't enter the city's political, economic and cultural centres. They graft and grind but are despised by city folks.

"Let's talk about something even closer still. There were three villages that used to be encircled by the Western Capital. Eastern King Village disappeared in March two years ago. When the village was flattened, the wrecking unit said the residents would be resettled according to an exchange rate of one-to-one. That is to say, for every square metre of old residence, they would be compensated with one square metre of new residence.

"However, after the real estate businessman got hold of the whole plot of land, he resold it to another real estate guy and this real estate guy changed it into a villa area, with not even one residential building for the households that were supposed to be relocated. The villagers went to look for the guy. He, of course, didn't acknowledge the past and the first real estate businessman had already run south with all the money. The villagers appealed to the Court, but when will the case ever be settled? Not for donkey's years. At the beginning of this year, Three Family Shop Village was demolished as well. Now only our Benevolent Lenient Village is left. It is a bachelor now. The leaders of the district government have asked me to go there twice. They have resorted to both harsh and soft words. I can tell you, I have drunk their wine and smoked their cigarettes. As long as they are not poisoned, I dare drink and smoke. Anyhow, it is a waste if I don't. If they try to stage a honey trap, I will meet this plot with another plot. But I have also hurled abuse, slapped the tables – my wrist is still blue from doing that – sweet-talked, begged, played rascals and wiped away tears.

"The District Head said I am a headstrong prick with a one-track mind. I, Chivalry, *am* a headstrong prick and a dog from Benevolent Lenient Village. Even if you beat me until my head is drenched in blood, as long as I'm still alive, I will pounce to bite.

"When he was backed into a corner, the District Head said he had considered the situation of Benevolent Lenient Village. How could he not care about the interests of the people under his jurisdiction? What had happened was that someone in the city government asked him to do what he was doing, so how could he not follow orders? His words were true, and true words are pleasant to people's ears. I asked him what the next step forward could be. He agreed that after I come back, I should gather you guys together to write a report to the city leaders. Good, this is a decent boss. A leader is not necessarily well-educated but, as long as he is an understanding chap, we will shout: 'May you live for ten thousand years!'

"Now, I have finished writing the report and you should put your signatures on the blank space below it. If you can do it, do it; if you can't, let another one hold your hand to do it. We'll try our best to let Benevolent Lenient Village not be wiped out because of our muddle-headedness."

Not until now did we realise the purpose of Chivalry's speech. I took the lead in clapping my hands and was soon followed by all the others, applauding and cheering how right they had been to elect Chivalry.

They also started to blame and curse the old Village Head, believing that if he had taken measures like this earlier, things wouldn't have become rotten to this degree. Chivalry appeared very excited, perched on the grinding stone with his knees bent and his legs folded. The top of his tilting foot impaled a shoe, which dangled there unremittingly. I went over and gave his foot a pat. He smiled at me, stood up, pulled out a pack of cigarettes from his pocket and asked a man to toss one to everyone. "You have one too," he told me. I pointed out that there was a large crowd here and it would vex others if a girl smoked. He then handed me a roll of paper. I moved a table over and let the others put their names on it.

A name is one's personal property, but it is always other people who call it out and use it. When these peasants wrote down their names for the first time on paper, they gripped the pen very hard so it leaked ink, dying their fingers. However, Bolt's second uncle – the chap who wasn't right in the head – was somehow seized with delight and used his blue-stained fingers to pinch Chivalry's nose, saying: "When the PRC was established in 1949 and the land was handed out, I signed my name. At the time of the Korean War, I signed my name too. Now I am signing my name for you." Chivalry's nose had become bluish-black. The others then all wiped the ink from their hands on to Chivalry's face, chortling: "Chivalry, stand still. This is good. We are congratulating you over a happy event."

There's a countryside custom that on a wedding day, for the sake of celebration, red, blue and black pigments are daubed on to the faces of the bridegroom and the bride. Now, Chivalry's face had been painted by almost everybody; some even poured out the ink on to their palms to rub it in. Chivalry had become a piggy or a dark ghost that had just clambered out of a charcoal kiln.

Brow also ducked over to daub and, when she came back, whispered to me: "His nose is so hard."

"What? His nose is hard?"

"It seems you're still a virgin girl – the last virgin girl of this century. Women's mouths and men's noses are both signs. You can tell whether a man is a tough guy or not by touching his nose to see if it is soft or hard."

"You slut."

Brow reached out and used her hand to muffle my mouth and we both giggled unstoppably. The others all looked at us and almost all of them tumbled about laughing. Then several descended to wipe blue ink on my face. It was only then that I realised that when Brow muffled my mouth, she had smudged my face dirty with blue ink.

The guys took the chance to spice things up, but Brow shouted loudly: "What are you doing? We are congratulating the Village Head, so why have you dirtied Plum's face? Is today their day for celebration?" Superficially, Brow was taking my side. In actual fact, she was making a rough sea stormier and poking fun at me.

"Brow, you're talking crap," I growled angrily. "Old Ran will come and beat you."

I observed how Old Ran's nephew was watching me quietly from a distance. On hearing my words, he turned his face and stomped away.

On 23rd December, according to the lunar calendar, before the Chinese Spring Festival, Old Ran insisted on accompanying me to buy clothes in a shopping mall. The glass door of the mall was wiped very clean. He walked straight forward and, *bang*, bumped into it head-on. I thought he might have gotten a bloody nose, yet nothing was wrong with him, except for a bump that developed on his forehead. He asked me to massage his nose. As I pinched it, it moved to the left and to the right as if it was made of dough. A small soft nose, no wonder.

I lifted my head to find that Brow was still smiling at me. I blushed. Chivalry came up and said in a low voice: "Let them carry on. Everyone is in a festive mood now. Benevolent Lenient Village is celebrating a happy event."

"Uncle Chivalry," I said, still peering at his nose. "You're a hero now."

Chivalry added: "The masses are lovable. There are only no-good leaders but never no-good masses. As long as a leader has made a small contribution, they will support him."

"A headstrong prick is just what the masses need."

"You mean I'm headstrong? A selfless man fears nothing. Long, long ago, before Chen Sheng[am] rose up, he wasn't a good peasant, but he did say: 'How can a sparrow know the ambition of a swan?' Zhang Liang[an] hired the strongest man to fling a heavy hammer at the First Emperor at Bolangsha, and Zhang Liang was strong-headed."

"Yao, comparing yourself with Zhang Liang?"

"Even though I can't hold a candle to Zhang Liang, I am a Han Xin."[ao]

I snatched away his sunglasses. "Actually, you don't look like an artist, but a gangster." One book, I faintly remembered, recorded the set of couplets inscribed on the gate of Han Xin's Temple: "He has one bosom-friend in death and life; survive or not, that's down to two wives."[ap] "If you are Han Xin, then who is that bosom-friend of yours?"

"*Ai*, why didn't you ask Grandpa Cloud Forest to come today?" I asked suddenly.

"He's gone to the city leader's home to see the patient again. He has almost become a royal physician now."

"You should thank him this time."

"This time? What do you mean?"

"If Grandpa Cloud Forest hadn't asked the District Head to escort him to see the city leader's daughter-in-law, the District Head wouldn't have allowed you to do as you have. He wants to climb higher and has taken the chance to suck up to a man who is his superior.

"He wouldn't dare say anything on our behalf unless he thought his position was safe."

"How do you know this? Did Uncle Cloud Forest tell you?"

"It just occurred to me now. I even got angry with him over it, complaining that he had offended the fat policeman, but he was prepared to apologise to him."

Standing speechless for quite a long time, Chivalry finally announced: "I will build a temple for him in the future."

"If an idol of Grandpa Cloud Forest is to be put up there, there should be idols of Golden Altar Boy and the Jade Girl too,"[aq] Brow cut in out of the blue.

I turned around to pinch her mouth and hissed spitefully: "Look at your mouth. Now, rip it back. Tear it as far back as your earlobes!"

Chapter Fourteen

The petition signed by all the Benevolent Lenient villagers was presented in person to the Mayor by the District Head. More than once, Chivalry went to ask what the verdict was and the District Head criticised him for being impatient, pointing out: "The Mayor is not just the Mayor of Benevolent Lenient Village. Are you the only folk he has to take care of? No result is perhaps a result in itself. When leaders come across something that is tricky to deal with, they resort to cold treatment and what has been done is done." Enlightened by the words of the District Head, Chivalry understood that a leader's work was a matter of artistry as well.

Through this conversation, he also learned that the Mayor's home-help had gone back to her hometown to get married. After returning to the village, he cajoled Liuhe's sister, who was then escorted by the District Head to the Mayor's house, to take the woman's place. Originally, Liuhe's sister had been a member of the pharmacy's purchasing team. She was earning a tidy sum and worried that being a home-help might be too tiresome. Chivalry promised that she could draw her old wage as usual and that sealed the deal.

After the girl had been with the Mayor for a fortnight, Chivalry dropped by to give her the wage envelope and, unexpectedly, the Mayor received him.

On that day, the Mayor was in a sprightly mood and had rice paper spread out in his study to practise calligraphy. Hovering about for some time, Chivalry heaped praise on him, not daring to rashly voice dissent over the redevelopment of Benevolent Lenient Village. That would be to risk cocking up a complicated matter. He only begged the Mayor to bestow upon him a precious piece of calligraphy bearing the characters "Benevolent Lenient Village". Surprisingly, the Mayor obliged. Chivalry returned, deliriously happy, and smoothed out the rice paper for us to appreciate.

"The Mayor's handwriting is like this?" I asked.

"You think it was easy for me to get this piece?"

"It was not easy to get, so it's not easy to discard either."

"You don't know a fart!" Chivalry concluded.

The three words prompted Chivalry to think big and build a decorated archway in the village.

According to Chivalry, since someone in the leadership of the city was conspiring with the real estate company against Benevolent Lenient Village, we should use the Mayor's calligraphy to exorcise the ghosts like Zhong Kui[ar] did.

By giving the impression that the rice had already been cooked and could not be made raw again, they could compel the leaders to change their decision to redevelop Benevolent Lenient Village. Even though we could not, at present, renovate the whole village, building an archway with the name inscribed by the Mayor at the entrance to the village would carry some significance.

I objected to this project. "A village isn't a castle. Why should an archway be built? In the past when an archway was built, it was usually because a rich household or prominent clan wanted to occupy a site with auspicious feng-shui or show off their power and prestige. Now, Benevolent Lenient Village has fallen so low that we don't even know whether the village can be saved. Why should we still spend so much money on superficial illusions? Can you use them to scare away a real estate company? Can you use them to force the hand of the city government? What's more, the village is a long way from being filthy rich. What are the residents' opinions about this large-scale luxury project?

"Peasants are used to poverty. When they can take something home, they roar with delight; when something is taken away from their family, even if it is only one cent, they feel they've had their flesh cut away or their hearts stabbed."

Chivalry answered: "You're still a woman, after all. Why is it that a woman can't be a high-ranking official and have a great career? They're near-sighted, that's the long and the short of it."

These words made me flip. Usually, Chivalry loathed how I didn't pay any attention to clothing and never applied make-up. He'd lecture me to the effect that a woman showed herself to be a woman by being the polar opposite of a man. But now he was lambasting a woman for being a woman.

In a fit of umbrage, I refused to attend the meeting of the Village Committee, but Chivalry forced my hand. I sat there with my mouth gagged and confronted him passively.

Chivalry's passion seemingly hadn't abated and he put forth sets of construction plans. Having wandered outside for many years and seen a lot, he fished out countless photographs for us to refer to, including pictures of modern parks and university campus gates, as well as the gates of some temples and ancient Ming or Qing Dynasty residences.

"I am of the opinion," he said. "That if we build a modern building, there will be better ones outside no matter how hard we try. Whatever I do, I want it to be the best. Let's build a stone archway modelled on a memorial chastity archway. No matter where in the world you walk, you won't be able to find another one like it."

Without allowing the others to beg to differ, he pulled out a photograph of the stone chastity archway in the Qi

Family Township at Hanzhou.

"Let's model ours on this. Once the stone archway is finished, it will be the scenic spot above all else in Benevolent Lenient Village. Later if our village is preserved, if it becomes rich – I have thought about that as well – let's build a Buddhist pagoda. Looking like a pagoda from the outside, it will appear to be the Number One Pagoda in China. Actually, it will house a hotel on the inside, equipped with all the facilities available in a big downtown hotel. If this place is to be regenerated, let's do it ourselves. Do we need others to commandeer our land and tear down our houses? Anyhow, one's own child is reliable. *One's sister's son is his maternal uncle's dog; when he is well-fed, he'll go out to slog.*"

Now, really unable to hold my tongue, I blurted out: "You want to build a feudal landlord's manor?"

"That makes sense. But this in this case, landlord doesn't mean the same thing it used to. It refers to the Lord of the land – or we can call it Mother Earth. With an area this size, what's wrong with us building such a huge manor? Isn't it better if we can preserve a plot of homeland in the Western Capital? It's a pity the city government doesn't have our foresight."

I stood up and pretended to go out to the latrine, but slipped back home instead, kicking the cobblestones angrily on my way. The chickens were riled and squawked and flapped their wings. At the entrance to the lane, A-Shun was pedalling a tricycle and was about to turn, but on raising his head and spotting me, he turned back again to go out. He was in such a rush that the tricycle hit the foot of the wall and jolted his passenger, First Cutter, down on to the ground.

"Sister Plum, Grandpa Lu wanted to go to Prosperous Hospitality Hall to stock up on medicine and I said I would send Grandpa there so that you needn't take a taxi back and can save the fare," A-Shun explained breathlessly.

"You want to take a tour of the city?" I asked. "Where did this tricycle come from? Can you handle it?"

"Borrowed from the stadium compound. I can ride it OK. How could I not be capable of handling a tricycle?" A-Shun rattled on, while peeping at my eyes. "Grandpa Lu, you take a taxi there then. If the Manager doesn't allow me to go, I'll return to the pharmacy."

"I'm not a tiger. How can you be afraid of me? You can go downtown, and I'll tag along."

"Ha!" His worry giving way to joy, A-Shun jumped on the vehicle and pedalled like mad out of the village. When the tricycle reached Northern Avenue, A-Shun's clothes were sweat-soaked and his dripping hair stuck to his forehead. Even so, he was feverish with excitement, surprised to observe how a high-rise had sprung up alongside a shopping mall.

Later, he screamed shrilly upon finding that the lane behind the hotel on Northern Avenue had been turned into a clothes market. Everything seemed a rarity in his eyes and he wanted to babble about anything that crossed his line of vision.

"A-Shun, shut up. You're making an exhibition of yourself by being so easily impressed," I said, jumping from the tricycle.

A-Shun's face reddened. "Sister Plum won't accept my ride. Have I made you lose face?"

I waved my hand, murmured that I had something else to do, and asked him to pedal to Prosperous Hospitality Hall. After they left, I regretted having come downtown. Standing at the crossroads, I stared around blankly. Should I go to the Institute of Agricultural Science and Techno-logy to look for Old Ran? I didn't want to. Should I go to a cinema to watch a film? I didn't want to do that either. I wanted to sit down, but couldn't find a place so just gawped at pedestrians who passed by. I was overcome with the sense of being a true yokel from head to toe; not even as good as A-Shun.

Keep on walking, keep on walking. I ought to just let my legs carry me wherever they wanted to go and let myself become worn out. Then my brain wouldn't be preoccupied with so many things. I reached the door of a fashion boutique in this frame of mind and, as I was combing and gathering together my soaking hair before the shop window, I bumped into Brow.

"Sister Plum," Brow shouted volubly. "Why don't you come over to my place since you're in the city. Buying clothes?"

"I want to buy a pair of trousers," I replied absent-mindedly. "This pair is too dark. They're presentable in our village, but look too grey once I come downtown."

"You should have changed them for another pair a long time ago." Brow dragged me into the shop.

Everyone in the store sneaked glances at us. They must have seen the gorgeous finery on Brow and the grey clothing on me. Brow heaved her chest and, her legs seeming to not even bend, soared straight ahead.

I uttered in a low voice: "Your chest sticks out so high. You'll hook their eyes."

"Yeah. Don't talk. If we talk, they'll be able to tell we are peasants from the 'burbs. Brush them off, take them all as stupid…, then you can relax."

I did manage to unwind. There were so many people in the city and no one knew each other, so what should I be afraid of? Still, I knew I wasn't as beautiful as Brow. The only way to drive away my embarrassment was to forget that I was a woman. What fortified and held me up was that I never latched myself on to anybody else; independence was mine and I'd educated myself well at home. Thinking like this, I grew more at ease, my legs remembered how to strut forward and my hands knew where they should repose.

Brow insisted I buy a pair of brand-name trousers, which she asked me to put on immediately and shove the old ones into a bag. She probed: "How do you feel?" Not bad. She was happy. "New clothes can really boost people's spirits. In a new outfit, I'm never tired even if I've walked the streets for a whole day. I will guide you to somewhere we can look around."

"What place? I won't go to your company. I shall start to fume as soon as I reach there."

Brought up sharp, Brow twisted me a bitter smile and bleated: "Sister Plum!"

"Huh?"

She held her tongue. After a while, wrapping her arms around my shoulders, she poured forth: "Since you're not willing to go to my company, we won't go there. In fact, my boss is a good guy. He does business simply to make money and never thinks much, unlike the guys in our village. I will escort you to see a shopfront in a street. Do you know, the boss has told me that after he's stitched up another bit of business, he will help me set up a copy shop. He'll stump up the capital and I will manage it on my own; the losses will be his and the earnings will be mine. How did I find such a good man? He is really kind. As long as I have a shopfront, I'm sure I can do good business and perhaps become a somebody after a few years. Our boss has set his sights on the shopfront in secret; he says it is Number 15 on Southern Avenue. Let's go take a look."

I followed Brow, feeling dubious. On the one hand, I didn't believe there was such a nice piece of cake in the world. On the other, I felt envious because if she really possessed a shopfront, Brow would no longer be the Brow she was now.

"A city guy is not always as good as his word."

In my vague envy, I started to query why the boss treated Brow so well. What was behind that? And what was the relationship between them?

"He is a friend of Old Shao's and he won't screw me over. What is more, I am doing quite well in his company."

We reached Southern Avenue and saw a beauty salon was still doing business in the Number 15 shopfront. Pointing at it, Brow observed that its trade would soon be wound up and the space rented out. Her boss had noted the prime location. We stood there talking. A row of female shoe-shiners crouched at the foot of the wall. Among them were some young girls and some middle-aged women with sallow faces. When they saw us, they rapped their shoe-shine brushes incessantly against the small iron water pails and whooped: "Shine, shine!"

"The city is too dusty and shoes become dirty within half a day," Brow reasoned. "Let's go and get our shoes shined. You see, you're sporting a pair of brand-name trousers and your shoes don't go with them."

"Yeah, a new pair of trousers corrupts us into needing a whole new outfit. Good trousers need a good blouse to match. When you have a good blouse, your shoes will not be a good match. When you have new shoes, your hair needs to be tidied. Then, you need a necklace and a gold ring. But where can I get so much money from? Chivalry has now stepped into the same trap."

"Chivalry? What's wrong with him?"

I told her that the village was going to build a stone archway. Brow responded: "We country cousins really have a different way of thinking from city slickers. Strain every nerve to run a pharmacy and build a decorated archway after making some money. Really, it is not as good as dividing up the dividend to buy a few suits in the latest fashion. Let's not talk about Chivalry anymore. He's a man and even he knows how to spend money. We are women so we should know even more about it."

She pulled me over to take a rest on a small bench in front of a middle-aged woman and she herself sat down on the bench in front of a little female shiner, shouting brusquely: "Use nice shoe polish. My shoes are made of top-quality hide."

When I lowered myself down, the middle-aged woman, still smiling profusely, immediately put down the sesame pancake she was gnawing, scooped up my foot with her hands and dipped a toothbrush into the water to swizzle away the mud and dust from the heel of my shoe. Straightaway, I came over uneasy and yelped a staccato "no, no" before retrieving my foot. I never had my shoes shone like this before. How could a youngster like me make a forty-something woman kneel down to serve her in exchange for just one yuan? This was too cruel and such cruel things only happened in cities.

I vented my embarrassment. "Brow, this is not proper."

Brow encouraged me: "Shine it, shine it; she is good at her work. Your shoes are old, but they will look brand new after she's worked on them. Don't feel uneasy. If you refuse her, this older sister will be unhappy. You have sympathy for her. If you show sympathy for her, you will do them a disservice. They do this job to make a living."

"In this case, is our exploitation a deed of merit?"

"Your way of thinking is out of date."

Despite my profound unease, I had my shoes shined and afterwards tugged at Brow to run away.

"Truly you do learn from the company you keep," I lamented. "I'm against Chivalry's extravagance and wastefulness, and yet I have come here to splurge."

It was already afternoon by the time I arrived home. The construction of the stone archway had been greenlighted and announced. Chivalry didn't say anything when he noticed me. He didn't ask me where I went in the middle of the meeting either. His eyes fixed on my new trousers and shiny leather shoes. He was brought up short, but kept silent.

Building a stone archway was not a simple task. Masons could be hired and the stones required were available in the Yucheng County seventeen miles away from the Western Capital. After doing the costings, we found that the building materials and the masons' pay amounted to 100,000 yuan. Since it was decided on by Chivalry and he was the Village Head, he informed me that there would be no sharing out of the dividend from the pharmacy this month. I endorsed whatever he decreed. Chivalry then criticised me for not being cooperative and asked me what I meant by pulling such a long face.

"Nothing. My hair is long and I am short-sighted, so what could I mean?"

He let out a quacking sound. "Good, during the fundraising period you should throw yourself into this work and not go downtown as your whim takes you. That way, I won't be able to find your shadow anywhere in the village."

He knew that I had gone downtown, that cunning Chivalry! "Benevolent Lenient Village is not an army barracks," I retorted. "Yet you don't let me even have a squaddie's freedom? Do the divvying as you like. The money was distributed to each house only last month and now you are asking for it back. You carry on undermining the villagers' productivity."

"That's right!" Chivalry boomed. "Here is my qualified team leader and this is the advice I want to hear from you. I have given it some thought too. Impositions are a problem. Let's take out a loan instead. It's said that you can't set up a lottery without permission from certain authorities, but we can take out a loan.

"Who doesn't have some money to hand? If a certain someone can put on airs by paying to have her shoes cleaned then she can cough up so the village can do something great."

I glared at him and growled spitefully: "Yeah, I've had my shoes cleaned. In future, I will go downtown to take a sauna." Having said that, I couldn't resist tittering.

Money was borrowed per capita, 200 yuan for each person. Although most villagers showed signs of reluctance, they all finally agreed. Soon, 70,000 yuan was raised, but there were still some villagers who only made verbal promises and dilly-dallied when they were due to withdraw the money. They tried to postpone it from today to tomorrow and from tomorrow to the next day. Shaved Head the grocer and his wife nearly killed each other. Shaved Head smote his chest before Chivalry, but he did not wear the trousers at home and, when he went back to fetch the money, he rowed with his wife. In his anger, he slunk over to Little Wei's home to learn how to play the *erhu*. *Yiyiyah, yiyiyah*, the tunes of *Little Cabbage*[as] and *Cold Cave*[at] were to be heard blaring out.

His wife continued to hurl abuse in front of the shop even when an outsider passed by selling tender, well-cooked corn on the cob.

Missus Shaved Head accosted him and said: "I've been a peasant all my life. Still, I haven't eaten corn on the cob for a fair few years. How much is one?"

She grabbed a cob and began to bite it, though quibbled over a ten cent discount when it was time to pay.

"Ten cents off and that's it," the seller stood his ground. "You won't become rich and I won't become poor."

These words grated on the woman's ears and she cursed: "Why should I care a fart whether you are poor or not? Is a shitting piece of cheap corn a gold ingot?"

She flung a roll of loose change on to the counter. The seller didn't say a word and counted the banknotes, finding he had been short-changed to the tune of ten cents. But the woman yelled: "How can the money be under when you come to touch it? Who knows why the money is short? How can I have swindled you? Have a look at this shop. Is your waist thicker than my finger?"

The seller became riled up and tossed the whole basket of corn on the ground, with the riposte: "You must have crawled into the eye of money. I will give you this whole basketful of corn! I suppose I'm feeding a pig with it!"

At Little Wei's home, Shaved Head could overhear sounds from the shop. He stalked out with the *erhu* and, on catching sight of the contretemps, bundled the corn cobs back into the basket and persuaded the outsider to leave. The woman brow-beat Shaved Head, again stoking up a set-to between them. Shaved Head at last found his balls and gave her a kick. The woman pounced and clawed his face so it became mangled. Then, slapping and beating her head against the ground, she threatened to commit suicide.

Someone ran to report the disturbance to Chivalry. Chivalry asked, "What about Shaved Head?" and was told that Shaved Head had kicked his wife. Chivalry flashed: "Do it again; aim straight at her arse."

At the stroke of noon, the couple was still embroiled in their drama. Someone ran to report it to Chivalry, saying that the woman was going to hang herself. Chivalry asked, "What about Shaved Head?" and was told that Shaved Head was weaving a grass cord at home. Chivalry advised: "Take this one. I have ready-made ropes here."

At dusk, Shaved Head's wife suddenly started to channel psychically the words of the dead. In the voice of A-Shun's late father, she ranted and raved that A-Shun and his mother were pitiful. A widow, who was already short of money and grain, still had to bear the burden of contributing to the building of a decorated archway. The First Emperor was building the Great Wall! Next, with dishevelled hair, she wailed and laughed.

A-Shun's father was a fiendish man when he was alive. Now, he swore and cursed through the mouth of Shaved Head's wife. Many stepped forward to pinch the ridge between her nose and mouth and pour soul-awakening soup made with peach wood into her mouth; some took out the white and red notice paper issued by the Court and pasted it on her head. The woman still didn't open her eyes and spittle dribbled out of her mouth.

Chivalry came over to intervene, recalling: "A couple of years ago in the Zhongnan Mountains, I saw a chap who cured this kind of speaking in tongues. Go and get a spoonful of urine. Ghosts fear urine."

Sure enough, somebody fetched a spoon of piss.

Chivalry said: "I need three guys to pin her down and then we must use chopsticks to pry open her mouth. Let me pour this slowly down her hatch." Shaved Head's wife instantly opened her eyes and stared daggers at Chivalry. She then ripped a wad of banknotes out from her bra and screeched: "Take them, take them!" She stood up and stalked home. She no longer stirred up trouble.

The money was ready at last. Chivalry beckoned Shaved Head to another county to hire the masons and subbed him for food and boarding. Shaved Head handed the money to his wife and hit the road with two pancakes.

Chivalry hadn't shown his face for several days. One day, when I was at Grandpa Cloud Forest's place consulting him about sending someone to purchase medicinal herbs, Chivalry entered, whipped out a roll of paper from his chest and spread it out with a rustle on the bed. I believed he had taken up collecting calligraphy and paintings as a hobby, when in fact he had gone to the City Design Institute with the purpose of asking the architectural designers to sketch the blueprint for the stone archway. Of course, the newly-designed archway appeared markedly different from a chastity archway, especially the words and carvings to be inscribed on it, which had nothing to do with chastity. The pictures to go on the dragon and phoenix plaques, the large horizontal tablet and the small horizontal tablet related three stories.

"This is my idea," he proceeded. "The three dragon and phoenix plaques on the main and minor archways will tell people stories about the Three Kingdoms.[au] This is *Military Council Hall*, this is *Plight Mutual Faith in the Peach Garden*[av] and this is *Three Visits to the Cottage*.[aw]

"A decorated archway in a village should not only be a symbol, but also something that educates the villagers. When attempting something big, unity must be found first. If the villagers want to stand united, they should follow the example of plighting mutual faith in the peach garden.

"Running a village is the same as running a country. After Liu Xuande[ax] had established his capital, Cao Cao[ay] in the North had the advantage of timely circumstances, and Sun Quan[az] in the South had the terrain in his favour. Liu only had the allegiance of his men. He sought peace with the western tribes and pacified the Li and Yue people of the South. He befriended Sun Quan, who was outside the country and ran the government well from the inside. He first made a firm stand for his tripod out of the southern lands[ba] and then campaigned for the northern heartland. Don't laugh. These are the original words from the novel.

"As to 'Plight mutual faith in the peach garden,' this refers to a peach tree with Zhang Fei[bb] standing on the top, Guan Yu[bc] squatting in the middle and Liu Bei sitting quietly at the base with his feet firmly on the ground. Zhang Fei suggested, with the tree as his witness, that whoever climbed higher should have precedence over the other two. With these words, he catapulted himself to the canopy of the tree, Guan Yu crouched at its middle and Liu Bei sat at its root. Inscribed on the big horizontal tablet will be a picture of the twelve signs of the Chinese zodiac: the Rat, the Ox, the Tiger, the Rabbit, the Dragon and the Snake being on the left; the Horse, the Sheep, the Monkey, the Rooster, the Dog and the Pig on the right; and the Cat in the centre. The Cat is not included among the twelve signs of the Chinese zodiac, but it was, in fact, the Cat that initiated the naming of the Chinese birth signs. He forgot himself, but was glad to be the commander in the command tent.

"Inscribed on the small horizontal tablet is a picture of meeting at the Magpie Bridge, the old buffalo crouching at the centre, the Cowherd and his children in two baskets on the left, the Queen Mother of the West and the Girl

Weaver on the right, and the Magpie Bridge behind the cow, where the Cowherd and Girl Weaver will meet.[bd] The traditional farming idyll in which the man tills and the woman weaves is admired by us peasants. I don't care if their love story goes smoothly or not. I set great store by buffalo. A peasant depends on his ploughing ox. There are no ploughing oxen in Benevolent Lenient Village, but they are a symbol of our land and we can't forget our peasant roots.

"The whole archway is made up of three four-pillar and seven-storey towers. The four pillars will be arranged like this: two on the outside and two in the middle. Each pillar will bear a picture of the stories of six filial sons, which all together make up the *Stories of Twenty-four Filial Sons*.[be] Throughout the whole of China, there is no Temple of Twenty-four Filial Sons. People don't even mention these tales anymore, but we will inscribe them on the pillars. Filial affection is also a part of cultural civilisation and, what is more important, is that one sight of this will tell people that this is the countryside."

Chivalry explained with such passion that two blobs of foam formed at the corners of his mouth.

His train of thought proved systematic and was something I had to admire. Obviously, though, I could sense that the pictures he had designed were brimming over with the cockiness and confidence that signalled he was Mr Big in the village.

"Liu Bei sits at the foot of the tree and the Cat initiates the naming of the twelve signs of the Chinese zodiac in the command tent. This might be a way of saying that a man's life should have a solid foundation. Benevolent Lenient Village is based on farming. It also shows that the villagers come first and you come last, but you are Liu Bei and the Cat."

Chivalry glared at me and his eyes gleamed with a kind of cold, ghostly light. Old Ran's eyes couldn't emanate such a light, nor could Old Shao's, even though his eyes were big and watery. When I was young, wolves sat on the field ridges howling like an old woman weeping. Mother shut the gate and didn't allow me to go out, saying that a wolf's eyes glint with green light at night.

Chivalry's eyes bulged, but weren't round, and when he knitted his brow, his eyelids folded into three.

"Yeah," he pronounced, his finger rapping the table loudly. "In this society, I make no bones about being an official because, only through being an official, can you do what you want to do. I agreed to be the Village Head because I wanted absolute authority in the village. I don't have this authority for selfish purposes. I, Chivalry, don't want to get rich – I don't even have a wife. What I want is to do something great."

He reared up and, with his head held high, unbuttoned his shirt. His was a chicken's chest!

"Grandpa Cloud Forest, look at Uncle Chivalry and see if he looks like a wolf?"

I recalled that he swaggered clumsily at ordinary times, throwing his head and chest forward while his body still lagged behind. Moreover, his eyes scanned around in an alert manner. Even when he was clean shaven, his chin appeared iron black, and his upper teeth were wide and protruding, though his lower teeth stayed closely bunched together and retracted backward. I felt proud of my sudden discovery. Still, Grandpa Cloud Forest sat with his eyes closed and snored, which more or less soured Chivalry's mood. I asked again: "Grandpa Cloud Forest, Grandpa Cloud Forest, have you fallen asleep?"

"I'm listening," Grandpa Cloud Forest responded.

"Do you agree with this design?"

Grandpa Cloud Forest opened his eyes to fumble for his water pipe, polished off a pipeful of tobacco, flicked the ball of fire on to the ground, refilled the bowl, picked up the ball of fire and pressed it into the bowl of the pipe to draw on again. "Chivalry is the Village Head," he enunciated. "Whatever he says goes."

Chapter Fifteen

Shaved Head transported a batch of stones to the village. Twelve masons settled down in a cluster of felt sheet-roofed bunkhouses in a corner of the pharmacy courtyard. These guys were all weirdos. Throughout the day, they chiselled stones on the empty ground on the other side of the cemetery. At mealtimes, they always fished out noodles from a cauldron. They straggled about the pharmacy, each of them with a big bowl, and chattered while stuffing themselves and tut-tutting audibly. According to the rules, when the pharmacy was in business, extraneous people were forbidden to chit-chat around the counter in case the counter-keeper made a mistake in dispensing herbs.

Once, Last Counter Keeper found himself unable to decipher a Chinese character written in running script on a prescription and asked a mason called Eighth Yang, who had a big bowl in his hand.

After telling him what the Chinese character was, Yang felt very cocky and asked Last Counter Keeper why the old gatekeeper in the cemetery always fixed his eyes on the spot behind his ears and reached out to touch there more than once. Last Counter Keeper knew why, of course, but only grinned. He had also heard the executioner explain what kind of people were prone to commit suicide and what kind of people were apt to being put behind bars or beheaded.

Presently, he told Yang that the indentations on both of his nostrils were configured in an ominous way. With most people, these ran down passing by the corners of the mouth, but his ran directly to his mouth. "Has your personal freedom ever been restricted? Have you ever been cross-examined, let's say, or put under supervision?" Yang asked him what he was driving at. Last Counter Keeper gave nothing away, but asked again if the father of another mason had passed away many years ago. Yang said "yeah" and felt very surprised.

Then he quizzed Last Counter Keeper about why he should ask him if his personal freedom had ever been restricted. One asked the question and one gave the answer. Owing to this distraction, the diner's food became cold and Last Counter Keeper made a mistake in dispensing the medicine. I criticised Last Counter Keeper severely, imposed a fine of several yuan on his bonus and forbade the masons from going to the counter to natter.

They then began to loiter in the inner slicing room, watching First Cutter cutting the herbal ingredients into small pieces. First Cutter was tight-mouthed and scrupulous. When these guys came in, he would tidy away the fine goods and gesture for A-Shun to slice up the medicinal herbs. A-Shun chopped motherwort, hemp-agrimony, perilla leaves and taxillus.

"Rough Cutter." The masons already knew A-Shun's nickname. "I can do that job of yours. You don't know how to cut them into slices. You only do them lengthways."

"You know a fart!" A-Shun lashed out. "Do you know the meaning of *'liquorice should be cut like willow leaves, an inch of white peony root should be cut into two hundred slices, monkshood should be sliced thin enough to float in the air and betel nut should be so thin that it appears untouched*'?"

"I don't, but I do know Chairman Mao said 'I like eating sweet potatoes'. You can also declare that you like eating sweet potatoes and may well be telling the truth. Does that make you Chairman Mao?"

A-Shun blushed. "You're good, but I've seen that your master's skill is for carving flowers in stone. So, why do you only grind stones from morning to night?"

"Think it's easy to grind stones and that anyone can do it? One fellow can only manage to finish grinding two slabs a day. When the finished slabs have water poured over them, the cracks stay dry, you little shit."

I couldn't help spluttering into laughter when they engaged in this tongue tournament. Eighth Yang no longer talked to A-Shun but came to me to heap praise on the affluence of our village. He was a smooth-tongued guy. After passing on his compliments, he sweet-talked me, saying: "Manager, can you find a home for me? I won't mind even if it means me having to marry into Benevolent Lenient Village."

"You've got your eye on our village?"

"It is a good place, near the city proper. Perhaps one day the city will suck you up and all at once you'll be city dwellers. Living in our home village for generations, you can't strip off your peasant skin. If I can come to Benevolent Lenient Village, any household is OK. My wife doesn't need have to be pretty; I only want to diversify the genes of my offspring."

I gave him the once-over. A snub nose. No, I didn't want to carry on with this conversation.

"This is a great idea," A-Shun chipped in. "Sister Plum, one branch of the Fang family at the southern end of the village hasn't got a son-in-law yet. He could marry into their family."

I couldn't bring to mind any girl in the Fang family; there was just an old man with a humped back.

Yang queried: "A widow or a virgin girl?"

A-Shun replied: "Everything is good about her except that her mouth is a little long and her ears are a little big. And she isn't a virgin either."

"Has she got babies already?"

"Eight babies. When she breastfeeds them, four crouch on either side."

Yang cottoned on, heaved a spiteful sigh and ignored A-Shun. I smoothed things over by adding: "We won't take in an outsider. You have no wife? Even our Village Head still doesn't have a wife yet." My words put a smile on Yang's face.

"Chivalry still doesn't have a wife?" he ejaculated. "But he's tough guy and looks so dashing. How could he have no wife?" Then he whooped joyously, saying that everything in Benevolent Lenient Village was good except for their women, who all had pale faces. But, of course, the Manager is the pick of the bunch.

"I don't blame you," I replied. "You set your mind on marrying into our village, but you look down on our women."

"The trees are not green, the flowers not red, the sky always greyish, the sun never bright, the roads buried beneath a layer of black coal ash, freshly-harvested grain is never to be had and the water is heavy with the smell of soda. Look at you, city guys."

"Our place doesn't belong to the city."

"*He-he*," Yang laughed. "Our home village is poor, but the water and earth are good and the girls are all tall and slim with peaches and cream complexions." He touched his own face. "The water and the earth in my hometown only nurture women and not men. If Chivalry really doesn't have a wife, I shall introduce one to him. We have Pretty Face, who declares she will marry the son of the County

Head if she gets married at all. Hmm, how can a county head there be as good as the head of a village here?"

I didn't know why, but I made no response. "Huh, I need to go to the miscellaneous room to air-dry those medicinal pills and powder." With that, I walked away and, from then on, couldn't abide the sight of Eighth Yang.

When most of the work of carving the stones was done, the foundations of the decorated archway started to be dug. The chosen site happened to be the entrance to the main lane in the south-west. We didn't know from where, but Chivalry hired a feng-shui master, who decided the position with the help of a pair of compasses, saying that it faced the dimly-visible main peak of Mount Tianzhu in the Zhongnan Mountains.

The hole was to be dug deep because the submerged part of the four pillars should be half the height of that which stood above ground. When a depth of thirty-two feet was reached, Gao Feng swung his pickaxe. *Clonk* – he bounced back, flailing over together with his digging tool. Believing that he must have struck a hard rock, he yelled: "Give me a crowbar." The crowbar was plunged in and he jerked his wrists hard. The corner of the stone that was exposed had a smooth surface and seemed to be inscribed with Chinese characters. Gao Feng guessed: "We've hit an ancient tomb."

An eight-pound sledgehammer was deployed, which cracked the stone slab into two. The pieces were then hauled up with iron wires. No tomb lay beneath, though after the two broken sections were joined together, the characters on top obviously formed the inscription of a memorial tablet. Chivalry bent over to inspect them. Many characters had been eroded, forming an indistinct blur. What appeared to be recorded were the origins of the Jia family. Jia was the commonest surname in Benevolent Lenient Village, for it was shared by almost seventy per cent of all the households. The stone slab must have been a relic from their ancestors.

Chivalry upbraided Gao Feng with foul words, saying that he shouldn't have used the eight-pounder. The skin of Gao Feng's hand tore when he was prying out the stone. Picking up a wad of chicken feathers from the ground, he applied them to the bloody bruise and groaned in dismay: "How was I to know that it is a stone tablet?"

On that day, I received word from Brow and went to her home to see the effects of her nose-lift. Originally, she had a pert nose. More than anything she wanted a nose like a foreigner and went through hoops to have it padded out. Following the operation, the organ was swollen. When I entered her courtyard, she closed the gate to prevent anyone else from catching sight of it.

After listening to her lecture about the demeanour and temperament of a modern lady, I heard someone knocking at the gate of the courtyard. Brow held her tongue and didn't allow me to go and open it. Then we heard someone shouting abuse: "Beat this horny dog! Raised by Benevolent Lenient Village? A sex-crazed beast, whoever he sees, he will take liberties with." Next, stones and fragments of tile showered down over the gate; one stone landed in the courtyard and smashed a flowerpot on the stone steps.

I ran out to open the gate. A-Bing was crouching outside. One of his hind legs was already beaten so he had a limp, but he didn't flee. He only barked. Three men, two women and a girl stood in the lane and, spying me go out, they took a few steps back, although they went on cursing: "Where did this horny hound come from? Who raised it?

And raised it to be such a beast?" Their words were unpleasant and I had an altercation with them.

It turned out that when I went to Brow's home from Grandpa Cloud Forest's place, A-Bing, who had nothing else to do, tagged along. When he reached her home, he clawed her gate, but we didn't go out to open it. Coincidentally, the group of guys from the stadium compound passed by. Maybe the tuft of hair standing up like a garlic stalk on the girl's head had triggered his playful streak? A-Bing had wrapped his forepaws around her waist. He couldn't have known that, when he stood straight, his not completely healed whip would be exposed. He earned himself a good beating for that.

If the guys' words had not been so harsh, I might have explained to them the ins and outs of A-Bing's condition. However, they just cursed the dog and hurt its master and I would not swallow this.

We started to cross swords. On hearing the racket, many villagers thronged to the lane, swearing and hooting uproariously. Little Wei's wife even swooped this way and let fly unrepeatable words like mercury was surging across the land: "The dog is never horny when he sees our villagers, so why is he turned on by the first sight of you? Is it that the horny creature has met another horny creature or has the dog sniffed another dog's pong?"

Old Ran's sister-in-law pulled me to one side and blamed me: "The dog might have come looking for Brow. Does it have anything to do with you? You scream abuse like this; an unmarried girl – you want the others to gossip?"

I retaliated: "I have screamed abuse. What am I afraid of? Afraid that nobody will marry me? Better if this were the case."

Old Ran's sister-in-law was choked and, though her mouth was open, was unable to say a word. I scraped up A-Bing and went back to Brow's home to chat. Liuhe ran over and said Chivalry wanted me at the entrance to the village to look at a stone tablet. I asked him, what tablet? He didn't know. I said I wouldn't go. Liuhe said the Village Head asked me to go and I wouldn't? I asked him if a Village Head's words were an emperor's decree? Nonetheless, I still went.

When I got to the pit, Chivalry observed that my face appeared amiss. I filled him in about the slanging match. He, seemingly uninterested, only murmured: "This Brow…", then picked off some dirt from the tablet and enjoined me to study the inscription. The text was very long, recording how Jia Wansan became the "richest man on the south of the Yangtze River" in the Ming Dynasty.[bf] One paragraph related his exploits as follows:

Zhu Yuanzhang established his capital in Nanjing. Jia Wansan helped him build one third of the city walls, a feat which made the entire country bewildered and envious. Jia Wansan then suggested that he reward the ranks of the three armies. Fierce was Zhu Yuanzhang's rage when he exclaimed: "If an ordinary person wants to reward the whole army then that will cause trouble to the public. He should be decapitated." The queen remonstrated: "Heaven will punish the inauspicious lout. Why should Your Majesty have him executed?" Later, Jia Wansan was transported to a distant place for penal servitude.

Aiyao! I let out a scream. We only knew that our ancestor was a drummer in the army of Zhu Yuanzhang, who contracted scabies and had pus flowing all over his body as he was fighting here and there. He was ditched, wandered to the village in poverty to multiply his offspring and left behind the *Drum Music of the Ming Emperor*. We never realised our ancestor was once the richest householder south of the Yangtze River and had such legendary splendour.

That night, I stayed at home with A-Bing and bathed him in medicinal waters as per the prescription from by Grandpa Cloud Forest. Then I sent A-Bing to sleep on a Ming-style wooden bed. I myself couldn't manage to drop off. An Asian tiger mosquito buzzed. Dung beetles crawled up along the foot of the walls. Was that the sound of earthworms exhaling or were land snails sighing? A-Bing *hmmed* like a man and kept tossing and turning left and right. I detected a flea inching its way to my belly from my ankle. It must have leapt over from A-Bing. Having sucked his blood to its heart's content, the flea had a noxious odour.

What did Jia Wansan, my ancestor, look like? A man could rake in money in this world if he was rough, simple-minded with thinning hair, a thick hide and shed oily sweat. When he was stinking rich, was that old lout of an emperor Zhu Yuanzhang perhaps still a beggar? You were wealthy and that's good, but why did you still want to be noble? Why did you squander several million kilos of silver to build a third of the walls of the capital? Why would you want to reward the three armies? Did you want to use this route to enter the imperial service and stand among the ranks of the ministers? A wealthy guy is never noble; a noble guy is never wealthy. What a simple truth this is.

Furthermore, the family name Jia meant "businessman". Surely destiny dictated that a member of this clan could never be a king. A-Bing again flared his nostrils. Could a dog get sinusitis too, or did he merely grunt because he was dreaming? No matter how pretty or smart a dog might be, these qualities were only sufficient to save him from the slaughterhouse. Once he exposed his whip, Brow kicked him and the outsiders threw stones at him. But a dog mustn't be treated as a man by humans. I still could not fathom: even if our ancestor was so proud of himself and overstepped his station why would Zhu Yuanzhang want to execute him? On top of that, why would the queen call him an "inauspicious lout"? Inauspicious lout!

The bright moonlight winked through the window, illuminating the dainty authentic Ming Dynasty sandal-wood box at the head of the bed. The four, green Chinese characters on it, "Flower Blooms in Spring", could be seen clearly. I dipped a finger into my saliva and, relying on my instincts, reached gently under the quilt to catch the flea in the sticky fluid. I failed, though my hand made contact with my coccyx. Mine protruded. This was an unmentionable secret known only to me and my mother. Ten years ago, I came across a piece of news in the inner margin of a news-paper, which reported that every inhabitant in a small African village had a small tail, which the press labelled "atavism." Was my coccyx also a small tail? Even though it only stuck out a little, I dreaded that it might grow into a mouse's tail in the future. I wore a pair of big, close-fitting knickers throughout the year and never allowed anyone to touch me there. Inauspicious lout. Did Jia Wansan also have a jutting coccyx?

All through the night, wild thoughts crowded into my mind until my head ached, and felt as if it had been filled with water. Whenever I moved, the waves crested painfully. After getting up at the break of day, I headed to the mirror. My face was black and, when I reached my hands out, they resembled chicken claws. Flesh; where was the flesh on my hands?

"Grandpa Cloud Forest!" In my grave doubt, I consulted Grandpa Cloud Forest. The monks in the temples were the modern incarnations of the ancients and Grandpa Cloud Forest could instantly create a bridge between modern society and ancient times. "The record on the stone tablet, have you seen it? What do you think of it?"

"A peach tree used to stand there," Grandpa Cloud Forest remembered from the past. "The peach tree was so old it was riddled with holes and just crawled along the ground. Every year, it came into blossom early but never had any fruit, so the villagers referred to it as a male peach tree. In fact, it must have been dropping us a hint about the stone tablet buried beneath it. A pity nobody ever thought about that. Later, when the road was being built, it was whacked by an excavator and snapped in two."

Grandpa Cloud Forest held a rubbing of the inscription in his hand. He pondered it at and ran his hand over the paper again and again before asking Chivalry to hang it on the wall.

"The stone tablet was buried so deep and, what is more, none of us knew that its history went back that far. Was it buried like this because our forefathers didn't want to mention it?" I still couldn't banish the expression 'inauspicious lout' from my mind. "We'd better bury it under the decorated archway."

"How brilliant the history of our ancestor was," Chivalry chuntered on. "If they didn't want to mention it, why would they have it carved on the tablet? It must have been buried underground because of an earthquake or something. The peach tree was either a mark or the revelation of a god, or it stood simply because the stone tablet was waiting.

"Just imagine: having been buried for so long, it reappears exactly when we are putting up the decorated archway. What does this mean?"

Increasingly, Chivalry was inclined to grow puffed up with pride and put a positive spin on anything.

"Close your eyes and think about it again," he continued. "A peasant, no matter how rich he was, had the guts to help build the walls of the capital city and even had the guts to suggest that the ranks of the three armies be rewarded.

"Our ancestor was a peasant whose personal wealth could rival that in the national treasury. If he had rebelled, he would surely have beaten Zhu Yuanzhang. If he were a fish, he would be a whale. Now the books all say that peasants are backward, conservative, selfish and mean, but which historical event in China was not achieved by them? After all, Zhu Yuanzhang was a peasant himself."

The old executioner was shouting raucously at someone nearby: "Your afterbirth was buried under the laundry stone in the courtyard!" Where was my afterbirth buried? When Mother combed her head, a lock of hair would always fall out, which was then coiled into a ball and poked into a crack in the wall.

"A peasant must know peasants best," I interposed. "So, Zhu Yuanzhang had our ancestor exiled." Inauspicious lout!

"If he were not exiled, how could there be the *Drum Music of the Ming Emperor*? How could there be Benevolent Lenient Village?" Chivalry speculated.

Grandpa Cloud Forest only smiled a fond smile that bared his gums. Today, he brewed tea for me and Chivalry with the snow water he collected in winter. He encouraged: "Drink! Drink your tea."

Since our ancestor's stone tablet was unearthed, Chivalry's confidence had been more conspicuous; he bragged everywhere about our ancestor's bold spirit, and it appeared as if he were born with the soul of this ancestor in his body. He directed the villagers to dig the foundations, while spewing dirty words at them. As to those masons, he capriciously required them to do their tasks like this and not like that. According to the original design, the main, minor, sandwiched and flanking parts of the decorated archway should have rising ridges and slopes with decorative animal figurines on the upturned roof ridges. Now he insisted that various decorative animal figurines should be added: a dragon, phoenix, lion, tiger, unicorn, heavenly steed, seahorse, fish, the *xiezhi*,[bg] the *hou*[bh] and the monkey. "We want a luxury item. It will be passed down for dozens or hundreds of years and become a cultural relic."

Thus, swimming dragons and fluttering phoenixes were carved in the sole horizontal tablet, the Three Sage Kings and the Five August Emperors,[bi] and three lotus flowers and five lotus leaves were introduced between the horizontal dragon gate tablet and the small horizontal tablet. The bottom of the pillars was decorated with skyward-facing lotus flowers, downturned lotus flowers, pendulous flowers and sea lilies.

"Plum," Chivalry crowed, "I have almost cracked it. Later, if we build a pagoda-shaped hotel, the pillars, doors and windows will all be painted yellow and all the furniture will be made of red wood. One exhibition hall will be left especially for you to exhibit those Ming and Qing Dynasty pieces."

"Leave it at that. Think about how to decorate your office first," I parried. "By that time, you will be the Manager, no, the CEO, signing a whole heap of documents for the village."

"I'm talking serious business and you always think I'm playing a child's game. In the village, I'm the King and you're the Queen. We should cooperate harmoniously."

"You are my uncle!"

Blushing, he started to rub his hands; the female member looking rather bashful.

When the decorated archway stood fully erect, firecrackers exploded and drums thundered, and people from near and far descended to watch the effervescent scene. Chivalry persisted in climbing up the construction scaffolding to gild with powder the three Chinese characters 'Benevolent Lenient Village' as written by the Mayor and later inscribed on the dragon gate tablet of the main part of the decorated archway.

After that, he draped a swag of red cloth along the topmost ridge. Actually, these jobs should have been done by the masons. He now turned to leap on to the ridge and a miraculous spectacle unfolded. First, he sprang upright, doffed his small straw hat and waved to greet the crowd below, after the fashion of Chairman Mao when he stood at the city tower of Tiananmen Square. Before the crowd knew what had hit them, he almost cried out in frenetic excitement.

Scared, I hollered out from below: "Squat down, squat down; it's too dangerous." He turned a deaf ear and launched into a somersault on the ridge, balancing on one foot like a golden rooster. My heart leapt into my throat, and everyone below was terrified. They blanched and unconsciously stretched out their hands as if to catch him. But Chivalry's frenzy intensified, with him jumping and swinging, pulling all kinds of stunts. Once, he missed his footing intentionally and toppled down. We screamed out. But when we looked again, his foot had hooked a corner of a stone slab on the ridge and, with a gentle swing, he pulled himself back on to his feet. Not until then did we know that he possessed spectacular kung-fu.

Where did he learn kung-fu? For as long as he had been back in the village, he had not shown even the slightest hint of it? Faintly, I heard someone whisper: "*Xiah*, quite a spirit."

"The stone tablet was destined to be dug out. Wansan has come back to life again!"

"How could Wansan be as good as this? It's Shi Qian the Flea on the Drum."[bj]

"You mean he is a thief?"

"Tell me where he learned this kung-fu from?"

Seeing that Grandpa Cloud Forest hadn't come, I ran to carry him over, but the gate of the shrine was open and no one was in.

I asked A-Bing, who was dozing under the gatepost: "A-Bing, A-Bing, where is Grandpa Cloud Forest?" A-Bing answered *Wow!* and hurried to the cemetery. Sure enough, Grandpa Cloud Forest and the executioner were playing five-in-a-row Go at the entrance to a lane in the underworld village. Behind them lay an unpainted toon wood plank, which read: "Do you know your home?" A bottle of liquor balanced on the plank and whoever lost a round must drink. The executioner was already high and, sweeping aside the counters, he carped: "The board is full of demonic aura. How could a man beat a demon?" But he persisted in going another round and asked me to sit down and take his place to drink. They romped like children and squabbled over a move, during which time I had already drunk eight big mouthfuls of hard liquor and felt merry.

"You won't go look at the decorated archway?" I burbled. "Eye-poppingly impressive."

Grandpa Cloud Forest asked: "Really? And is Chivalry eye-poppingly impressive too?"

Grandpa Cloud Forest must have been a deity. He hadn't gone there, but knew how Chivalry was flaunting his kung-fu!

"He has his fun and we have ours."

The executioner again brushed aside the counters. "Plum, drink another mouthful. I don't believe that I can't beat him."

I was duty-bound to drink another mouthful and the game of Go carried on with great interest.

That afternoon, I should have carried Grandpa Cloud Forest to join the fun, but instead ended up getting squiffy in the cemetery. In an alcoholic trance, I recalled the story of the *Rotten Handle*, which described how a woodcutter saw two elderly people playing Go deep in the mountains. Transfixed, he didn't know how long he had been watching and when the game ended, the handle of his axe on the ground had already gone rotten. I arose, observing that a stone nearby had liquefied without flowing away. And so, I sat on it. *Wow!* I had dumped myself on A-Bing. Then, I lapsed into unconsciousness.

Chapter Sixteen

We made a date to rendezvous at Solitary Tree. This was a place name. When I was in school, a tree – a willow tree – stood in this expanse of cornfield. I didn't know why a century-old willow tree would stand in a 25 *mu* cornfield as lush green as a forest, and why the place was called Solitary Tree and not something else.

Every afternoon, I went there to go over my lessons with a book, chanting "…knocking on the sun as if knocking on glass", while the setting sun was being pecked at by the birds on the limbs of the tree (the birds were, in fact, pecking at the tree – *boom, boom*).

Later, that quiet reading terrace was encroached upon by courting men and women from the city and, still later, the second ring road of the capital city swung past and the willow tree disappeared. But this station was still called Solitary Tree. We would sit on the cement benches alongside the pavement, the vehicles whizzing past behind the closed guard rails before us like running water as I handed Fan Jingquan a number of articles I had written.

It was I who suggested to Chivalry that we should seek out Fan Jingquan for help, but before I went, Chivalry eyed up my shoes and asked me how much they cost. I claimed 40 yuan. He disagreed: "You are lying. At least 160."

I retorted: "I'm a peasant. Even if I wear a pair of 300-yuan shoes, others won't notice. And, if I put on a pair of 40-yuan shoes, others won't believe that either."

"Then, as you've said, wear this pair, but you should

change your clothes. Change into your best finery."

I said with a smile: "You asked me to dress up like this. You want me to sacrifice myself for the village."

Fan Jingquan and I made an appointment to meet at Solitary Tree. I waited there for quite a while and he still didn't come. In a fit of annoyance, I turned to look at a not so distant hotel to kill time. It was an extremely luxurious hotel: the whole lobby was glazed with tea-coloured glass; the revolving door swirled one bunch of men and women in and another bunch out; and the several dozen columns of water in the fountain in front of the door vaulted up and down in a tedious way, making people feel drowsy.

Three girls, very beautiful, so beautiful that I was pricked by a sense of inferiority, stood by the fountain for a long time. A fat guy and two bony ones came out, laughing loudly about something, and then strode towards the girls, talking with them for an eternity. The fat guy then grabbed the waist of one of the girls to return to the hotel, but the other pairs of men and women seemingly had a falling out. The two men walked slowly towards me and drew to a standstill not far away. One moaned: "400 yuan for such a dark face?" The other one noted: "She's a newcomer." The first cursed: "Shit. You ask any one of them, they all say they are newcomers. She can fool you, but can she fool me?"

The man smiled at me and, not knowing why, I beamed back. With his hooked finger, the man beckoned me to join him. I immediately realised that they were a couple of whoremongers and spat out a gobful of saliva. Gao Feng once told me that there were professional escorts in the hotels of the capital city. Were the three girls on the game? At that very moment, to my astonishment, Fan Jingquan sauntered out of the hotel. At the sight of me, he apologised for being late and alleged he had gone to see a friend.

"See a friend? Or gone in to look for a working girl?"

"I wanted to, but now I feel the pinch and don't have that kind of money." He was all smiles. "Who else would I want when I have such a beautiful lady waiting for me here?"

"Huh," I heaved a hateful sigh. "Have you seen that pack of girls? All professional escorts, and I've seen them dealing with pimps. The men were all so evil-looking. The girls, though, they are so pretty and look so naïve. At the bottom of my heart, I really don't feel good. If I had money I would go buy them their freedom."

"Buy them their freedom? This is a hotel, not a brothel. There is no madam here," Fan Jingquan reminded me.

"Then I would give them each a large sum of money and let them go back home. A pity I don't have money."

"Plum has such a merciful heart. Circumstances might have forced them on to the game but, then again, they might not have. Needless to say, you have no money. Even if you had, you could dole out the money and send them back home today, but they might come again tomorrow."

"Don't they know what shame is? Don't they feel agony in their hearts?"

"Stop there, stop there. Plum, did you come here to discuss the city's whore problem with me? I don't want to sit on the street talking about such a heavy topic."

I quickly handed him my articles.

"If there is a wind," Fan Jingquan casually said as he browsed my articles.

"What wind?" My mind was still a jumble of thoughts and I turned to look at the door of the hotel again. The two girls were still there, and another man was already talking business with them.

"Wind?" Now cottoning on, I immediately knew that Fan Jingquan was commenting on my hat. I was wearing a small hat today, woven from Chinese wedelia grass.

Benevolent Lenient villagers always thought that Brow and I led the way where fashion was concerned. In fact, Brow led me.

After she had worn such a hat, she demanded that I also put one on. The day before yesterday, I met Old Ran and he didn't notice any difference. This Fan Jingquan was sensitive and he noticed, yet he mentioned it in a roundabout way. The garrulous writer!

"Is the hat attractive?"

"Very."

"You sure know how to praise a woman."

"Praising a woman can make a man noble."

He reached out a hand to remove my hat. I pressed down on it. His hand froze knowingly in mid-air, but he posed: "Why is there no wind?"

"Even if a wind came, I would pin my hat down and wouldn't let you see it."

"If the wind were to whip up your skirt, would you still try to protect your hat?"

"One hand would press down the skirt and one would take care of the hat."

"Then take care of your skirt now."

I bent my head, noticing that while I was sitting my skirt had ridden up to my knees. I swiftly dragged it down and tucked it in. "Don't let your fancy run wild."

"I thought you'd asked to meet me here for a nice reason."

"How could this not be a nice thing? The decorated archway has been built in our village. Hasn't Old Ran told you? Now we want to make much more of it. I came here to beg a favour. I need you to polish the articles and then try to find a way to get them published. Your labours won't go unrewarded."

I brought out a wad of RMB, rustled the notes and then tossed them on to the cement bench. "How much?" he asked.

"One hundred and fifty."

"Enough for us to have a square meal."

"If the articles don't make it into the newspaper, neither of us can take a bite."

"I'm full already."

"Huh?"

"Your beauty is a feast."

Fan Jingquan's words always managed to make you feel glad in your heart and shy in your face. They relieved you of your boredom and tiredness without you feeling he was an indecent guy. "Fan Jingquan, Mr Fan!" I exclaimed. "I don't understand: a man like you, how could you have befriended Old Ran?"

"Not only your Old Ran, but also Benevolent Lenient Village. I don't understand either. Way back, 'When Confucius travelled west, he was unwilling to go to the State of Qin'. Now the State of Qin has produced Old Ran and Benevolent Lenient Village. Look, you built the decorated archway because of those words inscribed by the Mayor. After building it, you started to generate popularity and now you want to publish your propaganda through the back door. The old tippler's delight does not in fact reside in wine. Step by step, you are trying to see which way the wind is blowing and to exert your influence."

"No matter how good we are, how can we be better than you? After all, you're a teacher. Do you think these articles are OK or not? Can they achieve the desired effects? If they are not good enough, please polish them. Whether they can be published or not all depends on you."

"The articles are good, but I can only talk about the articles themselves. That sentence on the seventh line is a little tongue-twisting. As to getting them published, I can't do anything."

"Why?"

"I have written many novels, though few ended up being published. I never go to the editorial offices to pull strings. How could I do this for such a report? I will give you 150 yuan. Please kindly exempt me from this errand."

Fan Jingquan's words were totally unexpected. He brandished a pen, spread out the manuscripts on his knees and corrected the sentence on the seventh line as well as three spelling mistakes and one punctuation mark.

"I might joke sometimes, Plum, but I really can't do you this favour. Last month, an underboss asked me to write an article for their company and the pay was 10,000 yuan. I didn't, and not because I have a holier-than-thou attitude. I was simply not interested and, if I am not interested, I can't write a word."

I looked at him and he looked back. He pulled a face and repeated: "Sorry."

"Give me a cigarette."

He gave me a cigarette and lit it for me.

"You mean, I, Plum, don't have the right face?"

"Plum, your face is as big as the sky. If it were your own personal business and you asked me to die for you, I would lie under the wheels of a car immediately."

"Then, you disagree with our struggle over the survival of our village?"

"No, I have been paying close attention to you, sympathising with you and showing understanding towards you. I support you in your struggle against those bureaucrats and businessmen.

"Even though I'm a city dweller, I am fed up with the city. The city folks are shrewd, arrogant, calculating, eloquent, never honest, xenophobic, indifferent to others, mean, selfish, faddish, frivolous and sly. They are fond of doing new things for the sake of being unconventional or un-orthodox, they pay too much attention to trivial things and are slack and lax in their discipline. But you and your Chivalry? As an individual, Chivalry is great. I respect and admire him. What is more, he is now the Village Head. The villagers have been counting on an almighty man who can reverse the course of events. Chivalry is just as stubborn and as crazy as a child. Even so, you always say 'no' to the city.

"Is it a good thing to preserve your village? Urbanisation is the means by which the industrialisation of our nation is shown in everyday life. This process is the mega-trend. Can a mega-trend be sidestepped?"

"Then what about us? What are we?" My anger mush-roomed. "In the past, there was the capitalist class and the proletariat, the working class and the peasant brothers. But now, the city slickers don't want us. Without a household registration card, we can't eat low-price grains, can't enjoy the subsidies on non-staple foods, can't receive free medical care, can't get an old-age pension and can't live in affordable apartments. In their eyes, we are peasants. But how can we be peasants in the true sense of the word? We are a pile of leaves in the wind and a mass of clouds scudding across the sky. If we lose this village, what do we have left? Should we go drink the wind and shit out farts? Should we winnow the ashes of our ancestors?"

Focusing on me, Fan Jingquan broke into a smile.

"What are you laughing at? Am I not right?"

"You come across like a left-wing orator from the movies about the 1930s. I have never heard Chivalry's speeches, but from your tone I can guess what he says, can't I? Your words are very inciteful. Really, if I were a Benevolent Lenient Village guy whose personal interests were at stake, I would be stirred up too, as if I had taken a stimulant. However, after you have been stirred up, after you have been stimulated, will you take action and stoop to violence? Can you swing into action? Is this still the age that can give birth to peasant uprisings like those of Chen Sheng and Wu Guang?[bk] Is it still the age that could foster another Cultural Revolution? In this era of the atomic bomb, you might be able to practise your horsemanship and archery until you can shoot a willow leaf from 100 paces, but can you conquer the world? Those words are opium, making the villagers intoxicated with their own sorrowful cries."

"If it goes on like this," I interrupted him, "should we invite the old Village Head to come back, let the village be redeveloped and scatter ourselves about the city to rove and beg? Should we become professional escorts like those girls?"

Fan Jingquan let out a sigh and his shoulders sagged then lifted again. It was obvious he was a little cross. He declaimed: "In a fit of bad temper, you quit the correspondence courses. In my opinion, you should go to a formal university to study. Everyone should recognise the difficult situation you are facing, though in today's society, of all the people, be they city dwellers or rural inhabitants, who doesn't face difficulties? We should start from scratch. Huh, Plum! Why must you emphasise the working class and the peasant class? In some places in the South, cities are already no different from rural areas. Township enterprises are industrialising the countryside. Peasants are workers and workers are peasants.

"We should not simply say 'no' to cities or deny the countryside. We should have a healthy state of mind. Even the climate of the world has changed and the boundaries between the four seasons are being blurred. You should walk out of turbulence, surpass indignation and bid farewell to revolution, which will do good to both people and things. Can't you see that thieves can never be stamped out? Proper etiquette can make enemies retreat. The best military strategy is never to resort to arms; baseness is the passport for the base; revolution is the victim claimed by revolutionaries."

Once Fan Jingquan spouted these quotations, he became so gleeful he lost control of himself. "Mr Fan?" I asked.

"Huh?" He was taken off guard.

"Are you reeling off passages from your novels or giving me tutorial lessons?"

"Hear me out. I think, if Benevolent Lenient Village has its own enterprises and develops its economy, it won't be demolished and redeveloped and the villagers needn't wage such a painful fight. But if Benevolent Lenient Village remains stuck in a rut, it will be rendered obsolete. Despite all your refusals and struggles, the village won't be saved. If you hadn't come to look for me, I would have gone to look for you and provided you with a piece of information. Do you know Magic Farm Tableland?"

"Yes. It is a picture-pretty place 50 *li* to the south of the Western Capital. A few years back when the villagers went on a spring outing, we cycled over there."

"Magic Farm Tableland is a township under the jurisdiction of Wen'an County, which is a part of the capital city. The expressway that leads southwards from the Western Capital goes through it. Nowadays, the Western Capital is regarded as the centre of the cluster of cities, and the counties around the Western Capital are also forming their own city clusters, but Magic Farm Tableland is building a new-style, urban-rural area. It is a city, with all the functions of a city, but without any of the drawbacks and disadvantages of the Western Capital. It is the countryside without rural backwardness. The traffic, communications, trade, life, cultural and entertainment activities are convenient, but the environment is beautiful, the water is not polluted and the air is fresh.

"Of course, its population lives under strict controls and not just anyone can live there. A friend of mine is now the legal counsel for the big real estate company and it is now cooperating with a group from Singapore. Since Benevolent Lenient Village will be demolished, why not try to relocate the whole village collectively?"

"Your tongue churns this way and that, but you still want to let the real estate guys wipe us out. One real estate guy wants to demolish our village to make a killing and then turns it over to another one, who still only wants to use our land to make a fortune. We're a piece of meat. In your words, you describe that place as paradise. Why don't you go there then?"

"Of course, I want to," Fan Jingquan said. "But I'm not qualified. My friend is encouraging me to study law in my spare time. When I've got my lawyer's certificate, I shall follow him to join the team of legal counsels for his company."

He took out two books from his chest, one being *The Art of Fiction* and one being *Legal Knowledge*. I gazed at the white-haired young man. Cars zipped past one by one behind the closed guard rails, the sun cast out shadows aslant on the roadway and numerous vehicles ran over the ridiculous silhouettes of our heads.

"What do you think?" Fan Jingquan shot me a prying question. My mind had gone blank. I didn't agree with all of Fan's words, but what he said happened to make sense. How on earth would Benevolent Lenient Village continue to exist? What would our fate be?

I didn't know what God had ordained for us and I didn't know how Chivalry would lead us forward. But, today, the only concrete fact was that I hadn't fulfilled the task given to me by Chivalry.

"Mr Fan, what you have said – and what I said – reminds me how you tutored me in Classical Chinese in the past: if I say I don't understand, I do actually understand a little; if I say I do understand, strictly speaking I don't. It is paradoxical. Can you repeat these things to Chivalry, or can you tell me why you can't help get these articles published? Otherwise, he might think that I didn't come to look for you."

"I won't go to him."

"You mean, he is Satan?"

Fan Jingquan started to laugh.

"How shall I put it? I disagree with some of his exploits, but if the village didn't have Chivalry, the situation would be unimaginable. I have been drawn to your village because I think God has arranged matters in a perfect way. He asked Grandpa Cloud Forest to be Jesus and Chivalry to be Satan. Life can't go on without Jesus, but life can't go on without Satan either.

"A man's heart is a true hell, like a primitive forest, only a very small part of which is illuminated by the light of civilisation. Nonetheless, civilisation follows its bigoted course and plays its part, believing that this small part is the entirety of the heart or its most rational part. Therefore, a big pile of self-deceiving qualities such as loftiness, beauty, kindness and the like are cooked up and some illusory questions are put forward so as to build a moral, orderly and rationalised internal world that completely ignores negative things and refuses to face the inner world of one's self.

"This is why we feel the city is disgusting, but at the same time are not satisfied with rural life; why existing civilisations become congested and stiffened and why people live increasingly uneasy and shrivelled lives. The progress of society and the perfection of civilisation require many catalysts and the true, the good and the beautiful can be perfected and completed only in these ghastly, spasmodic, wild and rude things. Well, I should stop now, or else you'll laugh at me again and say that I'm warbling out my novels. Chivalry is at the crest of his enthusiasm and won't listen to me. I can do no more than give you information; you must try and influence him and listen to his ideas."

I stood up. I could only say goodbye to Fan Jingquan.

"You really won't resume your correspondence courses?"

"No."

"Then this is my last time tutoring you?"

"Thank you."

"So, we'll just say goodbye?"

I reached out and shook hands with him. My sponge-like hand contracted within his grip. "It's said that if a man shakes hands with Chivalry, his hand will…" he said.

"This is the other Fan Jingquan?"

I retrieved my hand and pretended to lift my skirt to my chest in one go.

"Good, Fan Jingquan. Give an inch, take a foot? If you ask me to lift my skirt on the road, I will oblige."

"Press it down. I am chicken-hearted."

That was Fan Jingquan. If he wasn't warbling out his novels or lecturing people, endless ridiculous remarks would spill out of his mouth. You could listen to him while reproaching him, and still wanted to listen to him after you had cursed him.

Old Ran maintained he was his good friend. That guy was a dangerous fellow. One should not stay with him for too long. If friends stayed with him for long enough, no woman could step out of the shadow he cast over her.

I strolled slowly back to the village, frequently darting glances at the expressway, hoping that somewhere Old Ran would be tailing us and peering. "In this summer sun, your hat is really bonny."

Fan Jingquan still mumbled behind me. I didn't look back but was thinking: why was this place called Solitary Tree? Why had I made an appointment with Fan Jingquan to meet here? What about the three girls? Where did they come from? How did they get caught up in that trade? How would they live in the future?

Chapter Seventeen

I relayed what Fan Jingquan had described to Chivalry. Barely had I spoken a handful of words when he chortled, "Fan Jingquan has appointed himself as the strategic adviser to our village."

I carried on. His face darkened and his hand swished. "A man of letters doesn't know military matters." I held my tongue while I dragged on a cigarette.

He, however, said: "Go on, go on with your words."

I began to talk about Magic Farm Tableland and related, with some embellishment, what Fan Jingquan had conveyed about this earthly utopia. Chivalry listened attentively, though later his lips pouted like a nose and turned this way and that, and then his head bent too. I sensed that Magic Farm Tableland had stirred his heart, but, with his head still bent and his eyelids turned upwards, he asked: "Would they allow us to move as a whole and still live together? Still live like one village? Would they also allow our cemetery to be transferred?"

"I haven't asked in detail. But I think it's possible for us to live together and impossible for us to move the cemetery."

"My prick! Then why should we move in the first place? The water and earth of one place nurtures the people of that place. It's also written in books that the oranges that grow to the south of the Huai River[bl] are tangerines, while those to the north are bitter oranges. If they can build their village well, why can't we? You think that I, Chivalry, only know how to conquer the country but don't know how to run it? Fan Jingquan must have been belittling me."

He recovered the articles and went to enquire among the patients if anyone had any contact with the newspapers. As it happened, the uncle by marriage of the patient boarding next door to Brow turned out to be a newspaper editor and soon the articles were published.

By contrast, the petition signed by all the villagers still hadn't been ratified and Chivalry set about putting the lanes and roads in good order.

Presently, many rich villages in China were arranging for the peasants to live together in villas or apartment blocks. Our economic strength was not so great. According to Chivalry, doing things that way didn't constitute a rural village and a rural village should look the part. For example, every household should live in single-storey buildings and, outside the gate, there ought to be a courtyard. People should never turn their backs on the land but cling close to Mother Earth and, in this way, it would be convenient for them to drop in on each other.

Clay brick walls were the best material because the buildings would retain heat in winter and remain cool in summer, so there was no need to install air-conditioning and heating, contraptions which made it easier for people to catch a cold or succumb to fever.

Dustpans should be hung below the eaves so that sliced sweet potatoes and persimmons could be air-dried, and wooden pegs should be driven into the walls to hang strings of chillies and tobacco leaves from. Firewood and briquettes should be stacked up, a seepage well should be dug to carry away the waste water and a small swing in front of the door should be built for the children. A small latrine should stand in a corner behind the house and the cesspool should have a cover. No tree should be planted in the latrine because people were prone to wipe their arses against it – toilet paper, old newspapers or children's used exercise books should be made available instead.

A bamboo pole should be balanced across a corner of the courtyard to air-dry children's nappies and women's red underwear; any family that had women's underwear being air-dried on the bamboo pole must be leading a peaceful life. At noon, the chickens should flap into the air and the dogs leap and the chimney of each household belch out smoke. At mealtimes, everyone should walk here and there with a bowl – a huge bowl – in hand and all go to the big myrrh tree; your children should eat my rice and I should go to your home to get a plateful if I have no dishes at home. Grandchildren and grandfathers should forget the gap between their ages and test their strength, squabble and romp. A slobbering man, a water-pipe clamped between his teeth, should trade wisecracks with another man's wife, but they would never gossip, steal or commit adultery. All the children should attend school for free and the young of each family perform their filial duty.

Chivalry's ideal epitomised the ideal of Benevolent Lenient Village, which was ever harder to pursue nowadays, yet he wanted to pursue and build a utopia in the capital city. He convinced me.

Magic Farm Tableland in Fan Jingquan's words might be all well and good, but that was a pancake sketched out on paper, whereas Chivalry was distributing substantial pancakes to all of us. Chivalry ordered each household to clean up their own walls and courtyards: walls must be whitewashed, gate awnings must be decorated and, above the gate awning, a tablet must be fixed with words such as 'Family of Tillers and Scholars', 'Green Mountains and Clear Waters', 'The

Auspicious Star is Shining High' and 'Propitious Beginnings to the New Year'.

There should be no lawns. City slickers had started to plant lawns because they picked up their habits from foreigners. Chinese people were always fond of growing flowers and, in the countryside, grapes, pomegranates and kidney beans should be planted inside courtyards and in front of gates. Beautiful and practical.

The lanes should be designed anew. A main lane must be straight. Later, when the economy had become more developed and we were rich, cars would pass along them. All manner of cables should be buried underground. All the secondary lanes should have drainage ditches, trees should be trimmed and the tree trunks slathered with lime water.

These tasks sounded simple and trivial, but not all the households were able to put them into practice. The locals responded with a smile: "The boss is right." "Very good." But this family looked at that one and vice versa. Some mended their gate awnings and some swept their courtyards numerous times. But after a few days though, chicken muck and pig shit were once again everywhere in front of their gates or the brushwood was in a mess.

"This can't do," Chivalry roared. "My words have become farts!" He stayed at home to draw up village rules and his reference books included *The Story of the Peach Blossom Spring*,[bm] *A Collection of the Documents in the Yan'an Rectification Campaign*,[bn] A *Handbook for the Members of the People's Commune* and *Moral Maxims of Zeng Guofan's Family*.[bo]

He also gladly brought along a worm-eaten, hole-riddled central scroll. This he discovered in Old Ran's sister-in-law's home and was anxious for me to scrutinise. The scroll read:

Reaching forty-five, being naturally alive,
Hair turning white, teeth becoming slight,
Still high-spirited, never dull-witted,
Wind-like tongue, bellyful of song.
Read more books, hate foolish looks,
Have knowledge amassed, present and past.
Zizhan[bp] you befriend, Du Fu superintends.
Welcome your guest with care, host,
Drink free-mindedly, play Go wholeheartedly,
Love the scenery, fear no cadre,
Respect your parents, be joyful peasants.
Get up late, be early in closing the gate,
Follow Heaven's force, everything's on course.
Plead not poverty, broadcast not adversity.

I looked at the signature and the complimentary seal. It turned out that this was a piece of calligraphy presented as a gift to an elderly Mr Liu in the West Guanzhong Academy by my great-grandfather. How did it end up at Old Ran's home? The contents were interesting, despite it being a self-referential bit of writing created by a rich leisured man of letters. Of what instructive value could it be to a peasant?

Chivalry declared: "This is your great-grandfather's handiwork. He was a great Confucian scholar in the west of the Guanzhong Plain. The Ran family preserved it and so the Ran family too produced men of letters. Look again: 'wind-like tongue, bellyful of song', 'love the scenery, fear no cadre', 'respect your parents, be joyful peasants', 'plead not poverty, broadcast not adversity'. What fine words. If every household had a similar scroll hanging up at home, what would become of our village?"

She pictured Old Ran with his persimmon face and small nose. He was speaking softly with deliberate slowness and grinning shyly.

"What will become of our village?" I said sourly. "Zheng Banqiao[bq] once wrote that 'It takes effort to become dull-witted'. But some people are born dull-witted. If you ask people of that ilk to make the effort, they will become a bottle of glue or a pile of mud."

"That depends on the Village Head's leadership abilities. In the past, a County Head was called 'the learned man of the county' or 'the protector of the county'. Isn't it the same when it comes to a Village Head? The village rules are established for the villagers and it is the Village Head's responsibility to manage and supervise."

In total, he laid down 15 village rules, including that we should love the earth, be industrious, kind, filial and clean, follow the family planning policy and hand in our allocation on time. Each rule was to be strictly enforced. Those who complied would qualify to have a plaque stating 'New Ethical Household' hung above their gates. If a household failed on three occasions to meet the criteria for this honour, their electricity would be cut, their patients' registration numbers cancelled and perhaps have their welfare allowances invalidated. Worst of all, they might be fined or become pariahs in the village.

"The higher authorities haven't granted our petition. Is it really a good thing or not to be doing this?" I questioned.

Chivalry answered: "Look, look, look. Does every woman really have two ounces of pig brains? The petition was submitted so long ago and still hasn't been ratified, which means that the higher authorities have one eye open and one eye shut. The more you persist in this way, the less likely they will be to grant it."

On second thoughts, his words made sense. Brow once recounted a true story. Their company obtained a plot of land – 33 *mu* – which was originally bought at a very cheap price by the son of a Beijing big-shot to attract foreign investment and build a factory on. After he secured the land, he resold it to their boss at the market price and skimmed off a huge sum of money. Someone submitted a report about this to the respective leader. When the report reached the Secretary's desk, the Secretary asked the leader to give instructions. The leader said he wouldn't read the report and he should ask the related departments to settle it. He didn't read it, which meant he knew nothing about it. The knotty problem was put off and now many years have passed. If our business was also to potter on in this way, then Chivalry is free to muck around.

Still, Chivalry managed to issue a whole set of requirements with regards to the pharmacy. The main economic source of our village was selling herbs. As per his plan, Benevolent Lenient Village should be built into a huge hospital and pharmaceutical factory. He requested that I apply my brains to this rather than focus on trifles. From now onwards, I was to devote a great deal of effort to purchasing medicinal herbs, and to placing ads in newspapers and on TV to spread the renown of our village far and wide and enhance our influence. Next, we would manufacture medicinal pills on a large scale and operate a huge pharmaceutical factory.

You had to admire Chivalry's agile mind. If he rolled on like this, he might really knock the village into shape and then any kind of miracle might occur. I started a publicity drive in newspapers and on the TV and then organised hands to go to Northeast China and Yunnan to purchase medicinal herbs. For the time being, we couldn't mass-produce medicinal and herbal pills. Patients from all over the country trekked over to our village. Oh gee, there were so many people with liver ailments in the world! From then on, wherever I went and whoever I saw, I would habitually look at their complexion, thinking: "Has he got a liver problem?"

There were countless men and women in the Western Capital who were inclined to quarrel and trade punches and kicks on the street without provocation. Something must have gone awry with their livers. Newspapers frequently cried out in alarm that Chinese people were turbulent, and those experts and scholars proffered this reason and that reason. But they were just scratching the itch from outside the boot and didn't know that it was because the number of liver patients had rocketed up.

Come to our village – we had Grandpa Cloud Forest! We had single-storey buildings on the ground. Only the earth could accommodate the patients, and the power of Mother Earth could eradicate the pathogenic bacteria. City guys left the land behind and, with it, Mother Earth. Your livers must be damaged or dying.

Finally, I knew why Grandpa Cloud Forest was paralysed. This man who walked with his four limbs on the ground was following the will of the heavens and a revelation had been dropped down to the mortals by Him. If Grandpa Cloud Forest was a god, he wouldn't be the God of Medicine or the God of Drugs. He well and truly was the God of the Earth!

I shared my important revelation with the community and they all agreed enthusiastically. They worshipped the land more fervently and grew firmer in their resolve that they would never leave Benevolent Lenient Village, instead working to safeguard it. However, how were the real estate investors in the Western Capital, not to mention the Bureau of Land Management, the Bureau of Urban Construction and the City Mayor to know this? I loathed them – hated them – and flung myself into work regardless of whether it was day or night. I travelled to the medicinal herbs markets in Hebei Province to replenish our stock, during which time I distributed and hung leaflets advertising our village everywhere.

One month later when I came back fully loaded, the face of the village had changed greatly. The lanes were all paved with fine sand, flower beds had been created along the foot of the walls on both sides and stacked up with pots of blooms, and many trees were planted with their trunks coated with lime. The walls of some households' gate awnings had been repaired and tiles replaced. Pigs and chickens could still roam freely, but were followed around by people carrying dung buckets and piss scoops. Whenever a pig raised its tail, they would charge forward to catch the waste.

Almost all the patients strolling around the village wore their uniformly-distributed, loosely-fitting, clean hospital pyjamas made of rough, chequered, homespun cotton cloth. The handful of principal lanes had been kitted out with loudspeakers, through which Chivalry spoke three times a day and which were used the rest of the time for broadcasting music. But what frightened me was that Brow was no longer a member of the village, even though she still inhabited the courtyard with the grape trellis.

Things wound on like this. The gate awning of Brow's courtyard always went unrepaired. A rafter on the right corner of the gate awning had become rotten and the exterior walls were not whitewashed either. Moreover, she regularly quarrelled with her neighbours. Consequently, she was not entitled to have the 'New Ethical Household' notice above her gate. Next, her electricity supply was cut off and then her patients' registration numbers were voided.

Brow was not a lantern accustomed to burning without an abundance of oil. She had her pyramid selling agent Old Shao, she was thick with Fatty the policeman and, on top of that, she was an employee of a real estate company. She might have become muddle-headed. Brow actually brought harm upon the village. She told her boss about everything we were doing, and he then went directly to the city government and exhorted them to honour their promise to redevelop all the old buildings on this stretch of land, including Benevolent Lenient Village.

To begin with, the company had planned to build a forest of residential buildings after demolishing our village. Now, to allure and coerce the city government, they said they had decided to erect a large restaurant which, according to their former plan, ought to have been built in a city in the South of China. The Western Capital didn't look like a metropolis because it lacked top-grade highrises. Now, a modern, five-star, 21-storey restaurant was to be erected here. What an irresistible temptation that proved to be. The news soon swirled through the capital city and even the advertising hoardings on the City Square proclaimed this development. Benevolent Lenient Village panicked. Chivalry went to the district government to negotiate and got wind of the role played by Brow. In a howling rage, after coming back home, he expelled Brow.

Brow became a traitor and the shame of Benevolent Lenient Village and gossip about her spread everywhere. Her saving A-Bing was taken as evidence of the illicit relationship between her and Fatty. Some even questioned how A-Bing's whip should have come to be exposed when he was raised by her. A woman from the neighbourhood told everyone that Brow and the Shao guy cohabited before getting married. It might have been OK if they restricted their business to inside the house, but they also did it under the grape trellis in broad daylight and she moaned like a screeching cat.

"I stand by my words," the gossipmonger declared. "She is intimate with the fat guy and the Shao guy is jealous. Once, when they quarrelled the Shao guy threw this shoe into my courtyard." The woman wielded a leather stiletto in her hand, expressed repulsion that this was a 'slut's shoe' and only held it up by the laces. I recognised that it belonged to Brow.

I wanted to go and visit Brow. I couldn't understand why she had changed suddenly, but she was the only one I knew who would ever act like this. She had set her mind on developing her career in the capital city and coveted the fashionable clothes of city slickers, their luxurious housing, their temperament, airs and graces. Once she brought along Old Shao's mobile phone and spoke into it loudly while strutting along the village lane. She told me that she wanted to learn to drive a car and that she and Old Shao were grafting away towards the goal of having their own company and buying a private car. She was not suited to living on the land. Perhaps she was a city slicker in her previous life and reincarnated wrongly in this one. Or perhaps she was a foreigner in her bones, planted in Benevolent Lenient Village through some mistake and mutation.

"She is different from us," a woman called Xiuxiu commented after running into me at the entrance of the lane and knowing that I was going to see Brow. "Take the things between a man and a woman as an example. If we fall in love with someone, we will say 'I love him!'. But what will Brow say? She says: 'Old Shao is very good in that respect.' She is very practical. Why do you still go and see her?"

Nevertheless, I still went to see Brow because we were both women and it was impossible for me not to harbour a little envy and long to see how she made an exhibition of herself.

One blessing I had was the ability to immediately recognise my own narrow-mindedness. Being able to compare my heart to hers and placing myself in her shoes, I started to sympathise with Brow, who, like me, was a woman too. *Bang! Bang! Bang!* I thumped at her gate.

For a long time, nothing stirred inside and the hammering sound startled the pointy-mouthed neighbour. She was drowsing at her loom in the gateway and the knocking sound woke her up. Giving me a smile, she promptly rubbed her hands, directed her thumb at me and pointed her little finger at Brow's gate and – *pooh, pooh* – spat on her little finger.

The infamous gossipmonger amused me. I enquired: "You're still weaving cotton cloth?" She replied: "You don't know? Now it seems that city folks are sick of meat and fond of rough grain; the capital city has three restaurants selling rough grain and wild vegetables. They are tired of fine clothes as well and pure cotton cloth is now all the rage; quilt covers with a homespun cloth lining fetch a good price. Since our village had a little fame, my cousin's been lodging at my home to sell homespun cloth. I'm also taking the opportunity to weave some. When will you get married? I will send you a quilt cover with a homespun cloth lining as a gift."

I thanked her and lowered my head to squint through the newly-installed peephole in Brow's gate. Brow was the only one in the village to have had a peephole installed. I glued my eyes to the hole but could see nothing inside. Gentle movements were still to be heard within. I surmised that she must have come out of the main room and was now bending towards the peephole to look outside. What must I have looked like from the other side of the peephole? Why did they call a peephole a 'cat's eye' but not a 'dog's eye'? I guessed because people became snobbish when they peered at others with dog's eyes.

The door opened. It was Bushy Beard Shao.

"Where is Brow?" I pretended to be calm and not to know anything. "You took so long opening the door. In the cat's eye, I am a mouse."

"Brow asked me to open the door only because it was you."

Brow was in the main room and didn't come out to welcome me. I walked in. She was attired in the latest fashions (a Western-style black dress and a leather mini-skirt) sitting on a big genuine leather sofa with a Pekingese in her arms. The Pekingese was extremely tiny. His four legs were as short as the distance between one's outstretched thumb and little finger, though the hair on his head was almost long enough to cover his eyes. She reposed squarely there, like a noblewoman.

"Well, it has been a while and, look at you, all dignified."

"Why do you come?"

"To pay respects to Your Highness. You still don't offer me a seat? Do you want me to kneel down?"

Brow swept down briskly from the sofa to clasp me to her bosom and then cried spasmodically, saying, "Sister Plum, you still come to see me. You are the only one in the

263

village who will come to see me. This must be fate. I haven't lived here for a few days because living here is like being imprisoned and, barely had I come back today, when, against all expectations, you come. Where have you been? Why didn't you show up when they bullied me?

"Are you jealous of me? Many villagers are jealous of me. You too? Jealous of me that I have Old Shao, I have good clothes and I have so much jewellery."

She gripped and shook my shoulders hard, looking at me ferociously. A full-length mirror stood behind her. She was taller than me, and her waist was slimmer. Bushy Beard, what are you smiling at?

"I'm jealous of you?" I tossed her aside angrily. "You have Old Shao, but I have my research fellow. Is it that Old Shao is a man and my research fellow isn't? What is more, I haven't got married yet and I can fall in love with any man in the world. Is no man better than Old Shao? What's the big whoop about good clothes? How much is a good suit? If one thousand yuan is not enough, then ten thousand yuan can surely make you drip with jewels."

Brow lay insensible there again and, gazing at me, bleated: "I didn't think you'd be jealous. Don't mention the outside world. The Western Capital is swarming with rich men and even rich women are ten a penny, so why can't Benevolent Lenient Village find a place for me? How could I betray the village? Chivalry is over-sensitive and takes me as his doormat. You also know that my boss has promised to help me run a copy shop. He is nice to me, so why shouldn't I do my job well? Who wouldn't seize the opportunity? Chivalry can expel me and it is no big deal. I am sick of this shithole – it is not stylish, it's not comfortable, there is no tap water, no flushable loo, no gas supply, no hot water and no air-conditioning. What's wrong with the old houses being renovated and everything becoming modernised? We and our children, generation after generation, will never be peasants again and what's wrong with that? Does this mean I have forgotten my roots? Have I gone down?"

Brow flared up. This grievance and hatred must have been smouldering away for so long within her, though she wasn't able to find anyone to confide in. I didn't rebuff her. Nail polish and scissors lay on the table. Convinced that I wasn't angry and even managing to wear a smile, I sat there manicuring my fingernails. Remaining quiet and composed was a better means of defence than finding one thousand reasons to criticise and rebuke her. That way, I could watch her jumping here and there like a psychopath. I took a seat at the table. Bushy Beard Old Shao immediately laid the sweetmeats tray before me and hinted that I shouldn't lose my temper. This guy was reasonable. I didn't touch the nail polish, instead pouring myself a glass of water and watching the farce.

"Why don't you say something? You're the Manager. Tell me, where did I go wrong?" Brow roared and threw out her hands. A lock of hair fanned out in front of her forehead and the region around her eye sockets was blue. Old Shao, who must have been thinking that her face didn't look good, filled a basin with water and invited her to take a wash. "Why growl at Plum? She is not an outsider."

She dipped her hands into the water and cried out: "You wanna poach a chicken?" Old Shao then added some cold water and it ended up being too cool. She poured the water out and flung the basin on the ground. Embarrassed, Old Shao crouched on the threshold with his back to us to smoke a cigarette.

A woman was a piano, but the tune played by Old Shao was a cacophony. Old Ran was not a skilled pianist either. There are no skilled pianists in this world. I gathered up the Pekingese in my arms and twisted the long hair on his head into one small plait and then another one. Brow quietened down and sat there in the same posture for a long time. Then she went over to pick up the basin and, trying to find a means of retreat, said: "Give me a cigarette." Old Shao handed her one. She flashed him a smile. Old Shao grinned back obsequiously. She immediately mopped the smile off her face, flicked him aside, retrieved the Pekingese from my chest and plopped him on her lap.

"Where did you get this thing?" I asked.

"This type of dog is all the rage among city folk." Her tone of voice grew gentle and low. "A-Bing has a household registration card in this village now and I don't. The other day, I ran into him on a road. I called him, he ignored me and, in a rage, I went to buy this lapdog. He is not as beautiful as A-Bing, but look at how he clings to me." Brow finally smiled softly and her smile must have been worth a thousand pounds of gold. Old Shao's face became ennervated too. He took a bottle of XO from the cabinet and wanted to drink with me. I declined and he started to help himself.

I suggested that Brow should ease the tension between herself and the village. Though she had been expelled, I could still put in a good word for her with Chivalry. At the end of the day, we were all residents of Benevolent Lenient Village. Chivalry did what he did, not because he had it in for her but only because he wanted to run the village well. How else could he expect to maintain his prestige?

"Live here," I proposed. "I will come to see you frequently."

"Of course, I will come back," she answered. "Chivalry

might not recognise me as a member of the village, but he can't torch my house. Old Shao's flat in the city is 100 square metres, but I will come back every three or five days. I'm waiting for the renovation of this place and then this house should entitle me to a new flat with three rooms and a hallway."

She was evidently still hoping Benevolent Lenient Village would be demolished, which made it tough for us to find common ground in our conversation. I begged to take my leave. She insisted on seeing me off and we went out with the lapdog. The weaver next door looked at us in surprise. Brow spoke to me loudly on purpose to demonstrate that we were on very intimate terms. Despising her hypocrisy and not wishing my closeness to her to become a topic for idle gossip, I did not talk too vehemently about her chosen topic. We stepped forward and the Pekingese tailed us. At the T-junction, from which I ought to head southwards, I waved goodbye.

When I turned around to look, Brow was still there, apparently at a loss, her gaze locked on me. The Pekingese continued to follow me.

Brow also detected that and catcalled: "Lap! Lap!"

"Why does the lapdog follow me?"

"He's got short legs and can't see high, so he only recognises shoes. Today, your shoes and mine look the same. He must have mistaken you for me."

"The doggie recognises people by their shoes!" I grinned.

I was on my period and my body was not clean. When I arrived home, my underwear was already soaked in blood. Hurriedly, I shut the door and windows to wash and change. I accidentally touched my coccyx again. Many times, I reminded myself not to touch it, much less think about it because many diseases are spawned out of people's imagination. Added to this, the more frequently I touched it, the more rapidly the coccyx would grow, like a mole on the forehead. Even so, my hand would always unconsciously reach down to my buttocks. Sticking my bottom out before the full-length mirror to take a look, I felt unbearable agony. My body might fairer and smoother-skinned than my face. Sly Brow knew which part of hers should be beautiful: the skin of her body was swarthy and coarse but, from her neck up, was refined and smooth.

I could see my coccyx. Panic-stricken at my own behaviour, I shot a glance at the door, which was shut. Again, I sidled up to give the window curtains a tug. The radio cassette recorder belonging to the new patient boarding in the lean-to was still on. His face seemed sallow like yellow touch-paper, yet he still liked music so much. Had he found out my secret?

I peered through a crack in the door. The patient was balancing on a bench near the courtyard wall, hanging laundry on an iron wire and striking up a conversation with my neighbour. He couldn't see me. Would my secret ever be brought to light? There were mice and mosquitoes in the room even though the door and windows were shut, and beetles skittered along the foot of the walls. Maybe the wok, basins, bowls, glasses, tables and chairs, and especially the Ming and Qing Dynasty furniture, had some intelligence?

A stream of irritation and depression coursed through my heart. I wrapped myself up with a sheet and lay on the bed.

On the spur of the moment, I thought about whoever would end up rubbing down and cleaning my dead body before it was cremated and who might change my clothes. They would surely gasp in surprise: "Look, she's got a tail!"

Would Old Ran be around then and be so greatly surprised that his glasses would topple off with the shock? He was no tough guy, but what was I?

Did Brow have a tailbone? Did every beautiful woman in the world have one or was it only those of us in Benevolent Lenient Village?

"You like music so much. Are you a music teacher?"

"A man can't stand loneliness. I like any sound. At midnight when nothing can be heard, I listen to my heartbeat – *bang, bang, bang* – agitating like a drumbeat. Did you hear any stirrings from my home last night?"

"First an *ah*, next an *hmm* and finally a long *ohh*. What's going on?"

"*Ha-ha-ha*, you could be a spy! The *ah* came from my son's room. You still haven't got it?"

"I've got it, I've got it. You let out an *hmm* and perhaps your wife gave you a kick and you again *ohhed*. You randy old dog!"

"Your ears are so sharp. You know, you should go to the cemetery at night."

"What's wrong there?"

"The old executioner says there is always a sound like arguing as soon as night falls."

"Ghosts are quarrelling?"

I buried my head under the sheet and, dangling before my eyes, were all the tiny, top-grade pieces of real silk underwear that hung out to dry beneath the grape trellis in Brow's home. "The city women are very fond of small underwear, but yours are so sloppy and so thick. Out of fashion!" They were jeering at me.

Chapter Eighteen

Chivalry soon found out that I had been to see Brow and bawled at me. Were he to ask me about it calmly or to scold me in the pharmacy or in the office of the Village Committee, I could have explained myself. But, not caring about the possible repercussions, he growled at me in front of the old executioner and so many others, complaining that I didn't adhere to principles and was a dunderhead without shame. Furthermore, he made these criticisms when we were burning touch-paper and incense sticks to our ancestors in the cemetery. To make matters worse, when he growled at me, the old executioner's eyes were fixed on the back of my neck.

I lost my temper too. I remembered Fan Jingquan's words and cursed back that he was Satan; a ghastly, cold, erratic, crazy and rude demon.

"You curse me as a demon?"

He stared at me in surprise and that hand – the female hand – lifted up.

"So what? Not only me. Loads of people are cursing you."

"Who?"

"Fan Jingquan."

"Fan Jingquan?" he smiled coldly with a snort of distain. "If I, Chivalry, am not cursed by others as a bad guy, I haven't been successful. He, Fan Jingquan, has a bellyful of theories, but what I want is to save the village and for every villager to have food to eat, so they can live. I only need to make it big and, wait and see, he, Fan Jingquan, will come out to sing my praises. In my opinion, the more correspondence courses you have taken, the stupider you have become. Follow Old Ran obediently. Don't follow Fan Jingquan like a tadpole follows a fish to flirt with the waves. Careful, you might lose your tail in the flirtation."

Maybe he threw that out unintentionally, though it reminded me of my jutting-out coccyx and I blushed instinctively. When I raised my head, I saw Old Ran's sister-in-law standing under the wooden stake with the yak's head on top. I lashed out furiously: "What qualifies you to interfere in my private business? What's wrong with me and the Ran guy? What's wrong with me and the Fan guy?"

I could see Chivalry standing there choked, that woman's hand waving, and then he whisked up a bottle of sacrificial wine to pour into his mouth – *glug-glug-glug*. A bystander snatched the bottle from him and shouted "Chivalry! Chivalry!"

Gao Feng blocked me and said in a low voice: "Plum, he is the Village Head and we should have the sense to protect his authority and honour."

"Is he Grandpa Cloud Forest?" With a bang, I flung the fencelike gate of the cemetery open and left in a fit of outrage.

When my footsteps had already carried me to the earthen ground before the shrine, I changed my mind and decided not to go to Grandpa Cloud Forest to air my grievances. Grandpa Cloud Forest was our god. If I go to the shrine, I should go there to purify myself. If I turned to him whenever anything went wrong, only taking things from him, that would make me appear mean. Yet, since he was godlike, how could he not be all-knowing? Was there any need for me to bend his ear?

I walked back home with a black face. Many in the lanes caught sight of my facial expressions but no one dared to ask why, only gazing at me instead until I reached my home and kicked the gate of the courtyard open. The sallow-faced patient was following the tape-player, singing "The birds all pair up in the trees. Husband and wife together return."[br] Before he had finished singing the next word – "home" – he clicked off the recorder.

I shut myself in the room in the afternoon. Up until that afternoon, I had not understood that a house was originally used to imprison people. A man built a house, which meant turning one's self in and being banged up. Then I thought of the Western Capital and all we had done for Benevolent Lenient Village.

When I took a bath, I sank into a state of still greater panic, for I discovered that my tailbone was sticking out even further. Did becoming stimulated cause people to develop a disease? Did the jutting-out coccyx mean that I really was sick? In the two years before Mother passed away following an operation for stomach cancer, the doctor said if she could manage to make it through one year, she could live for two; if she could manage two years, she could pass the hurdle of the fifth; and if she passed the five-year hurdle, everything would be OK. In the first year after my mother's operation, I too fell ill and felt constantly dizzy. I knew that I was worrying about Mother and my nerves had been strained too taut.

Mother made it through the first year, though she didn't survive the second. She passed away. I no longer suffered on her account and my illness healed. If a jutting-out coccyx really was a disease, that disease must be inevitable.

Since Chivalry became the Village Head, the village had been shrouded perpetually in a nervous climate and each morning I felt increasingly stifled and terror-stricken. Whenever I opened my eyes and whenever a sound entered my ears, I wondered if some drastic change was in the offing. The pressure of life had seldom been so evenly and so heavily distributed across each day. Was it because of these extreme conditions of nervousness and panic that my protruding tailbone had mutated? And had the altercation with Chivalry worsened it still further?

I warned myself that I should relax and calm down, but how could I? Fate caused me to be born in this village and fate again had dictated that I should live here among such people.

"Plum, have you fallen asleep?" the sallow-faced patient called me gently from outside the window.

"You haven't been out the whole afternoon and it's dark already. You still haven't cooked either. I have eaten some noodles, but I can't invite you to join me in case you get infected. You really should cook and eat something."

"I know. I have some leftovers."

"Then you're not going to watch the football game? There is a football match in the stadium tonight."

"I won't. You can go if you are able."

Another football game was being played in the stadium tonight. After the last football riot, the Western Capital was disqualified as a home ground. To rebuild the image of the city and regain the right to host, the city leaders had pointedly invited two away teams to compete in a match.

This lunchtime, Chivalry prattled on and on about football and asked me to buy some small trumpets to hail encouragement. I reminded him that he should not be impetuous and that if a riot broke out, he should not participate in it. He said gloatingly: "You mean my life doesn't belong to me alone?"

But now waves of football chants emanated from the stadium and Chivalry was sitting in the stands. A man has too many places and ways in which to vent his wrath. Wine will make his indignation evaporate through his pores along with his sweat, and crying in a stadium might make him leave his unhappiness behind. But I myself was still burning with a furious rage, which again exacerbated my disease.

Chivalry! Chivalry! Wolfish Chivalry! I repeated this spiteful name in my mind and wanted to channel the powers of my mind to cause the one in the stadium to have a telepathic response. I wanted to make him suddenly aware that I was still angry with him and thus be stricken by conscience. But I soon realised what a ridiculous loser I was. How pathetic!

After turning several times and heaving a long sigh, I lay semi-awake on a reclining chair with a blurred mind. Somewhere Little Wei was sawing away at his *erhu* – "*Who will get drunk with me. Bosom friends for all time we will be – twang!*" "Time" was stopped abruptly when a quivering *erhu* string snapped in two. At this moment, a man slipped in without a sound. A thief? According to past experience, whenever there was a football match, our village would be visited by thieves. Sallow Face had gone to watch the football game. He didn't ask me to shut the gate of the courtyard and he did not lock it from the outside.

The thief just breezed in. The murderers who entered the artist's house abseiled from ropes hung down from the roof and then climbed in through the window. They were thieves first and foremost, not murderers. Why didn't the artist surrender his fortune to save his life? If he could, he should have been unwilling to part with his fortune. Fan Jingquan said you could never arrest all the thieves in the world, but they would leave if you were polite to them. I closed my eyes and pretended to be drowsy, while keeping my ears and all my nerves alert to see how the thief pulled off his job.

However, the thief only sat quietly on the other side of the bed and didn't move. This was a strong-nerved thief. After a while, the thief stood up as if to leave. Even a thief was unwilling to walk away with something of mine. I grew angry and exclaimed: "Leaving? Shut the door behind you."

The thief stopped and asked softly: "You've woken up?" The voice sounded familiar. I opened my eyes and standing there was research fellow Ran.

I began to giggle, but Old Ran was a humourless man and I didn't want to share my illusion with him.

"Why did you come? And then why did you leave soon after that. You are a thief."

"I came back from the institute and went to the pharmacy," Old Ran said. "A-Shun told me there was a football match tonight and most probably you'd gone there.

"I didn't find you in the stadium, though did see Chivalry. He said you are at home and not in a good mood and asked me to come and have a look. Sure enough, you don't look fine. Seeing as you were sound sleep, I decided that I would come back again later."

"Chivalry asked you to come, did he? What an obedient little man you are."

"The situation in the stadium is fairly calm tonight. The police presence has been doubled compared with before so there won't be a riot."

"No riot? Then you can't see a woman being stripped naked. Is that why you don't want to watch the game?"

"How could that be?"

He was an honest man, and I couldn't bear to make fun of him anymore. I said: "You're good. Tonight, all the villagers have gone to watch football and you still came to see me."

I jabbered on like this, trying my best to forget my misery.

For whatever reason, Old Ran dropped by at this particular time, which meant we were still joined by fate. Chivalry, you just watch the football and Old Ran is still mine.

I stretched myself lazily and felt all my joints snapping loose and all my vexation being shaken off. I told Old Ran that his hair was combed very smoothly today. Old Ran came over embarrassed and ruffled his hair. I repeated that I meant what I said. He again patted his hair back into place.

I knew Old Ran really loved me, but I was normally so stubborn he got cold feet and was unable to tell which of my words were sincere and which were ironic. Biting my lower lip, I gazed at him. Had my eyes rested on another man, he would know the signal and pounce despite any consequences. Old Ran wanted to come over but wouldn't risk it. He abided by his routine, which entailed the debilitation and gradual development of passion. His indecisiveness affected his self-confidence. Veins stood out on his hands, which wriggled nervously along the edge of the bed before he retracted them and balled them into fists. He stood up and walked towards me, bent at the waist to haul up the vacuum flask and poured himself a glass of water. He then walked back and sat down on the bed with the water. He didn't drink, instead putting the glass at the head of the bed.

Tonight, I had experienced the entire psyche of being a woman. No matter how dignified, tough and stately she might be, she hoped in the bottom of her heart that a man would praise her, appreciate her and, perhaps, play with her.

If a man was too forward, she would curse him for being a hooligan. But if a man was too reserved, a woman would hate him and look down on him because she couldn't stand the loneliness. Tonight, I didn't know why I needed Old Ran. I was surprised at my bravery and a thought flashed in my mind: I was hungry for him because I wanted to banish the worries of this afternoon. I needed Old Ran to help me forget the worry.

"Do I look beautiful in this skirt?"

"You are beautiful in anything."

"Come over and sit. You don't love me now?"

"I love you." When he said this, his face changed colour and his features no longer occupied their ordinary position, seeming to become uglier.

He pounced like a monkey and scooped me up in his arms together with the cooling mat on the reclining chair. I glimpsed the back of his shoulders in the full-length mirror and my face on his shoulders. I didn't want to see myself. My facial features must also be gross. My face felt like it no longer belonged to me. My neck moved like it was swivelling on a pivot, moving this way to receive sloppy, watery saliva.

I heard him murmuring: "I love you, Plum, I love you to death, but I'm afraid to make a move. I worry that if I do, you might loathe me. You are not in a good mood and I can't take advantage. But if you give me an inch, I will advance bravely ten feet. You try, have a try. I can do it."

He grabbed my hand and put it on the spot between his thighs, whereupon a bump rose.

"You can manage it today?" I asked.

"Last time I was too nervous," he replied. "The heavier the psychological burden, the more I believe it needs the courage of a hooligan."

I started to chortle.

Old Shao had such a bushy beard. When he came to our village for the first time, the children followed him to observe the rarity, shouting: "He has no mouth, he has no mouth!" Old Shao was angry and parted his beard and cursed: "This is not a mouth? Is this your mother's…?" Chivalry's nose was hard. The goal was so big, but those stinky old feet could never drive the ball home. A chick nearby said to her father: "It will be so good if there is no goalkeeper."

"Do you know," I continued, "I'm six months older than Brow? She has had more than one abortion, but I still haven't experienced anything. Tonight, I will give everything to you. Have you shut the courtyard gate?"

He immediately stood up to close the gate while saying: "Then I'm leaving." Coughing loudly, he opened the gate and closed it again, tiptoed across the courtyard, shutting the door of the main room after he came back in and drew the curtains tight.

I laughed. "You're an old hand at this. Do you say those words for the patient's ears even though he is in the stadium?"

He raised his voice immediately: "You're the team leader of the village and I won't give others the chance to gossip."

Everything was relaxed. Relaxation makes people become ingenious. When making love you should compare notes with your lover. Old Ran carried me to the bed while tearing at my upper garment and skirt, but he couldn't find the buttons and the belt which fastened the skirt. The spittle that brimmed up in his mouth dropped down and his glasses fell on to the quilt. I picked them up and placed them beside the pillow.

I said: "Come. If you want to do it, let's do it for real. Do it at ease but not like a thief."

I lifted aside the old bottom sheet and swapped it for a brand new white one.

"Pour out some water and have a wash."

He promised as obediently as a child and when he pulled the basin out to get the water, he gave my backside a pat. His pat alerted me to my tailbone. Unwilling to clean himself before me in the bedroom, he took the basin to another room. I was even more reluctant to wash in his sight, so took my turn when he came back. At that moment, my heart leaped. Was this the feeling people went after? My audacity caused me to blush, yet at this moment Brow flashed in my mind and I found an excuse and comfort for my shame: I was doing what was right. Such a mature girl, I should have a man.

Then I felt myself hot and burning throughout my body, especially in that spot, which was swelling unbearably, puffing out hot steam and streaming hot water. As a girl, I set great store by this day, not because I was very traditional but because it should be remembered forever and pined after for as long as I lived. It should be a solemn occasion because it was the time when I would find myself most in need of consolation.

I walked out with my body drawn bolt upright. I should bravely expose my whole body to Old Ran, but when I stepped into the bedroom and was illuminated by the white lamp light, I bent intuitively and didn't peel off my underwear. Wrapping a big towel around my waist, I pressed my hand to my coccyx and the two ends of the big towel rode over it.

Old Ran hadn't yet burrowed under the quilt but sat on the edge of the bed in his birthday suit, looking like a spider. After exchanging a glance, neither of us could pluck up the courage to look at the other again. We shut our eyes and became fused crazily in each other's arms. In spite of my perplexed state of mind, I was still on the alert. Whenever his hand reached my back, I dodged or grabbed it. I slanted myself and wanted to tug at the pull cord of the electric bulb. He stood up, eager to carry me to the quilt. "I will go myself."

I asked him to go to bed first and, lowering my head, found a round, yellow mark on the white bottom sheet where he had just been sitting. Believing it to be dust, I used my hand to pat it. The yellow didn't disappear and seemed to become messier. "What's this?" I asked and bent over to inspect it. To my surprise, it was shit. A sense of instant disgust attacked my heart and all my desire vanished into oblivion.

I shouted: "You haven't wiped your arse clean!"

Old Ran stood there petrified, his face changing dramatically, and reached out to wipe it clean, murmuring: "How could it be, how could it be?"

I asked: "What the hell is this?"

He explained: "I have haemorrhoids. I went to the bog just now and thought I'd wiped it clean. But…"

It would have been OK had he not described it like this. The franker he became, the deeper my disgust. I raised my foot to kick his arse and cursed: "Fuck off! Off!" Then I yanked aside the bottom sheet and – *wah, wah* – bent over to vomit.

Old Ran still stood frozen to the spot. Then he started to put on his clothes. Next, he announced: "I'm leaving." When he went out, he forgot his glasses. He eventually found them at the head of the bed, put them on, repeated "I'm leaving", opened the door and walked away.

A wave of din flooded in from outside like a tidalwater. Noise from the football stadium. Had a goal been scored? No, the footballers were still running relentlessly. Go there excited and come back disappointed? My fate was just as bitter. My tears streamed down. May another football riot erupt tonight. May all the vehicles be overturned, all the guard rails be stamped on and broken, all the women be stripped naked, their lower halves clawed and mangled and their nipples ripped off. Let the armed policemen fire volleys of shots and batches of men drop dead and then more batches of men drop dead. Chivalry should be mowed down with them. Tonight, he would once again strip himself topless and paint the emblem of the football team on his face. After he had fallen down, all his chest muscles would distend and one hand would still be raised in mid-air – the woman's hand. When the woman's hand gripped his thing, did it never loosen its hold? That transplanted hand must have belonged to a slut. Brow was such a slut. Tonight, would she once again be having a whale of a time? Was she in the stadium or in bed? She was right. What she wanted was a man, not the honour of the village or a professional title or knowledge.

Today, 27th July 1995, I had changed the most beautiful festival into the most heartbreaking day of mourning. I cursed Old Ran and I cursed myself more harshly until the break of day.

When morning came, I felt too lazy to get up, but then someone was thundering at the door. From the way the person at the knocker breathed, I knew it was A-Shun. I always arrived at the pharmacy at seven but was late today and A-Shun and the others must have thought that something unexpected had befallen me.

"Why knock? Why?" I snapped impatiently. "I haven't died yet, you know."

From outside the door, A-Shun said: "Manager! Sister Plum! Get up and hurry. A patient has come. In a critical condition!" I rolled off the bed, below which lay the dirty bottom sheet that had I ripped apart and flung down there last night. I stamped on it twice, kicked it under the bed and ran to the pharmacy after A-Shun without washing my face. The old lady living diagonally opposite was sweeping the ground with a broom. She piped up: "Plum, last night…" I raised my hand and wanted to say something, but I had already turned around at the head of the lane.

Three men had drawn a handcart to the pharmacy and the man lying on the cart was frantic and restless, bellowing like a mad bull and struggling to pounce. One of the men held the cart steady like grim death, while the other two tried desperately to hold the patient steady. But when the patient's head was pinned down, his feet kicked, and when his feet were nailed down, his head rose up. It seemed like a duel between man and leopard. One man used his body to weigh down the patient. Another started to rip the padding sheet into shreds to twist into a rope to hogtie him. I shot a glance at the patient. His face was burnt-yellow, his mouth and nose parched and cracked and his five sensory organs twisted in great pain. He looked rotten. I had heard tell of a patient in such a condition but had never received and treated one.

It was a kind of liver spasm and the severity of the pain might cause the patient to lose his sanity. If he deteriorated further, he might develop hepatic necrosis and become comatose or die. Panic-stricken, I didn't know what to do. "We can't cure such cases." The three men all looked at me in disappointment, and then knelt down and beseeched: "If Benevolent Lenient Village can't save him, he will surely die today. Please think of a method and treat the dead horse as a living one, Doctor."

I wasn't a qualified doctor, though I knew that the duty of a doctor was to save people. "I shall go and carry Grandpa Cloud Forest here," I said. But barely had I turned around when A-Bing ran in from the entrance of the lane and then

Grandpa Cloud Forest appeared, edging towards us with his four limbs paddling against the ground. This was a miracle! Grandpa Cloud Forest, who had never gone out so early, had come to the pharmacy today. He must have had a kind of premonition. Sure enough, he instructed me: "Go concoct 'Three Star Herbal Soup'."

I lifted Grandpa Cloud Forest to the handcart while, at the same time, asking A-Shun to prepare the soup. After examining the patient, Grandpa Cloud Forest said: "No need to tie him up. Does he really still need to be bound when he is already cut down like this?" The three men released their hands and stood aside. *Pooh!* Grandpa Cloud Forest spat a mouthful of water on to the patient's face. He hadn't sucked any water into his mouth before, but still the water being spewed out looked like a mist. Then he gave the patient's rib cage a stab. The patient's raised hand stood there still and then fell down gently, his eyes closed and he heaved a long sigh, sweat beads rolling down like beans. Grandpa Cloud Forest turned around and again edged towards the lane with his hands paddling against the ground. I wanted to give him a piggyback back to the shrine. "No need to bother. You see that he drinks the 'Three Star Herbal Soup,' arrange for him to settle down and ask his companions to go to my place for the prescription," he informed me. He then paused and picked up something from the ground. It was a one-cent nickel coin, which he placed in the pocket of his upper garment.

I didn't ask the patient's companions to go to the shrine but went there myself for the prescription and medicinal catalyst. When I arrived, I asked Grandpa Cloud Forest what miraculous medicine he had prescribed to cure the frantic restless patient. "How can I know?" He was unwilling to tell me yet asked me if there was 'All-Powerful Tonic' in the pharmacy.

I responded: "Yeah. To be given to the patient?" He clarified that the earth needed it, that he had gone one circuit around the village this morning and detected that the earthly aura in the southeast of the village was a little weak and needed some tonic. He asked me to dig a hole about ten paces from the back of Lianben's home to the left front of Five Springs' home and to bury ten parcels of 'All-Powerful Tonic'.

Grandpa Cloud Forest was no feng-shui master. It was said that the feng-shui masters thought that burying ploughshares or millstones and weights could suppress evil when inauspicious signs were evident in a particular place. Now, he was suddenly asking me to dig a hole and bury 'All-Powerful Tonic', which I thought was very fishy. He wouldn't repeat what he had said and only tilted his head to look at me with a smile.

On seeing that smile, I came over weak-hearted, feeling that I was already a woman of glass standing before him, that he must know what happened last night and has known the secret about my tailbone for a long time. My face blushing bright red, I didn't know what to do.

"You don't have noodles? What about vegetables? Have you finished eating the Chinese cabbage?" I asked, wanting to escape to the kitchen to have a look. Grandpa Cloud Forest waved his hand, insisting he had eaten instant noodles and ready-made marinated beef slices.

Something horrible happened in Benevolent Lenient Village while I was talking with Grandpa Cloud Forest in the shrine. I trusted Grandpa Cloud Forest too much, believing that he had premonitions but, save for when a patient's disease was concerned, this was not the case. Or perhaps it was true he had a premonition about and knew everything, but was unwilling to pay any attention. I tried to persuade him to eat instant noodles less frequently.

Whatever he wanted to eat, couldn't he just tell someone in the village and have them prepare him a delicious meal?

Brow's neighbour ran in with unsteady steps. The man, who wore a big scar on his face, was an honest sort but, after barging in, was rendered mute. He swung his hands, stamped his feet and his face was smothered crimson. "Clawed Face," Grandpa Cloud Forest reassured him. "No need to worry."

Clawed Face opened his mouth, but still couldn't say a word. His childhood nickname was Stone. At the age of six, he was white-skinned and chubby like a lump of dough.

One summer, the whole family went to the threshing ground with straw mattresses to sleep out in the cool. To start with, the adults slept on both sides and Stone was sandwiched in between, but he woke up in the middle of the night, his bladder close to bursting, and went to one side to relieve himself. After that he tottered back with a dog on his tail. He called out: "Doggie, doggie!" The wolf drew closer. His calling the dog also roused his parents who, after opening their eyes, cried out involuntarily: "Wolf!" The wolf had been unmasked and dared approach no further. With a swish of his paw, he scratched Stone's face before running away. This left a scar. From then on, the villagers no longer called him Stone but Clawed Face.

"Uncle Stone, is the wolf coming?" I teased him with a grin.

Grandpa Cloud Forest glared at me and Clawed Face still couldn't spit out a word. He pointed outside. Simultaneously, I heard shouts come from the village and, knowing that something had happened, got to my feet to run over. My first thought was that the policeman, Fatty, had arrived and, while looking for Brow, was bickering with the villagers, or that people from the district government had come to look for Chivalry again.

When I dashed out, every lane was teeming with villagers wielding shovels, pickaxes, brooms and sticks of firewood, giving chase to a gang of people. Many households had opened their courtyards. Some guys were holding water smoking pipes in their hands and some of the women were sticky-handed with wheat flour. They enquired nervously: "Where? Where?" That gang then stomped this way and people by the gate shouted in unison: "Beat them! Beat them!"

A woman flicked the basin in her hands and water splashed on to their feet. Realising suddenly that she had flung out rice together with the water, she leaned forward to pick it up while cursing. I knew none of these people. One of them was a stub of a man with a thick waist and short legs, running as if he were a duck paddling in the water. They ran for their lives while looking back over their shoulders to curse. After hurling a hail of abuse, they lowered their heads to run again.

At the same time, a number of other guys were being chased out of the eight lanes and collided with each other. They turned towards me, their heads in their hands as they were hunted down fiercely by a crowd of villagers and showered with clods of earth and fragments of tiles. A broken shoe flew towards them with a swishing sound and hit the shoulder of the club-headed guy three metres away from me. He threw aside a small iron bucket and the China ink inside spilled all over the ground. The fastest pursuer – Chivalry – shouted loudly: "Drive them out! Drive these bastards out! If they dare come again, let's break their legs."

That gang surged past me. Afraid that I might halt them in their tracks, they stood firm at first, shot glances at me and then suddenly started a stampede. I didn't try to stop them. I only asked Chivalry what was going on when he caught up.

"Sons of bitches!" Chivalry cursed. "They invaded our village early in the morning. They measured up everything and wrote slogans on the walls without saying a word. I asked them where they came from. As proud as peacocks, they declared that they were from Great Prosperity Real Estate Company. I argued with them. Fuck Great Prosperity Real Estate Company! What right do they have to measure and doodle freely in the village? If they are tough enough, ask the Mayor to come."

His words fuelled my rage and, as I looked back over my shoulder, I saw the pack of men had reached the entrance to the lane. One of them hid behind the wall and stuck out his head intermittently to peek this way. I tried to gouge out a piece of tile fragment but the tile couldn't be dislodged. I gathered up a handful of dirt and tossed it over. The head did not stick out again.

"Go to Uncle Five Springs' home to get the gong, strike it and let all the villagers know that someone is going to demolish our village. If anyone dares to come again, we'll take on these sons of bitches."

Before I reached Grandpa Five Springs' home, he had slogged unsteadily this way with the gong. Little Wei snatched it away and thrashed at it, shouting: "People of Benevolent Lenient Village, come out! All of you. Snatch up anything at hand. No one should straggle behind. The critical time has come. Rise up and defend our homeland!"

Chivalry stood on the steps in front of one household and boomed: "Listen up, everybody. Now I, Chivalry, tell you in the name of the Village Head: Benevolent Lenient Village belongs to Benevolent Lenient Village people. Without our consent, nobody is allowed to enter our village to measure our land; nobody is allowed to touch a single clod of earth from our walls or a piece of tile from our roofs. Today, we've driven those bastards away. If one dares to come again, that one will be driven away. If two come, that pair will be driven away. If they can't be driven away, beat them and, if they have been beaten to death, I, Chivalry, will take the responsibility. The public security forces won't come to surround our village and shear us down with machine guns."

Those in the lane promised in chorus: "Fight! As long as they are not afraid of death, we'll pin our heads on our cloth belts. We stay; the village will stay! If no lives are lost, nobody will bother to come over and take care of this business. If one life is lost, our village might be saved." They raised their shovels, brooms and sticks, the very picture of a peasant uprising.

At that moment, I thought this might become an accidental trigger. A pupa was trying to bite a hole in the cocoon to fly out as a moth. It was by this chasing and beating that they were creating our hole. Back when Chen Sheng and Wu Guang rose up, did they launch their peasant uprising in this way too? And our ancestor, that rich merchant Jia Wansan, what was he like on the battlefield after he was exiled? The drum music our ancestor used to boost morale had a musical score and yet we just plied our gong frantically.

"Give me the gong. Let me bang it." I snatched the gong from Little Wei's hand and beat out an ear-deafening noise.

Although the riot in the village did not turn out to be very serious, the men we drove away lost their measuring tapes and notebooks as well as their ink buckets and the broad writing brush used to write the word 'Demolish'. A few guys were hit on the head and feet by tile fragments and a little blood was shed, but the upshot of the event was no less serious than that of the football riot.

How much land and how many villages had the Western Capital swallowed up and still the only one brave enough to resist was Benevolent Lenient Village.

After leading the villagers to chase out the gang, Chivalry organised people to dig a hole at each of the four entrances to the village, placing rafters across them to prevent vehicles from entering. In fact, the village lanes were too narrow and with the exception of one of them, they were not accessible to vehicles. These measures only served as a warning to those who had the nerve to encroach. Throughout the day, almost nobody in the village took a meal or did anything other than congregate below the decorated archway in case those losers came back to retaliate. It may be that this company had a strong backer behind them and would call upon the public security forces for assistance.

By this time the weather was already becoming cool, the sun was hiding in the clouds and a wind kicked up at dusk. We sat there and started a campfire for warmth. When the stadium guys went past, they picked up speed. A child spotted the fire and wanted to come over. The adult prevented him, shouting: "Don't you value your life?" After they had entered through the fencelike iron gate, the lock clicked shut. His condescension humiliated us. Gao Feng and Mangy Head cursed: "His mother's…, what do they think we are?"

Chivalry was smoking a cigarette. "This is good," he said. "Let the city folks fear us." But he bent his head sideways and asked me in a low voice: "Why is your brow knitted into such a lump? Morale can only be boosted, never undermined. Go buy some liquor and let's drink, then we won't feel cold."

I bought five bottles of liquor and seven cans of drink. Men and women, old and young, then proceeded to help themselves. Our stomachs were grumbling already and alcohol stirred us up easily. We played finger guessing games hysterically and startled the residents in the stadium compound. Even though they couldn't fall asleep, they didn't attempt to stop us. Perhaps because the wine had taken its effect or perhaps because we felt lonely and bored after shouting and yelling for some time, the raucous racket gradually died down.

Before the spluttering campfire, some started to twitter and make remarks, some cursed indignantly and others heaved helpless sighs. As the bundles of sweetcorn stalks were being burned, a cob that was overlooked in the harvesting process now started to be roasted in the flames and let off a delicious fragrance. The children vied to get a share and churned up the ash and dust. This rained down on our heads and shoulders.

Chivalry had drunk until his eyes were bloodshot. Sitting on a stone, he finished smoking four cigarettes in succession. The smouldering fire blistered his yellowed lips. With a roar, he ordered the children to step down. The others all looked at him in silence. He too must have sensed that he shouldn't have lost his temper like this. The villagers were all simmering with rage. If he couldn't control himself, who knew what his flame would generate. Pressing his lips together, he murmured: "It has got to this time, but still nothing stirs. They are on the wrong side and their hearts are weak. Why should we all stay here? Let's do it like this: a few fellas stay behind and the rest all go back. If the real estate company bastards come again, strike the gong and when we hear it, we will come out and gang up on them with arms. If the Bureau of Public Security sends folks to arrest us, let them go for me, Chivalry. Even if I'm made to stand before the court, I still have a mouth. Perhaps none of them dare come again."

Chivalry went on like this, but nobody left. On the contrary, more congregated, including many sallow-faced patients in their hospital pyjamas, who shouted: "If the police arrest people, let them go for us, as long as they are not afraid of Hep-B."

Chivalry immediately took a roll-call and asked households to escort their respective patients back home because a liver disease patient ought not to become angry and shouldn't be stimulated. "You might not care if your recovery is delayed, but that could damage our village's reputation for herbal treatments." Some then led their patients back home and then another batch went back too.

Unexpectedly, I saw that Old Ran was standing in the crowd, leaving in the last batch. He was participating in this operation as well, which took me aback. Before he turned to walk away, he sneaked a glance at me. I deliberately turned my head to talk with Chivalry. Chivalry tugged the hem of my blouse and said in a low voice: "That gentleman of yours, ask him to leave. If anything goes wrong, a peasant has nothing to lose, but he holds a government position."

"So what?" I replied. "Isn't he still a member of Benevolent Lenient Village?"

"Maybe he is here to look for you and yet you still don't go over there?" Chivalry pushed me.

I flung the length of stick in my hand over to the foot of a wall, whereupon it bounced back and dived into the campfire. A cloud of ashes rose like a black mushroom. "Fuck off!"

Old Ran, who must have witnessed my every move, didn't come over but just stood there. He took off his glasses and wiped them for quite a long while.

Chapter Nineteen

That day dragged on and so did the night, but nothing went wrong. For the next three days and nights, no one stood guard at the entrances to the village. Instead, Chivalry patrolled to and fro about the lanes carrying that bronze gong in his woman's hand like a soldier on manoeuvres. Maybe because walking like this made him feel lonely, he gently patted the edge of the gong with the mallet at intervals. The brisk staccato sound crawled into the ears of everyone. The pigs were attentive, as were the poultry, the trees and the stones. It was, indeed, the sound that signalled the coast was clear.

I had sworn that I would never talk to Chivalry again but, while we chased and kicked the arses of the guys from the real estate company, the contradictions between us – I couldn't pinpoint when and how – dissolved naturally. One evening, I took his place to let him enjoy a whole night's sleep. With A-Bing in tow, I strutted one circuit around the village and then sat under the stone archway where, out of the blue, I ran into Fan Jingquan.

Seeing him made me feel mildly embarrassed. He criticised Chivalry and our village and now something like this had happened. I didn't know how to open my mouth to say one thing to him. Fan, however, claimed that he had heard about it all. Today, he audited a legal seminar and on his way back he made a point of coming to our village to have a look.

"If you have no objection, I would like to keep you company pounding the beat."

"Things have reached this stage and you still want to risk siding with us. Are you here to gather source materials for your novels?"

Fan's flaw was that, when the creation of novels was raised, he would come over eloquent like a roaring river, saying that novels were the polar opposite to reality and should abide by a different set of rules. Nevertheless, a novelist had everything to do with the realities of his own life and only by living amid certain social and political circumstances could he possibly express his viewpoints on day-to-day political events.

"What do I have to fear? The real estate company did this and I shall expose how they conspired with the respective corrupt government officials. I have written a disclosure report to the City Disciplinary Committee. Whether it will work I can't say, but as a citizen, I should speak out."

He also told me that he had written a novel based on our village, an outstanding one that not only contained stories but fable-like morals as well. He asked if I was interested in reading it. I declined with a smile. With regret, he swept up A-Bing to comb his coat and, after catching sight of his exposed whip, asked me in puzzlement what disease the dog had got. I told him A-Bing's story. He sighed and reflected on how this disease was hard even for Grandpa Cloud Forest to cure. According to one book, after World War II, ninety-nine per cent of survivors from the Nazi concentration camps were impotent, incurably so. Even though A-Bing was not a human being, he had been subject to a similar terror and ordeal.

Fan Jingquan didn't leave that night until he had accompanied me on patrol for a long time. He slipped into melancholy when he learned that we wouldn't be moving to Magic Rice Tableland. Even after he departed, his words about the Nazi concentration camps rattled around my mind throughout the night. Benevolent Lenient Village certainly wasn't a concentration camp, but would the villagers end up being impotent? Would all the men turn out like Old Ran? And yet Old Ran didn't shoulder much pressure. If they were not rendered impotent, would their coccyxes start to jut out like mine?

The next day, I suggested to Chivalry that since nothing was stirring, the villagers should let out their pent-up stress as much as possible and resume their normal lives. Chivalry agreed and the Sunday film was screened as usual. While watching, the elderly folks began to recall the long-forgotten Bodhisattva Temple Fair. Counting their fingers, they discovered that 4th August – the day after tomorrow – was the date the temple fair should be held. Three old ladies put up an incense table under the myrrh tree, kowtowed and burned incense sticks to the bodhisattva. A-Shun's mother smeared a little cinnabar on her cheeks and began to sing a ditty in a shaky voice. A small temple used to stand below the myrrh tree. During past temple fairs, the village would stage operas and organise all kinds of rural festivities. People from nearby villages would all come to join the merriment.

It was almost an established rule that during the half month before the four days between 4th and 7th August, each household would write or pass on an oral message to their relatives, telling them that the famous star of such-and-such opera troupe would be invited for the temple fair. Their relatives would respond by counting off the days on their fingers. For the duration of those four days, the relatives would lay aside their farm work – no matter how pressing it might be – and come along dressed in new clothes from head to toe and carrying colourful steamed buns, red sugar and rice wine. Now the City God Temple Fair in the Western Capital had gone. No longer could incense smoke be seen snaking around those ten halls and eighteen courtyards and no longer could those various magic tricks be seen being pulled off by the roadside stalls.

When A-Shun's mother started to sing, Grandpa Five Springs was enticed over. Even the vendors from outside the village, who sold cold, sliced dough strips, oil-fried cakes and deep-fried cake balls, felt compelled and tantalised to follow suit, bellowing about the streets and the lanes.

More and more people assembled before the incense table. Those who could sing joined the chorus, and those who could play musical instruments picked up small drums, small gongs, *pipa*bs and *erhu*, pumping out a melee of metal, strings and voices. Hearing the news, I ran over. Shaved Head the grocer was scraping away at his *erhu* as his wife belted out *Flowers in the Twelve Months*. The woman had a shrill, ear-prickling voice and her eyes roved around as she performed. After the August flowers had been presented to the bodhisattva, Little Wei, who was rapping dishes to keep the rhythm, glimpsed Grandpa Five Springs cutting a watermelon and lost his pace.

A-Shun's mother raised a hand as if to slap him, though upon noticing me, said: "Plum has fine voice. Give us a few lines from *Cutting Paper to Decorate the Window*."

I didn't know how to sing it, but gestured for Shaved Head's wife to continue and picked up a fan to cool her, thinking: now the bodhisattva has no temple, she will come to our village if she hears the sound of the singing. I looked at the canopy of the myrrh tree, at the roof ridge of the front courtyard of the Jia family and at the screening wall of the middle courtyard, believing that bodhisattva was now everywhere in the village, blessing and guarding us.

It shocked me to recall one detail. The other day Grandpa Cloud Forest had asked me to dig a hole and bury 'All-Powerful Tonic'. Since then, I'd been so busy I had completely forgotten about it. Had Grandpa Cloud Forest sensed that things would go wrong and requested that I bury the medicine in the south-east in order to reinvigorate us?

I put down the fan and walked to the pharmacy. A-Shun's mother was still shouting: "Plum, can you beat the rhythm of the *Drum Music of the Ming Emperor*?" "I will go invite some canny guys." Before these words had left my mouth, I was around the corner. In the pharmacy, I asked A-Shun to go to Grandpa Cloud Forest's home to fetch the stone Buddha and to bring it to the myrrh tree and to ask First Counter Keeper, Second Counter Keeper and First Cutter to go and sing the bawdy strains of the local flower-drum opera. I myself brought ten parcels of 'All-Powerful Tonic' to bury.

Beyond everybody's expectations, the traditional temple fair was authentically recreated on the first day. On the second, the spectacle was taken up a notch as a dozen or more men began to play the *Drum Music of the Ming Emperor*. Nobody stood underneath the decorated archway as a sedan car approached. Because a ditch had been dug and covered over with rafters, the vehicle could not pass through. The passengers got out. They were Fatty the policeman, Brow and a woman in a red overcoat. The first one to spot the trio was Lianben's little nephew, who immediately hurried to look for Chivalry but failed to find him. He then asked a bunch of kids to go over. They walked around the small car and tried –

and failed – to tip it into the ditch. They then drove a nail into one of the tyres and *chi* – it went flat. The three visitors advanced along the lane as far as Grandpa Cloud Forest's shrine, surprised that they hadn't run into anyone else.

A-Bing then scampered to the pharmacy. At that moment, Chivalry, who had completed several circuits of the village, was inside asking about the turnover of the business. When A-Bing entered, we had just brewed some tea. His arrival generally meant that Grandpa Cloud Forest was summoning us. So, Chivalry and I went over there.

When Chivalry bumped haphazardly into Brow, they both put on unpleasant faces and fastened their tongues. Politely, Chivalry nodded to Fatty and then sat on the cattail hassock. Since I had previously quarrelled with Chivalry over Brow, it was inconvenient for me to say anything. In the end, I just asked Grandpa Cloud Forest what was the matter. Grandpa Cloud Forest replied: "For the moment, there is nothing here that concerns you. You can leave."

I became suspicious that Fatty and his gang had come for Chivalry. They must be here because he beat and drove away the real estate company guys. After departing, I swung swiftly by the myrrh tree and told those visiting the temple fair to wait on the earthen ground in front of the shrine in case they attempted to haul Chivalry away. If this transpired, we would surround them and whisk the prisoner off. I dared not say that Fatty had come in the company of Brow. She had already offended Benevolent Lenient Village and, if this time it was she who had guided the policeman to apprehend Chivalry, the angry mob would undoubtedly clobber her to death. Brow, Brow, I mumbled hatefully in my mind, you must have lost your head. Although you wanted to take revenge on Chivalry, you cannot act so flagrantly as this. And, anyway, Benevolent Lenient Village is your hometown. Would you sacrifice the chance of ever being able to come back and live in the village again for the sake of one moment of glee?

The crowd roosted quietly on the earthen ground like sit-in protesters; not even the cawing of the crows and the chirping of the sparrows could be heard. We tried our best to figure out what they were talking about inside the room, but the door was closed and not a peep was audible.

I experienced first-hand why people found a world without sound intolerable. The great quiet terrified us and when we tried to catch any stirrings from inside, the least extraneous sound became unbearable. Now, the breathing of everyone involved in the sit-in demonstration could be heard. Whenever a part of somebody became itchy or someone stood up or swivelled their heads, when they opened and closed their eyelids or their clothes rustled, giving off a noise that was sharp, granitic and fragmented as if ants were crawling about in their bones, it was unbearable. Unable to stand the torture, I exclaimed: "Who will go to our ancestors' domain to pray with me?"

Three others stood up. We went around the wall and entered the cemetery. An alternative Benevolent Lenient Village spread out before our eyes. First, we kowtowed in front of the great grave mound in the centre of the under-world village and prayed that our ancestors would protect us. Then we each bowed and knelt before the residence of every subterranean household. I invited all the people under the myrrh tree to gather in front of the shrine. We wanted to summon the spirits of the dead belonging to each household. Those entities could render us support and courage covertly.

After we had paid our respects to the residence of the last ghostly household, a breeze gushed past the more than thirty-foot-tall, one-thousand-branch cypress and sent it swaying. I looked up at the sky. Dark clouds massed there, very low and very heavy, metamorphosing into all kinds of images, so it appeared as though all the spirits were convening on top of them. Chivalry had once been to the historical ruins of the Kingdom of Kugê. What kind of castle could have been built on a mountain summit? One snowy morning 300 years ago, a cruel war was fought without the accompaniment of drums and horns. Swords and halberds were snapped, human heads rolled, blood coagulated in the extreme cold and snow covered the war steeds, whose crania had been split open. A kingdom with a history of 700 years was obliterated.

I walked towards the fencelike gate step by step, feeling as if I were the king of the Kingdom of Kugê. My crown was gone and the long empty sleeves, which should have covered my now-fractured arms, flapped about in the wind. I ambled my way to the edge of a cliff, pronouncing "Heaven doesn't want me to exist!" I prepared to jump down, but was held steady and heard someone gasping: "Plum, Plum, what's wrong with you?" Standing before me was the old executioner.

"Grandpa," My tears rolled down and I immediately wiped them away. "Look at the spot behind my ears."

The old executioner cackled and suddenly gave my neck a chop. I staggered but still stood straight. I stated: "If Uncle Chivalry is dragged away, I, Plum, will be the Village Head. If I'm beheaded, Grandpa, make sure there is a house set aside for me here."

I put on the air of someone willing to endure a violent death. Later when I recollected this, I found it to be ridiculous and comical, though I spoke those words with sincerity at the time and my three followers were all moved to sob profusely. Even the old executioner grew tender-eyed in an unprecedented way. He pinched up a mite of earth from the ground and sprinkled it on my head and forehead. He said: "Go, child."

But when we got back to the shrine, the sitters-in were nowhere to be seen, the gate of the shrine stood open and Grandpa Cloud Forest and Chivalry were not around either. Grandpa Cloud Forest and Chivalry ought never to have been taken away, I thought. If this were the case, wouldn't we hear the sound of arguing? But, where were they?

We headed to the lane, where the crowd had moved to. Fatty and the driver were busily changing a tyre, Chivalry and Brow were sitting in the car and Grandpa Cloud Forest, borne aloft by others, was talking with the woman in red. Finally, the car was ready to roll and the red-clothed woman bade goodbye to Grandpa Cloud Forest. With her palms pressed together, she bowed deeply and he planted a hand on her head. Without warning, she knelt and pressed her forehead on the ground. The scene moved the people of the village greatly because, in the dark and gloomy lane, her clothes appeared impressively bright and she herself was an incandescent beauty. She came in a deluxe and glamorous car and showed respect to Grandpa Cloud Forest in such a manner as to convey her special sense of friendship with Benevolent Lenient Village.

Someone in the crowd cursed in a low voice, asking which son of a bitch sabotaged the tyre. It was really a shame that the usually upright Benevolent Lenient villagers had lowered themselves to such a narrow-minded thing. The shame-faced little nephew of Lianben hid behind the crowd and faltered: "Not me, not me."

Yet who was this woman? Why did she come here? Why did Grandpa Cloud Forest see her off in person? Why was Chivalry going away with her in the car? When the car took off, Brow did not leave with them and quickly walked back home. In front of the gate of her courtyard, she filled me in on the ins and outs.

"She is the city leader's daughter-in-law who Grandpa Cloud Forest cured. She works in the Performance Section of the Culture Bureau. The city is going to hold an economic and trade meeting and the Performance Section will organise some cultural and artistic activities. I told her all about our village's *Drum Music of the Ming Emperor*. They said this sounded very interesting and reported back to the city government. Today, she came first to thank Grandpa Cloud Forest and secondly to ask Chivalry to discuss the performance."

"She was in the football riot," I shouted out in astonishment.

"That's right. Isn't she stunning? When she was ill, Old Shao and I went to see her and we are good chums now. I strongly recommended the *Drum Music of the Ming Emperor*. Though the village doesn't want me, I still keep it in my mind. It is understandable that the others hate and envy me. What I can't understand is that after she has been humiliated, Grandpa Cloud Forest is still so nice to her when, at the same time, he never asks anything about my circumstances. Even A-Bing is indifferent towards me."

I managed to restrain myself from saying: "Brow, when two armies are in a pitched battle, what they hate most is a traitor." I gazed at her as she entered her courtyard and then reported the red-clothed woman's origins to the villagers. They shouted out whoops of surprise, ran after the car and wanted to have a good look at the woman. However, the car had already left. In days past, we didn't know the woman and, when we talked about the riot, we regarded her humiliation as a tall story or a joke. Now the humiliated party had come to our village and shown such friendliness. We were pricked with deep regret about our former lack of care and sympathised with the woman. We even believed that her arrival heralded good tidings for our village. Was this a piece of divine revelation or our destiny? We were all victims humiliated by the city.

Eighty per cent of the villagers went to watch the football match and they all took great delight in talking about the riot after their meals. They even laughed at the woman, insinuating that her clothing must have been too revealing, her make-up too gaudy and her behaviour that of a hussy. We ought to shoulder a share of responsibility for her humiliation. Was it retribution that we were now being humiliated and victimised?

Suddenly, I empathised with Brow. I could see that we had gone a little too far in its treatment of her. I revealed my thoughts and got vehement criticism in return. "Plum, have you gone soft on the traitor? Your heart is too tender. A woman like her is not worth your sympathy; there is no need for us to relent. She should feel guilty about what she has done to us. Isn't it a fact that she recommended the *Drum Music of the Ming Emperor* because she wanted to flatter the city leaders? Then she ferried them here to let us know her sterling deed? We know her mind. Perhaps she came to show off. Plum, you are too tender-hearted, but you should know that the city slickers look down on us country cousins and, once a country cousin has become a city dweller, they despise the village bumpkins ten times worse than the city slickers do. You see, she was not a city girl in the real sense. She came back here in a little sedan car and didn't talk to us mere mortals. Such a fake foreign devil is even more foreign than a real foreign devil."

It was hard to argue against so many people and I could no longer say anything.

When he returned, Chivalry summoned everyone together and announced that he had seen the city leaders. They had told him that we should arrange meticulously the performance of the *Drum Music of the Ming Emperor*, but didn't mention a word about the relocation of our village and our hunting down of the real estate company men. "This is a chance and we should grab it like a drowning man clutches at a straw. It must be a success. It mustn't fall flat."

Chivalry then organised and selected the members of the troupe, thinking through its formation and training. He didn't mention Brow, and she wasn't awarded a position in the ranks. When Brow's father was alive, the village performed drum music every Chinese New Year and on festivals. He was a renowned drummer and one of the eighteen big cowhide drums was still stored in the wooden-planked loft of Brow's home. Chivalry sent a man to fetch the drum, but didn't allow Brow to accompany him.

"We should ask Brow to join us," I proposed to Chivalry. "She is a good drummer and she was always in our corner."

"She can't go. She can't represent our village now."

I was desperate to have a serious talk with Chivalry, so I asked him to put himself in Brow's position, or in any woman's position. and think about it. I even disclosed the reason why Brow still worked in the company, to obtain a private shop. Chivalry glared at me. When he glared at me, his eyes looked like a wolf's because they displayed more white than black. "Her crime may not be that serious, but

I will use her head to appease the wrath of the world, just like Zhuge Liang.[bt] He wept when he had his favourite general Ma Su[bu] decapitated."

I was stunned and dumbfounded.

On the earthen ground in front of Grandpa Cloud Forest's shrine, 18 drummers, 18 cymbalists and 18 gong players were familiarising themselves with the drum music and repeatedly rehearsing the changes in formation.

The drumbeat represented the roaring God of Thunder.[bv] Day and night, so many Gods of Thunder drilled and yelled in the village that every one of us forgot our tiredness like we had been pumped up so much we started to bulge. This had become the piece de resistance on the temple fair programme. Chivalry also announced that from now on, at the Bodhisattva Temple Fair every August, we would no longer stage dramas or organise rural festivities but perform the *Drum Music of the Ming Emperor* only. Everyone should join in, old or young, and generation after generation would work on it. The rowdier the scene became, the more pitiful I felt about Brow not having a role in it. True enough, she had this and that shortcoming, but if she could come here to listen to the drumbeat and beat the drum, the roars of the God of Thunder would shock her awake. It would be just like an iron can coated with mud. If struck with a drumstick, the muck would plop off *pitter patter*.

When I implored Chivalry one last time, he rebuffed me with extreme impatience and the stubbornness of an ox. He even changed his face and ordered me not to join the band. I returned to the pharmacy in a huff.

After I left, I thought Chivalry would come over to invite me back and apologise. He was born flint-hearted though. Gongs growled and drums thundered for a whole day. At dusk when A-Shun returned to the pharmacy following the rehearsal, he said that once they finished, Chivalry took out money to stand them a drink and now they were all rolling drunk on the earthen ground. He asked me to go have a look. I didn't and, instead, trod back home alone quietly.

My home being intolerably cheerless, I walked out of the village. Passing the guest house of the stadium, I was all at once in a trance. I again clambered through the same window I had gone through with Chivalry. On reaching the football stadium, I parked myself on the empty stands and let the moonlight illuminate me.

On the day of the performance, the few dozen members who made up the band all put on their costumes: a white shirt with buttons down the front, a red cloth belt and long black trousers with legs bound with silk ribbons. Everyone's face was daubed with red, either heavily or lightly so. All the villagers who weren't performing tagged along behind the band. Long beforehand, Chivalry gave the order that everyone should join in, providing they could walk, and those who did would be given an allowance of twenty yuan a day per head. On the other hand, the able-bodied who refused would be fined 50 yuan.

People holding up two tablets that looked like the decorated archway walked at the front of the peasant procession. One tablet was supposedly made of stone and the other crafted out of silk and paper. The tablets were emblazoned in gold with the words 'Drum Music of the Ming Emperor – Benevolent Lenient Village'. Behind the silk tablets were four rows of red, white, yellow and blue flags, which were all decorated with the Auspicious Bird, the Soul of the Sun, the God of Thunder and the God of Wind. Next came four long-necked bronze trumpets and two blunderbusses.

Further behind, a tricycle was loaded with a drum more than three metres in diameter, bearing 168 bronze studs in three rows.

Chivalry clasped the conductor's drumstick. Further behind were three rows of people with the eighteen drummers and their drums in the middle. The eighteen cymbalists and their cymbals formed flanks to the left and the eighteen gong players and their gongs to the right. At the tail of the procession came the motley gang formed by us. The procession commenced from the shrine, strode one circuit around the village, returned to the cemetery then advanced along the lanes to the capital city to perform along four avenues.

We knew we were actually staging a mass demonstration and taking the opportunity to show our resolve to survive forever. A capacity crowd was in attendance and wherever we marched, the traffic became jammed. Originally, we hadn't planned to process along Liu Lin Road on Northern Avenue, but because that was the location of the office of the Great Prosperity Real Estate Company, Chivalry insisted that we make a detour, stop in front of the building and hammer out a sky-shaking round of *Break the Enemy Battle Formation*.

Our leader was over-reacting somewhat, yet I was not really dissatisfied with his decision and even rued the day I quit the band on the spur of the moment. I couldn't release the sorrow and depression that had filled my chest through pounding on the drum and gong. Sensing my heart was anxious and my hands itchy, I sprinted forward from the tail of the procession and signalled for A-Shun to lend me a cymbal. Unwilling to do so, though having no alternative, A-Shun pretended that he didn't understand what I was saying and worked the cymbal more energetically. Not until his face glowed ruddy and his head was soaked in sweat, did he hand the instrument to me. Something unpleasant unfolded at this juncture. When the band pounded out the *Break the Enemy Battle Formation*, the tumult was impassioned and stirring. The combination of the bronze trumpets and the blasting blunderbusses made it sound as though consecutive thunderclaps were rumbling in the sky and as if molten lava was surging across the ground.

Many spectators clamped their hands to their chests, feeling panic-stricken and wishing to leave. Nonetheless, they could not tear themselves away. When one round of music ended, the whole street cheered. Innumerable pedestrians stood by the windows of on both sides of the street, some letting off firecrackers and some rapping washbasins or raising their hands, stretching out the middle and index fingers while screeching towards us. We didn't know what this hand sign meant and exchanged whispers to ask those in front, who relayed to us Chivalry's words: "That means victory." Yeah, we were victors. The procession copied the hand signal. We waved and waved.

A head stuck out from a window on the second floor of the office building of the real estate company: "Brow!" Sure enough, it was Brow. A green gauze kerchief was wrapped around her head. No matter what covering she used, she was still identifiable at first glance. Surveying the procession from Benevolent Lenient Village, she neither smiled nor showed any sign of hatred, but bore a mournful look in her eyes. Her sudden appearance in the office building of the company that we hated with every fibre of our bodies infuriated us.

The villagers spat at her, stuck out their tongues at her and, during the intervals between drumbeats, the percussionists pointed their sticks at her, pretending to stab her while cursing rhythmically: "Traitor – shameless. Shameless – traitor."

Brow's face altered and after a *wah*, the window was slammed shut. It was a terrible pity such an incident happened. I couldn't blame the villagers nor say they were in the wrong. I couldn't understand why Brow stuck her head out to watch at that moment. Didn't she comprehend her status and the situation? Brow, were you wilfully fighting against Benevolent Lenient Village? Or was it that you couldn't sever your bond with the village and so couldn't help sneaking a peek? No matter what the reason, she shouldn't have done it. You've got a wet brain, Brow. Stupid Brow!

The performance lasted three days. The government used culture to build a stage for a great economic drama and we took the chance to publicise ourselves and solidify our status. We won a notable battle and everyone was in the tight grip of frenzied excitement. Chivalry, of course, got drunk again. A bunch of rogues seized their chance to find out how and where his woman's hand had been transplanted. They even asked him to take a leak in public to see if it would grab the organ and not relinquish it.

At nightfall, when A-Shun and I were depositing a batch of herbs in the storeroom, Shaved Head ran here and informed me: "The Village Head sent me here for you."

"He is a hero now. Why does he want me?" But I still went.

Chivalry's courtyard was far from spacious, with three main rooms standing inside – one bright and two dark – and an old-fashioned wooden ladder leaning against the party wall where a wooden plank loft was to be found. When I entered, a dozen or more men and women were lolling around drinking, each with fiery red eyes. An old cracked table groaned under the weight of rice, dishes and liquor. Smoke was billowing, and the miasma of alcohol hung heavily all around.

Lianben was well on his way to being drunk. Raising a bottle of wine, he insisted that Little Wei's wife should drink some more.

"I can't, I can't," the woman replied, her tongue a little stiff.

"A woman can't be ignored," Lianben retorted. "As long as she drinks, she can drink like a fish. Enough liquor to fill an ocean. The others toasted you and you obliged. I drank to you, and you refused. I am not allowed to save face? Lianben is a trashy, good-for-nothing, but what about Lianben's drumbeat? I'm the number one or, at the very least, number two drummer in the village."

The woman conceded that Lianben was a fine drummer. "Of the 18 drums, only yours has been beaten until it is broken."

"I was so excited. I imagined the drum was the head of the real estate company's biggest boss and it was mine to whack. You still won't have a drink?"

Unable to decline and driven into a corner of the room, the woman saw me entering and said: "Let Plum drink. She hasn't drunk a drop yet."

Lianben came to toast me with the liquor bottle. I stood there and downed a single cup.

The others responded: "One cup doesn't count. You didn't come until we'd already emptied eight bottles. You should be fined. Drink, drink six cups one after another. Six and six, and all is fixed."

It seemed that I couldn't refuse. The drinking custom in our village was that if there was wine to drink, one should drink to one's heart's content. Being inebriated showed you'd had your fill. I tossed off six cupfuls and felt my stomach being burned by fire. I asked: "Where is the Village Head?"

Lianben pointed the wine bottle upwards and mouthed

inarticulately: "Upstairs. Why is he the Village Head? Drink just a little and pretend to be drunk. Boss, boss, come down. You haven't had your fill. Let's carry on."

He staggered upstairs. Someone propped him up, and while he was being held in that position, he thudded towards the ground, depositing the wine bottle on the table on his way. The spirits spilled out.

"Arsehole, you've spoiled the wine. Anything can be spoiled but how could you spoil the wine?" Somebody else cursed while lapping up the wine from the table – *slurp slurp*.

I climbed upstairs. The banisters were carved and almost half snapped. The hand rails were rickety. When I raised my foot and moved upwards, the stairs squeaked. Chivalry was curled up in a big round-backed armchair and two young men were persuading him to drink some vinegar, saying that vinegar was the hair of the dog that bit him. Chivalry ranted: "Why should I take vinegar like someone who's envious? I'm not drunk. How could I be drunk? Go ask Plum."

I chimed in: "I'm here. You're so pie-eyed you can't recognise people. Why do you still want to drink?"

Chivalry looked at me and, feeling sheepish, suddenly smiled, slapped his forehead and admitted: "I might have had one drop too many. Plum, come and take a seat. Today I'm happy and have stood the guys a drink. It's good to get drunk. I'm telling you, don't be angry with your uncle. You're too emotional and your uncle is not wrong. Don't look down on your uncle for being a peasant. Your uncle's fate has not been good. However, he is a politician and a revolutionary activist as well."

"You're also a good drinker," I replied. "Why should I be angry with you? You're the Village Head. What mistakes have you made? Isn't it down to your leadership that our village hasn't been demolished? And haven't we worked off some of our anger one more time?"

"That's quite true," Chivalry stood up and once again had the bearing of a wolf. "Son of a bitch, he can demolish anywhere and he can renew anywhere, but he can't demolish our village. The city is urbanised, but not our village. Benevolent Lenient Village won't be brought down. It won't be wiped out. You've read some books and I've read some books too. The books say that the Kingdom of Qin wiped out the other Six States.[bw] It's not that they were wiped out by the Qin. They wiped out themselves. I know this clearly. That why I hate traitors and moles. Brow is a mole."

"Don't bring others into this. You asked me here for this?"

"Don't think that Uncle Chivalry takes pleasure in bugging you. Today the guys are happy and want a drink. When I found you weren't here, I sent for you. Now you don't thank me but look at me with those fierce eyes. Let's see if you're still that fierce in a while? Puppy Egg, Puppy Egg, bring out that thing from the bedroom."

Puppy Egg was now a grown up, though still had a pair of peach blossom eyes. He winced: "You are gripping my hand so tightly. How can I go fetch it?"

Bolt, who was holding the vinegar bowl, said: "Your hand has grown on Uncle Chivalry's crotch?"

Chivalry cursed, kicked each of the bad arses to scatter them aside and went into the bedroom to pull out a single bed. The bed was not large, yet proved awkward to manoeuvre through the doorway. His legs weakened, the bed plonked down and, conveniently, he ended up lying face-down on it, inebriated.

It was a single-planked, purple sandalwood arhat bed with three sideboards. The sideboards were sawn from thick planks without any carving and only the back board had a narrow protective strip on it. The outer edge of the bed looked like the cross-sectional outline of a plate and had only one sideline. The legs were fashioned out of four big thick round logs, complete with protective wrappings and horizontal and vertical linking battens. The structure and ornaments of the bed could not have been simpler, giving people visual satisfaction and enjoyment. I hadn't clapped eyes on a better piece among all the Ming and Qing Dynasty furniture I had collected.

I asked Puppy Egg where it came from. Puppy Egg replied: "After Chivalry got to know the woman in red, he spotted this ancient bed in her home and exchanged it for a handed-down blue and white porcelain vase. He meant to send it to you." Looking at the roaring drunk Chivalry, I gave him a helping hand while shouting: "Uncle Chivalry! Uncle Chivalry!"

Chivalry hummed and hawed without opening his eyes, and then hurled out vomit all over the bed.

Chapter Twenty

Chivalry sent me the wooden plank bed made at the beginning of the Qing Dynasty, and I was grateful. It was so precious to me that he had the heart to send me things I'd been hoping for. However, the bed spelled the end of my engagement to Old Ran.

I no longer slept on a clay brick *kang* when Old Ran came to my house, instead opting for a bed constructed from three or four narrow wooden planks without a headboard. That day we failed to do it on the squeaky bed, Old Ran proposed that he buy me a sofa bed. "If I want one, I'll buy it myself. Do I like the things that belong to you?" Old Ran asked me when I would purchase it. I replied that he should wait and see. When I got married, I would buy a decent bed. After I had carried the Qing-style bed back home, he ran over to see me. I didn't know who had told him about it.

"You've bought a bed?"

"So what?"

"But you said that…"

I knew what he was implying. "This is an old-fashioned bed. I'm afraid I shall never buy a modern one."

Old Ran froze and repeated: "I'm also an old-fashioned man."

It was not easy for him to spit out this gobbet of humour.

When people get on with each other, you sometimes feel a sense of kinship on first sight and then are disgusted with them on another occasion. Especially where looks are concerned, there aere those you never grow accustomed to.

Old Ran was standing before me, but the smell of his body seemed different from that of days past. His hair had been dyed, though no matter how I looked at him, the hair was not as attractive as his dishevelled, uncoloured greying mop. I told him we no longer had that kind of relationship and we were now only fellow villagers. I welcomed him to drop by whenever he was free. The Ming and Qing Dynasty furniture we collected before should belong to him, so I asked him to take them back. He refused, asking why he ought to take the furniture when the person behind it didn't even want him.

"Well, then," I said and brought out sweets for him to eat. He took some and chewed them to a pulp without swallowing. His cheeks bulged outwards, and tears trickled down.

Old Ran and I broke up for good, our separation becoming major news in Benevolent Lenient Village. I didn't skirt around this taboo topic and told others in public we'd split up after I acquired the bed. What kind of destiny was that? Our courtship began with old furniture and ended because of it. A bed is indispensable in a woman's life. Whichever family's bed she sleeps on, she is a daughter-in-law of that family. This couch, on the other hand, belonged to the Ming or Qing Dynasty and it was an old piece.

I sang the following song about the village:
The sun goes down the western mountain,
And the moon climbs up the eastern mountain.
After the sun goes down, it will climb again the next day.
Flowers will come out again the next morning after they fade.
Beautiful little birds have flown away without a shadow.
My little bird has gone and will never come back.
Never come back, oh, gone and never come back.

According to my life's experience, the only way to maintain a sense of dignity was to mock yourself in a self-deprecating way. This allowed a person to avoid being played and being put in an awkward position. I wasn't very attractive so stated directly that I was ugly. I broadcast my ugliness, so that others would not laugh at me for being plain. By deliberately lowering their expectations, I could goad them into seeing aspects in which I was beautiful. Consequently, since I was fully at ease with myself, I wouldn't become touchy and think they were talking about me, making insinuations whenever someone observed that a crow was black.

When I was in the village lanes or in the pharmacy and, later, when I had a gallery for my Ming and Qing Dynasty furniture in my home and was describing the pieces to others, I hummed this song. Sure, after I had been crossed in love, there were young men who worried that my spirits might slump and that I would be inclined to behave abnormally. Instead, noticing how everything continued as before, they praised me for being strong. Ladies advanced in years didn't blame me for giving Old Ran the push. They pointed a finger at him, accusing him of not cherishing me. "Poor Plum, how can you be old?" This was how they consoled me. "You are not old. You can find a better one than that Ran guy."

Who was to know that after disowning Old Ran, I had finally shaken off the endless sense of vexation that dogged me. I sang the song because I was tickled by the hilarious rhythm and it became a means of conveying my ease and excitement. These, I thought, must be my happiest days: The village was intact, my relationship with Old Ran had ended and my tailbone seemed to be gradually contracting.

"Plum, I strongly disagree." The most vehement dissenter was Chivalry.

"Really?" I asked. "Uncle Chivalry, you loathe the fact that I said it was you who sent me the bed?"

"Why do you put it like this?"

"But this is true."

"I'm the Village Head," he lectured me in the name of the Village Head. "You're getting on in years. Won't you get married in the future? If you find an outsider, you will no longer be a member of the village. But in this village, from the south to the north and from the east to the west, which man is suitable except for Old Ran?"

I lost my temper and answered back loudly: "Does this also fall within your jurisdiction as Village Head? I have the freedom to choose who I can marry. You want me to stay with Old Ran, who is neither a city slicker nor a country brother, neither a man nor a woman, because you want me to suffer."

After hearing my words, Chivalry got angry. He slapped the table hard, flaring his nostrils. I could see that the transplanted, tender, fair-skinned hand had turned sauce red. He left and I suddenly realised that the expression "neither a man nor a woman" had wounded him. Everyone has a sensitive spot that should never be touched: there was the face of Clawed Face, the psoriasis of Shaved Head and my coccyx. I regretted my slip of the tongue and wanted to clarify my meaning, yet I couldn't go to him because that way I would have to mention his hand again and so hurt him once more. This had become something of a load on my mind and, from that day onwards, I no longer tussled with him. Whether consciously or not, I tried to be amiable and forthcoming towards him. I felt myself more or less humble.

Seven days later, we were all sipping tea in Grandpa Cloud Forest's shrine, mulling over the current situation faced by the village. A line had been drawn under the incident in which the real estate company men were bashed and driven away. I asked the gathering if we could fill in the pits at the entrances to the village and remove the roadblocks improvised out of rafters.

"For the time being we shouldn't provoke the outside world. Benevolent Lenient Village is now like a man passing along a street with a carrying-pole bearing two baskets of eggs: we are not going to squeeze past others because we are afraid of being squeezed."

Chivalry slapped me down: "You know, a woman can't make it big because she is too soft-hearted. How can there be no squeezing on a street? If you don't squeeze people, they will squeeze you. If you don't want to be squeezed, then grasp the nettle and squeeze others."

But how could we squeeze others? He proposed three ways. First, fight fair but firm with the bureaucrats and business-men. We would arrange hands to gather evidence about how the real estate company buys up and uses petty officials to take our land by force in the name of the government and send this data to the City Disciplinary Committee and Provincial Committee. Secondly, we would further develop our relationship with the leaders concerned in the district government and cosy up to the Mayor using the woman in red, who could encourage him to develop a liking for our village. Thirdly, build the village in a thorough fashion. If the work was to be thorough in every aspect, even someone who wanted to demolish it wouldn't be able to find a pretence.

When it came to the development of the village, Chivalry was fired up. His blueprint was extremely ambitious. It was his determination to make our village the most characterful in China, which not only preserved a plot of country land in the face of nationwide urbanisation but also become a beacon that was unified, upright, especially adept at fighting and capable of achieving common prosperity. He even pronounced cockily that sometime in the future a new '-ism' might be engendered in the village and asked Grandpa Cloud Forest to cooperate by putting forward some propositions.

"You will become a source of honour and a symbol for our village," he predicted. "Some of your words might be compiled to form *Quotations from Benevolent Lenient Village*!"

"I only know how to cure disease, Chivalry." Grandpa Cloud Forest sat there, a quilt draped around his shoulders because it was already cold.

"Yeah, there are too many patients in this modern society. Why do people get diseases, especially liver disease, and why are so many liver disease patients cured when they come to our village? Our village exists for eradicating human liver disease. This is *disease-curing-ism*, this is *Benevolent Lenient Village-ism*! I have wandered to the southernmost end of the skies and to the northernmost end of the sea and my soul was purified and found quiet when I reached Tibet and found this stone Buddha. As long as we have Uncle Cloud Forest, we can purify and find quiet for the capital city because het can purify and quieten down Benevolent Lenient Village. You're our Buddha."

Grandpa Cloud Forest sipped his tea and pinched the tea leaves with his fingers to munch on them. "I'm nothing but your uncle. Chivalry, show me that hand of yours."

Chivalry reached out his hand.

"The lady donor was not only shortlived," Grandpa Cloud Forest discerned. "She was a divorcee as well and rated herself too highly. You can go and compare your arm with Plum's. Only Plum can tame you."

I didn't look at my own hands. I didn't know what the lines on them represented. I slipped my hands beneath my bottom. Chivalry shot me a glance, his hand rose up and balled itself into a fist. Grandpa Cloud Forest's words might have been an ingenious criticism or perhaps only a jape. Neither of us laughed or added another word. "Has the tea been finished off? When the tea has been drunk, you can re-boil the leaves and drink some more," Grandpa Cloud Forest said.

"Ha!" Chivalry finally let out a laugh as an excuse for making a comment. "It's true that Plum can tame me. In our village, I daresay all the men will follow my words and my policies and my orders will go smoothly in all quarters. The only ones who brazenly disobey me are women; first Brow and then Plum. If Plum and Old Ran cannot get married, I'm afraid my days of really being gossiped about have not yet come around. I must have indulged her too much. A peasant; why of all things does she collect Ming and Qing items? Why of all the things I could have sent her in my muddleheadedness did I send a bed?"

"Uncle Chivalry, don't draw the quilt and drag the felt sheet at random. I can't tame you, and how do you imagine Brow could tame you?

"I'll say something I'm not really keen on sharing. I think you are too cruel to Brow. She hasn't been seen in the village for many days. How can she come back again?"

"You needn't scratch that boil again. I'm the Village Head and I'm not in the wrong here."

Once more our conversation ended on a sour note.

It was my turn to get blotto that night. I singlehandedly emptied at least half a bottle of hard liquor. With superhuman energy, I dismantled my former bed and put the new purple sandalwood arhat bed into use. Lying on it and thinking about how I hated Chivalry, notwithstanding the fact that I was sleeping on the bed he gave me, I was overcome with absurdity. Who had slept on this bed since it was made? Who would sleep at my side? Hovering between sleep and wakefulness, I sang: "The sun goes down the western mountain." But what came next? I couldn't recall the words no matter how hard I tried.

The woman was asking her husband, the patient: "Do you still want to eat?"

The husband answered: "No."

"Drink?"

"No."

"Maybe we can…?"

"You lift me on top of you and be gentle about it."

Grandpa Cloud Forest had drilled it into their ears that they shouldn't engage in intercourse, though the couple simply wouldn't follow his advice. The patient would have been cured in one month, but now he must stay for two more months.

Two months. I slumped into a dream. I was on my way to a remote place where there were snowy mountains, rivers and a gateway built out of flagstones. A notice was hanging on the gateway. I examined it, and it seemed to be the rules of the city or something similar. I couldn't decipher the words.

A man carrying a rafter on his shoulder wanted to go in but failed. Another man, also carrying a rafter, wanted to go out and failed too. Someone shouted from the gateway: "Turn it vertical. Vertical!" With the rafter tilted upright, sure enough the man could enter the city. The streets inside the city were very narrow. Some pedestrians were missing a hand and others an eye. I recalled how in this city those who committed theft would have a hand chopped off as punishment and those who fought would have an eye gouged out.

Every 100 metres or so, you could see a wooden tablet or a patch of wall whitewashed with lime upon which various quotations were written. Pedestrians were frequently accosted and required to recite the quotations and the rules of the city. I could never intone them correctly, dropping a word here and forgetting a sentence there. The examiner bawled loudly: "Don't use Standard Chinese!" They pronounced "two" like "do" and "folk" like "fuck," their tongues rolling further and further inwards. The king of the city rode past and set his eyes on me. I clamped a hand on my coccyx and leaned against the city wall to cover my shameful humiliation. Many others did likewise. Did each of them have a tail too? The king turned his face impassively, cantered past me and hung his horsewhip on the bronze knocker of a household gate.

A woman nearby informed me: "Pocky Wang has fathered a beautiful daughter and the king will stay at her home tonight." She tweaked her daughter spitefully.

I didn't know why but I had sunk into gloominess. Doctors stated that those who suffered from depression were inclined to methodically plan their own suicide. So, I contemplated how to end it all. My first plan was to jump from the decorated archway of the village, but I couldn't find it and later it dawned on me that this was not Benevolent Lenient Village. On second thoughts, there was no sense in jumping because it could prove too painful and it would be unsightly if my body was mangled in the fall and then seen by others. My Plan B was an overdose of sleeping pills; 88 tablets (because eight was an auspicious number). After taking the pills, I turned my head to look around to see my father and mother, Brow's mother and Chivalry's father. I was dying and when one is dying, you are supposed to be able to see spectres. How could there be no spectres? I started to write my suicide note, which dragged on and on. After I had finished it, I tagged on another sentence: "Death is not fearful." Then I lay on the bed ready to die.

Clonk – I heard a loud noise. The husband was asking: "Did the piss basin drop down?"

The woman answered: "I thought there were three steps."

I woke up. I wasn't dead? The windows brightened up.

"Cuiqin, is it cloudy?"

The woman answered: "Sunny."

Sunny days were good for drying herbal pills. Suddenly feeling unbearably itchy all over, I reached a hand underneath the quilt to scratch and discovered patches of small bumps on my legs and waist. I got up and lifted aside the quilt and mattress. Stinky lice were crawling about in the cracks of the wooden planks of the Qing-style arhat bed.

The most ancient insects in China had been hibernating and lain hidden in the cracks of the bed since the beginning of the Qing Dynasty, and they were still alive. As soon as they picked up the smell of a human being, they sprang back to life.

I dismantled the couch, hauled it out and boiled water to take care of them. A-Shun came to call on me again and stopped to talk to the patient's wife: "Are there still stinky lice nowadays? Such a good bed and it is infested with stinky lice?"

I squashed some insects to death, my hands dyed with blood. This was my blood. Stinky blood at that.

Chapter Twenty-One

Not only did Chivalry's attitude towards Brow fail to improve. He actually grew to detest her more with every passing day. In seeking to realise his ideal, he became more arbitrary and, step by step, put his plan into practice.

Meetings were held in the village and at every assembly he referred to Brow as a sobering example with which to warn the others. He made uniform arrangements for all the families' houses and required that all the patients' rooms be white-washed, sickbeds designated, quilts and coverlets kept clean and that there should be no discrimination among the patients and none of them ignored. That way every one of them would become a voluntary propagandist for our village after they left, and we were bound to see a growing number of customers.

This was a preposterous argument. In the past, we cursed, asking why there were so many patients with liver disorders in this world and, when we had to accommodate them, hoped their number would decrease. Yet now we scrambled after them until we were red-eyed. Our ads fluttered at the gate of every big hospital and we even sent hands to intercept patients on their arrival, wishing anxiously that all the people in the world might contract hepatitis and come to our village.

A crematorium stood at Tianzhao in the eastern end of the Western Capital. Tianzhao had come to be seen as the symbol of death, whereas the name of our village had become a pronoun to replace the word 'disease'.

When close acquaintances ran into each other in the Western Capital, one would say: "Hi, the chairman of our country can be seen on TV every night, but I haven't seen your soul for months. Have you been over at Benevolent Lenient Village?"

The answer was: "Not to Benevolent Lenient Village but a place not that far from Tianzhao." It was obvious that there were now twice as many patients in the village as there ever was before. Originally, each household kept all the income from providing food and board to patients. Now, Chivalry imposed a new rule that 20 per cent must be handed in. The money would be used to build a courtyard of collective sickrooms. The income from the collective sickrooms and the pharmacy would be saved up and used to fund the development and renovation of the village. Everyone grumbled but no one begged to differ at the meeting. They only proposed that, besides raising the number of patients accommodated by each household every month to three, they should also be allowed to rent out the rest of their unoccupied rooms.

Chivalry responded: "Of course. It's high time this was done." He even made a draconian decision: board up the gate of Brow's house. "Those who come to our village to see the doctor or rent a room, we shall take great care of them. Those who betray us, however, will never be shown any mercy." He kept a tight and meticulous rein on every piece of work. He was a livewire and required the others to follow his lead.

Many guys then came to look for me, looking for work in the pharmacy. The best position was being sent to buy medicine. Lianben chuntered on about how he was as busy as if he was being hounded by a thief. "I don't even have time to empty out my bladder and my crotch is always wet." But Lianben couldn't come to the pharmacy. None of those who wanted to come had their wish fulfilled. Chivalry named and reproached them at the village meeting. He then asked Lianben to stand before the table and required the others to pass comments. A few said he was lazy, and a few others said he joked about having to hand in 20 per cent of his income, not only in the public lavatory but also before the residents of the stadium compound. Gao Feng stepped up and said he had heard Lianben was in favour of rehabilitation. He wanted to replace Chivalry with the old Village Head. Lianben was pissed off. "Bullshit!"

Gao Feng questioned him: "When Brow's gate was boarded up, wasn't it you who sent two chicks of hers to be raised by the old Village Head? Wasn't it you who sent the eggs they laid to Brow in the city? Have you or have you not drunk wine at the old Village Head's?"

"Yeah. So what?" Lianben replied. "Is he our class enemy?

You want to be a deputy Village Head and you lick Chivalry's arse, but Chivalry doesn't know how many pounds and how many ounces you weigh? Be a good team leader and that's it."

His sense of disgrace giving way to rage, Gao Feng jumped up to deliver Lianben a slap across the face and then assumed his former seat. The slap was impromptu and everyone was taken aback. Not even Lianben knew what hit him. When he mopped his mouth, the edge bled and he pointed at Chivalry, yelling: "Why did he beat me and why did you watch wide-eyed?"

Chivalry stood up and asked: "Who beat him?"

Gao Feng answered: "I did."

"You shouldn't. A gentleman argues but never fights. Why did you beat him?" He downplayed the incident and dismissed it as nothing.

After the meeting, I interrogated Chivalry at his home: "What do you think about what happened at the meeting?"

Chivalry hunkered down on a bench smoking a cigarette, a smile hanging at the corner of his mouth. "Nothing."

"Nothing? I could see that you indulged Gao Feng. You want to create your own dictatorship in the village?"

"The old Village Head is very active. Plenty of folks go to his home to drink at night. What's behind that?"

Not until then did I know that Gao Feng's devious actions had been plotted in secret by Chivalry. Gao Feng might have slapped Lianben, but the true target was the old Village Head.

Sure enough, on the third day the old Village Head fell sick. Really sick.

He had got a fever, vomited and was soon totally out of sorts. Even Grandpa Cloud Forest had been deployed to diagnose and treat him.

Strangely enough, Chivalry came searching after me with a big sack of fruit and nourishment and instructed me to accompany him to see the old Village Head. We spotted Lianben in the lane behind the old Village Head's courtyard and Lianben ducked his head to retreat into a nearby latrine.

Chivalry didn't hasten away. He waited instead at the exit of the latrine. Lianben, who neither shit nor peed, stuck out his head to take a look and found himself standing face-to-face with Chivalry.

Chivalry probed: "You don't want to see me?"

"I'm a bad guy."

"Who said you're a bad guy? Why be fussed with a guy like Gao Feng?"

"Am I fussed with him? If I wanted to, I could despatch ten of him."

"I believe you. Come to my home and drink tonight."

They exchanged jokes and laughed. I made no comment.

More and more patients came to the village, and ten families also rented rooms. After the Village Committee accumulated a sum of money, we built a courtyard of single-storey sickrooms in the winter as well as my emporium of furniture.

Brow didn't come back during this period. When he heard about me exhibiting my furniture, Bushy Beard Old Shao visited once. During our conversation, he told me quietly that they had already acquired a copy shop and, moreover, they officially announced their marriage on the day of the opening ceremony. "Good news," was my reply. "Now Brow has fulfilled her deepest wish." I then asked him with a smile what was the difference between an official marriage and an unofficial one.

"I feel a sense of responsibility." His words made me splutter into laughter, though his talk about their marital life made me feel gloomy. After the shop opened, Brow became a workaholic. Day and night, she threw herself into the job. She wanted to enlarge the shop within the year and develop it into a company in three years. But their marital life was increasingly unhappy. Her character changed greatly and she grew maniacal, impulsive and apt to slip into a towering rage. Whenever they bickered, her face darkened and her limbs turned icy-cold. It was as if she were suffering from an acute disease and required a fortnight to recover. Throughout the day, her eyes were dull with black shadows beneath them. If they didn't know better, others might assume she was overindulging in nocturnal activities. In fact, she was becoming more and more sexually frigid and only doted on her lapdog.

Old Shao's words pained me, but I didn't offer any soothing sentiments for him to relay to Brow. The sudden change in her character had everything to do with village. The more her hatred for the community intensified, the more madly she flung herself into running the shop. And yet her health couldn't withstand the overburdening work and she was subject to rapid mood swings, which served to aggravate her animosity towards the folks in the village. Still, in her eyes, I was an important figure in the village and I must be an accomplice to her tormentors. I couldn't begin to imagine how she must be cursing me.

After visiting the emporium, Old Shao dropped by again with great interest in my collected items and also brought along two pieces of Ming furniture. One was a small scented rosewood box, 42 centimetres long, 20 centimetres wide and 16.7 centimetres tall, shiny and unpainted throughout. Beading the thickness of a lamp wick ran around the lid and the body. The four outer corners were clad in bronze protectors and the four corners on the lid had bronze ornaments. The foremost bronze plate was circular and the lock hanger resembled a bank of cloud. A haul loop was fixed on both of its sides. The other item was a tall, carved wash-stand. The towel-rest stretched out at both ends and each was carved with a round *Lingzhi* mushroom. A string of hanging teeth was carved beneath the towel-rest on both sides and looked like thriving, tender shoots. Both ends of the four battens that formed the frame to hold the central board stood at 45°angles and butted against each other. There were four supportive battens with a cloud design as well. These were two pieces of precious Ming-style furniture. I was startled to learn where Old Shao got them from and why he was willing to send me items of this kind.

"To be honest," Old Shao admitted. "These were collected by a friend of mine. When he heard that you like such things, he entrusted me to send them to you. He asked for nothing in return. He is a big shot, who doesn't care about money and only wants to make friends."

"Why didn't you bring him with you?" I enquired. "Now, I can't say 'come to Benevolent Lenient Village' without sounding like I'm cursing him to come down with a disease. You should have invited him to come and have a look at my collection."

"He will. He knows everything about your village and says he had never thought that Benevolent Lenient Village was able to perform the *Drum Music of the Ming Emperor*, let alone that someone would collect Ming and Qing furniture."

"Our village can boast many ancient ruins. The cemetery and the well are just two. Chivalry found some old genea- logical books in a crack in a party wall in Grandpa Five Springs' courtyard. They revealed that the Jia family fostered a painter, a scholar who met the qualifications for the highest level imperial examinations,[bx] not to mention my great-grandfather, who established the West Guanzhong Academy and was a prestigious Confucian scholar back in the day. Do you know about our village ancestor? Have you ever read the stone tablet that stands under the decorated archway? If I were the Mayor, I would never demolish Benevolent Lenient Village, only preserve it further. It is a rare cultural site."

"Exactly so, Plum," Old Shao shouted out, clapping his hands. "How can it be? Your words are precisely the same as my friend's? He thinks just the same."

"Our plan had been advancing, but now we've temporarily found ourselves strapped for funds. Next year – maybe in two years' time – you will be able to see how our village has been changed into a totally different place."

"This friend of mine went on to say that if your village can be renovated, all the houses should take on the Ming Dynasty architectural style so as to create a Ming-style village. This would then become a tourist honey-pot. He means that if you are short of funds, he can cooperate and singlehandedly fund the project. It's OK as long as the future tourist income is divided between the two parties, according to their respective shares of stock."

This piece of unexpected good news aroused my interest and I passed it on to Chivalry. He believed it was a good idea as well, and no doubt represented a way of preserving our village forever. Considering our current economic strength, he also agreed to cooperate and went to look for Old Shao in person. Chivalry's strong point was that once he reached a decision, he didn't have any scruples and could not even bring himself to consider the potential embarrassment and harm. I didn't know how Brow would treat him when he went to look for Old Shao, since he would inevitably encounter her. Would she snatch up a broom to sweep the floor frenziedly? Or pour out a basin of waste water? Or lean against the door frame and say: "Who are you? I don't know you." Or make a meal of noodles for him but half fill the bowl with wheat straw? How would he sit in Old Shao's living room, and what would he say?

He returned that afternoon and, as expected, was the losing party. He descended on my home in an almighty fury just as I was helping the patient build a stove fire under the eaves to decoct the medicinal herbs. The flames refused to flare up and the black smoke choked me.

He asked me which two pieces of furniture were sent by

the Shao guy. I pointed them out. He kicked them. The tall, carved wash-stand toppled over and the hanging teeth beneath the towel-rest snapped. The nail of his big toe cracked at the same time, releasing blood. He carried on by raising a modern-style chair with the intention of wellying it at the shelf. I restrained him with both hands and yelled loudly: "You're the Village Head. If you dare smash my personal belongings, I'll report it to the police."

The lifted chair was suspended in mid-air, then was flung out hard into the courtyard, where it smashed into a heap of splinters. "What a charitable thing you've done!" he roared. "Are they helping us? They are wolves trying every means to swallow up our village. I am not going to trash those two pieces, but you must send them back. You must."

He was out of his mind and terrifying to behold.

It went on like this. When Chivalry had gone to look for Old Shao, he saw Brow, but the scene wasn't as grisly as I had expected because Brow and Old Shao were still trying to make a contribution to Benevolent Lenient Village. Seeing the floor was carpeted, he wanted to take off his shoes on entering, but Brow didn't allow him to. Chivalry even ate a bowl of dragon-beard noodles cooked by Brow. While he was eating, Old Shao invited his friend over and the big, portly man turned out to be Brow's biggest boss, that is to say the General Manager of the real estate company who had been plotting unremittingly to demolish our village. Chivalry immediately grasped that he was being taken for a fool. He lost his temper there and then, cursed them roundly and went away with a flick of his sleeve.

"They can't get our village in an open way, so they resort to an underhand trick. This is the favour done by your good brother and sister Brow! No matter how impoverished we are, we can't cooperate with these people. If he is invited to build a Ming-style village, won't our village become his personal property?"

I couldn't avoid becoming furious with Brow and Old Shao. I was trying to help them improve their situation, while they were just pulling my leg. A man shouldn't be too magnanimous because magnanimity is rarely paid back in kind.

Unwilling to see Brow again, I asked A-Shun and others to send the two pieces of furniture back to Old Shao with a tricycle. I also copied down a length of an ancient adage on paper, which I hung on the wall to warn myself. It read:

Tillers toil, but they mostly have no food for the next day.
Silkworm women moil, but they seldom have enough clothing to keep the cold away.
When I have my three meals, I should recall the hardships the peasants have suffered;
When I have a stitch on, I should remember the hard labour the girl weavers have contributed.
For one inch of silk, one thousand silkworms have sacrificed their lives;
For one grain of food, an ox got one hundred strokes from the whip.
Receiving an undeserved reward, I will feel uneasy when sleeping and eating.
Befriend virtuous people and disown ne'er-do-well acquaintances.
Take deserved wealth and stay clear of reasonless liquor.
Always examine oneself critically and shut the gossipy mouth.

After A-Shun had returned the furniture, he came back and reported to me: "Brow has gone crazy."

"Brow has gone crazy?" I couldn't believe my ears. When? Chivalry saw her only a few days ago and everything was fine. How could that be? "How could she? She was only a tad weird. Perhaps on realising that I had given the furniture back, she was not in a good mood and said some cranky words to you."

"She only laughed," A-Shun recounted. "Laughed without stopping. Her face was covered thickly with powder and her mouth was red like she'd been eating raw meat. How could she do herself up in such a queer way? She just laughed without stopping. On one of her feet, she had a high-heeled shoe and on the other a flat-soled shoe. She walked like she had a some sort of disability. If that's not a mad woman, what is?"

I related A-Shun's words to Chivalry, who was busy arranging tenants at the homes of Lan Cheng, Gou Sheng, De Lun and Gen Ben. After his humiliation, he had drawn upon all kinds of connections to solicit a bunch of outsiders who had come to the capital city to make a living. They would board in our village. Having heard me out, he snapped: "Why should I care a fart whether she is mad or not? Why always bring her into things? Worry more about how to find extra patients and extra renters and, when we are rich, let's humiliate them. Then they will go crazy, whether they like it or not."

I hadn't believed that Brow could go crazy. Now she had a shop and was doing her damnedest to develop her career. Why should she go crazy? I no longer let this linger on my mind. Brow's neighbour, the pointy-mouthed woman, hung dyed, homespun cotton cloth at the entrance to Brow's courtyard and a piece of baggy red underwear on the knocker to dry out. When I passed by, I tugged down the red underwear and threw it into her gateway.

The woman asked: "Plum, do you think you can you give me a few more registration numbers?"

"This should be done according to the rules."

"That slut won't come back to live here, but we are still neighbours and my family should take her numbers."

"Good. Does that mean because we're fellow villagers, I should be able to scoff all the food in your home?"

The woman chortled and went on: "Plum, the guys in the stadium compound say that Brow is doing such-and-such with that dog, but I don't believe them. She hasn't been around for a long time. A-Bing comes every day. He puts his front legs on her gate and howls. That long whip of his is back on show."

I growled spitefully: "If you have the nerve to mock the village like this again, I'll ask Chivalry to slap your mouth."

Another month passed by and everything was fine and dandy. Snowflakes started to dance in the sky and every household was busy building a stove and chimney and making preparations for the coming winter. Early one morning, the briquettes for the jerry-built heating stove in the pharmacy had been used up and our mouths and faces were frozen blackish-blue. Second Counter Keeper and I transported several cartloads of loess to make briquettes in front of the gate. A-Shun used the chopped-up willow branches to fuel the stove for warmth. As the smoke billowed, he ran out, coughing.

A tooting motorbike and sidecar breezed across the snowy ground. Believing it was a peddler come to sell us caterpillar fungus – they put in an appearance a number of times – I told A-Shun to welcome the guest. A-Shun coughed until he was unable to straighten up and the motorcycle screeched to a halt before me. A voice intoned: "Through all the capital city, your village is the sole polluter. Stand on the bell tower and get a bird's-eye view of the whole city: a mass of black cloud can be seen gathering in the southeastern corner of the sky. If one single match was struck, the black cloud would explode."

The guy who dismounted from the bike was none other than Fatty the policeman.

I explained: "Hoh, Brow no longer lives here and you don't come over either. We don't have a heating system like you do in your buildings. Would you rather we didn't burn coal in our stoves and freeze to death? What official business are you on today? Which leader's wife is sick again and has brought you here to invite Grandpa Cloud Forest to go over?"

"I'm here for you. In Brow's absence, the village still has another beauty – Plum!"

"Plum should never fill your eyes; she's a country bumpkin."

The smoke in the room dispersed slowly. I led Fatty back to the pharmacy and poured him a cup of boiled water to warm his hands and drink. Fatty asked where Chivalry was. He had gone to Chivalry's home and wondered why his gate was locked. I suggested that maybe he had gone downtown again. After that row of single-storey houses had been put up, there were beds aplenty to hire out but not always enough patients to occupy them. He must have organised some folks to go and solicit renters.

"The renters must be checked carefully," Fatty reminded me. "The migrant population in a city is complex. Many criminals are renting houses on the urban-rural fringes or in villages in the city proper like Benevolent Lenient Village. Some are the bosses of on-paper companies, some are fugitives, some are thieves and some are drug-dealers."

"Fatty, shut your thick-lipped mouth. You're suspicious of us. If our renters are bad guys, then are the buildings in the capital city clean? Free of criminals?"

"Don't be swayed by your feelings. The public security situation is bad and the city has thrown more police into it. I'm in charge of the south-eastern area and at ordinary times I will come to the village to do my rounds. This is part of my job too. If there is anything fishy, you should report it straightaway."

"You're telling me. We fight for our own interests. Don't think we are fighting against the city in every way or our village is a den of iniquity, or we just want to start riots."

Fatty emptied the cup of boiled water. I refilled his cup, but he didn't drink again.

"I can't drink anymore."

"I won't charge."

"If I drink again, I'll contract a disease. So many hepatitis-stricken patients live here and viruses are everywhere. Can you tell me that the trees, doors and cups on the benches haven't been touched by them? You persuade me to drink. Are you hoping that I will catch a disease and have to board here?"

I snatched the cup from his hand.

"Fatty, do you want to put a wire mesh around our village and plant a plaque that reads 'Virus Zone'? We cure diseases for city guys and you talk like this. If there are viruses, who is to blame? You city guys!"

Fatty chuckled, retrieving the drinking cup, but bent his head sideways to say in a low voice: "Will Benevolent Lenient Village really change into a landlord's manor and has Brow's home been boarded up?"

"What landlord's manor? You really should talk responsibly. Anyhow you're Brow's friend. Old Shao doesn't come along and yet you do."

"It's not what you are thinking. Chivalry is flint-hearted.

How can you be like this too? It's been such a long time; why have never gone to see Brow?"

"She is a city person. I don't know how much grief I have suffered for her. She should come to see me."

Fatty looked at me quietly for a while and said: "You really don't know what has happened to her?"

His countenance was mysterious. As he spoke those words, he kept an eye on the gate, clearly apprehensive that A-Shun and others might overhear. "She has gone insane."

"Really?"

"She has well and truly gone off her rocker. After Chivalry made a scene last time, she behaved a little abnormally and played with her Pekingese every day, talking to no one except for the dog. One day, she went out on to the street with the dog. A woman happened to be wearing the same shoes as she was. The dog pursued her by mistake. She didn't detect it at first. When she found out that the dog was not behind her, she shouted: 'Lap! Lap!' The dog was following the woman across the road. A car came over. The woman stepped to safety and the dog jumped too. Unfortunately, it managed to pitch itself directly under one of the wheels and was killed. Brow half cried herself to death. She dug a pit to bury the dog together with one of her stilettos and then became quite mad."

First Cutter was slicing medicinal herbs on the steps, the cleaver swishing soundlessly and the slivers of herbs flying up like an orb of light. Second Counter Keeper and A-Shun were mixing the coal and the loess, the shovel slapping the black heap once and then one again. I remembered the time, back at the entrance to the lane, when the Pekingese had tailed me for a while. The animal was not as good as a man, recognising only the shoes but not the wearer. *Such a big window and such a big gate, such a grown-up woman but she doesn't have a mate.* Brow had married Bushy Beard. Bushy Beard was a hedgehog. "Any cigarettes? Give me one," I yelped.

"Where is A-Bing?" Fatty asked again.

A-Bing was fine. Did Fatty mean that he and Brow had saved A-Bing, but A-Bing no longer recognised him and Brow. Now that Brow's Pekingese was dead, did Fatty intend to retrieve A-Bing for her? "A-Bing belongs to Grandpa Cloud Forest now and he is does the work of a man in this village."

"That's just creepy," Fatty observed. "Brow is a Benevolent Lenient villager, but she is not regarded as one. A-Bing is a dog, but he is regarded as one of you."

Chapter Twenty-Two

On the morning of 9th December, according to the lunar calendar, the sirens of police cars could be heard wailing as the dim sky brightened. I was already awake but still lying in bed. I found myself reminiscing about how at noon yesterday the villagers, following the local custom of eating eight-treasure porridge,[by] walked with rice bowls in their hands, placed a small lump of cooked grain in the crotch of each old and newly-planted tree along the village lanes and sang:

Tree, Tree, eat the eight-treasure.
Next year bear fruit without measure.

Chivalry had consulted me: "Plum, how do you write the character 'measure'?" I didn't know. Benevolent Lenient Village had so many local expressions. How come that one had to be written down?

Shaved Head the grocer put a grain of rice on a bead tree and also sang the same line.

A-Shun's mother asked: "Bear so many bitter beads to do what, I wonder?"

Shaved Head changed his words to: "Tree, tree, tree, chew, chew, chew and scratch the sky till it chirp, chirp, chirps."

Fatty had laughed at us many times because in our particular pronunciation we didn't distinguish 'chews' from 'chirps'. More than once, Shaved Head mixed them up and we all laughed.

Chivalry declared: "Well done! This is the tongue of

Benevolent Lenient Village. Why should we learn Standard Chinese?"

I recalled immediately the dream I had. I climbed out of bed and raised the cloth curtains over the window that faced into the lane to look out. A number of motorcycles were parked up and a gang of men were running around, panting and calling rapidly: "Hurry, hurry, five to the east entrance and four to the west entrance. The rest, follow me!" Next came the confused sound of receding footsteps. My heart skipped a beat and my first thought was that the wrecking crew was on its way.

This time the real estate company had arrived in the name of the city government and was adding bite by involving the police. It was December and the Chinese Spring Festival would soon be here. They must be taking advantage of our slackness by catching us on the back foot. Believing that Chivalry must not yet know and driven by a strong sense of responsibility, I hastened to get dressed without even putting my bra on and sped to the second floor of the lean-to occupied by the patient to fetch the bronze gong. In such a fluster, I dropped the gong so it bounded down the ladder and clonked on the ground. The startled patient, who was squatting in the latrine, asked gruffly: "What's up? What's up? Plum, you're not hurt are you?"

"I dropped the gong. The wrecking guys have come and I want to drum up the folks to drive them away."

"I'll go too," he replied. "We patients will fight them as well."

I hotfooted it to the lane with the gong and started to bash it. Many flung open their gates and demanded to know: "Where? Where?" The peal of the gong was a signal that hadn't been heard for a long time in the village and many thought that their swords and spears could be put away in storage. Now, it was to be heard again. People caterwauled in surprise and came to the lane with shovel handles, sticks and firewood choppers.

"Who has seen the Village Head?" I demanded loudly. "Somebody, hurry and call him. They are coming again to destroy our village. Let's go drive them out. Nobody will bury his head like a turtle. If we do, our village will be finished."

The folks cried: "Plum, the Village Head is not here and you should lead us. Give your orders."

I was truly brave, not to mention having great presence of mind. I asked A-Shun's mother and Bolt's wife to lead a fist of women to stand below the decorated archway. If anyone tried to undermine the wall, they should lie under their pick-axes. Bolt's wife possessed a sharp tongue. She messed up her hair and called the women to the entrance to the village, while shouting the filthiest words.

A-Shun's mother went to carry Grandma Five Springs on her back. A good idea. An old lady guttering like a candle in the wind, who dare lay a hand on her? If a life were to be lost, let the murderer face the consequences. I divided the men into three teams, each overseen by headstrong chaps: Gao Feng and Baicheng led a gang to the eastern lane; Lianben, De Lei and Clawed Face led a gang to the middle lane; and I headed yet another gang to the western lane.

The patient boarding with me at my home really did come. I enjoined him to summon up more patients, all of whom should put on their hospital pyjamas and go to anywhere where they could hear quarrelling and stir up our morale. "We welcome their arrival. A boil needs to discharge pus. Better do it now than hold back until later. The government fears disturbances and unrest. These real estate companies are the ones creating unrest and we don't care about the consequences. When a riot breaks out, someone will be alerted to goings-on in the village, and the problem will get solved." The crowd separated and thundered on its way, shouting, crying and cursing all the way. However, when I took my group to the western lane, we did not run into any strangers. We surged to the middle lane, and only then did we spy from a small alley at the crook of the lane a parade of eight policemen, all armed to the teeth, tramping past us, frogmarching four guys, who, it turned out, were not our fellow villagers.

Taken aback, we had no idea what to do and stepped to either side, giving way without a sound. "What have these four done?" I wanted to know. "Do they live in the village?" The eight policemen ignored me. Another bunch of people strode from the head of the lane with boxes of liquor on their shoulders. Among them was Fatty, who upon catching sight of me asked: "Plum, where is Chivalry?"

"What's going on? Have these men committed any crime?"

"What's the matter with you – you didn't report this to me!" Fatty's face came over all serious. "Since Chivalry is not here, you should take charge. Order that nobody is to go to the seventh courtyard, which has been sealed off already. When Chivalry comes back, tell him to check out all the renters within the next three days in case anything similar happens. We will sign an agreement with you that Benevolent Lenient Village is to take the blame if any renters are found engaging in illegal activities here."

"What crime have these guys committed?" Greatly worried, I collared Fatty to press him about it.

Fatty explained that the markets of the Western Capital had seen a lot of fake liquor recently, the source of which could not be traced, no matter how hard they tried. At 3am today, when he and his colleagues were patrolling the streets, they saw a tricycle fully loaded with *Wuliangye*.[bz] Wondering why two shabby bumpkins were hauling so much expensive brand name liquor so early, they stopped to question them. Did they work for a hotel that had just taken delivery of a batch of stock from the railway station?

The liquor haulers might have slipped by if they had spouted some fluent lies, but they faltered ambiguously, saying these were commodities ordered by the Shangri-La Hotel. When they were asked where Shangri-La Hotel was and why they didn't pedal north but south, they couldn't relay accurate directions for their destination. Fatty smelt a rat and the men and liquor were brought to the police station. After some bluffing, they ascertained that the liquor was all counterfeit and had come from Benevolent Lenient Village.

They reported it immediately to their seniors and sent some officers to the village. Sure enough, they discovered that the three lean-tos in the seventh courtyard were the black den for bottling fake liquor. A search unearthed a great number of used bottles, ten bundles of *Wuliangye* labels and fifty-two boxes of ready-made fake liquor.

My face red, I gestured for the other villagers to disband by fluttering my eyelashes and then apologised to Fatty, pointing out several times that we didn't know anything about these criminals. Chivalry wasn't here but I could guarantee he didn't know anything. Had we detected the slightest sign of what they were up to, we would never have offered them refuge.

"I trust you," Fatty said. "But these guys have made so much fake liquor and you don't actually know anything about it. This means that you just care about making money and your morals have gone to sleep."

"A lesson that should be learned. Fatty, you really are a model policeman. Another deed of merit performed."

Chivalry was not home this morning. Yesterday afternoon, he went to negotiate with the General Manager of a travel agency to bring foreign tourist groups to visit our village. If the guests bought any herbal medicine, they could claim a fifteen per cent commission from the sales.

After the negotiations, the General Manager introduced him to the tour guides, who in turn told him what the foreigners' favourite Chinese herbal medicines were and how to wrap and publicise them. Feeling very appreciative, Chivalry dipped into his pocket and stood them a drink, but got plastered before drinking the tour guides under the table. Sleeping in a hotel in an alcoholic stupor for the night, he came back – still shitfaced – after breakfast. When he learned about the fake liquor thing, his anger erupted into a growl and he combed through all the renters' homes. To our astonishment, ten of the forty renters checked by us had changed their rooms into storehouses, where fake cigarettes, seeds and cakes of poor quality were deposited. Seven were scrap dealers and twelve were vegetable peddlers. Their businesses were not illegal, but when they first boarded here, they were alone; now they had all collected their wives from their native places. One family had a three-month-old baby, another a no-more-than-one-month-old baby and the other women's bellies all bulged. They had relocated here to avoid being penalised under the family planning policy and to give birth to children outside the state regulations. Four renters were single women. When we investigated them, they were still sleeping, each one with a sizeable sum of money in their rooms and condoms in their small handbags. Needless to say, they were singing girls or professional escorts, who plied their trade at the song and dance halls of the capital city every night.

"So much dirt is hidden in our village," I exclaimed. "This is our humiliation. Thank goodness the liquor fakers were caught this time, or else who knows when our village would be ruined at the hands of these guys."

Chivalry said: "To reiterate, these are all sins committed by the city. Why does Tibet never see these offences? Why has our village never seen these? The Western Capital is becoming bigger and bigger. More patients have appeared and more criminals too."

"But these guys all live in our village. Where can they find digs except for here?"

His eyes glaring, Chivalry barked at me: "You mean we are in the wrong? These guys should be handled by the police, but if you make a report to them, how will you save face? It is strictly between us and is our duty to settle it – fine them and drive them out after they've been fined."

Chivalry's decision was final. We fined them severely. They ranted and cried, kowtowing to me and acting rascally. Chivalry grew especially ferocious, shouting that they would be marched to the Bureau of Public Security if they didn't pay the fine. He even used his booted foot to kick them out of wrath. One working girl didn't want to leave and, even though her clothes had been tugged apart during the tussle, she didn't bother to cover up her chest. Chivalry slung a handful of condoms in her face and bellowed: "Benevolent Lenient Village doesn't want sexually transmitted diseases. Fuck off!"

Now, all the renters except for the patients were subjected to strict examination. The villagers were also on full alert and would report to Chivalry whenever they sensed anything dubious. Many who contacted us cancelled their plans and many who had already settled down chose to move house.

The village lost a bundle of income and Chivalry was put on a knife-edge when it came to his ingenious plan: The tour guides led the foreign travellers to our village several times. Apparently, the foreigners were less than satisfied, thinking there were few things to see and few souvenirs to buy. As for medicine, hepatitis had to be treated in courses, which varied according to the patient and the severity of the disease. They set little store by Chinese herbal pills and powders. In our eyes, all the foreigners looked the same and, in their view, we were all the same too.

No matter how wonderful we told them Grandpa Cloud Forest's medical skills were, they would retort: "You Chinese are fond of talking big, blowing your own trumpets while drinking, tooting your horns while playing Chinese chess, overselling yourselves while telling fortunes and reading faces and hyping up your Chinese medicinal herbs." They were only curious to know if our village had love potions to sell. Get your arses out of here! Not buying our medicine? You foreign foxes reek unbearably. We hadn't earned money so couldn't give the tour guides a kickback. Gradually, they no longer brought their tourist groups. I had never seen Chivalry in such low spirits. He sat in Grandpa Cloud Forest's shrine to pour out his bitterness, bemoaning that if it went on like this, he would lose the loyalty of the people like the old Village Head had.

"Why hasn't a football match been put on in the stadium for such a long time?"

"Need to relieve yourself?" I asked. "The football stadium is the public loo of the city."

Grandpa Cloud Forest turned the mattress to look for his radio. He had no TV and the small gadget had kept him company for ten years. He said it was Shaanxi opera time and today's broadcast was *Three Drops of Blood*[ca] with the County Head being played by Wei the Third, the third great uncle of Little Wei. Benevolent Lenient Village had also nurtured a renowned clown. Chivalry interposed: "Uncle Cloud Forest, I'm talking serious business with you. What's the good of listening to Shaanxi opera?"

"Everything is serious in your eyes," Grandpa said with a beam. "How could there be so much serious business in this world? Now spit it out."

His brow knitting into a lump, Chivalry himself beamed too and didn't know how to continue.

"OK, let's talk about the opera," Chivalry suggested. "None of the County Heads in operas presents a good stage image; every one of them has a white forehead, nose and chin. It's said that when Wei the Third was young, a phrenologist read his bumps and predicted that he would change his blue gown into a red one so as to be a County Head. Later, however, he became a clown on the stage. How could the County Heads in operas all be clowns?"

"So, Chivalry is afraid that he might become a clown," Grandpa Forest Cloud whooped. "Weren't operas all composed by scholars? Though they wanted to portray the emperor as a bad guy, how many of them had ever seen an emperor? But a County Head dealt with the little people every day. Whether he did good or bad, people all knew. In the past, there were no football matches and when hate and anger welled up inside them, the masses went to watch operas to get it out of their systems. If they couldn't aim their abuse at a County Head, then who else?"

"Oh!"

"Plum, why did you say oh?"

347

"I was thinking that at the time of liberation, many County Heads were shot and many Township and Ward Heads[cb] were suppressed. All the while, those Nationalist Party big-shots still lived a good life and had a position in Beijing. It seems to follow the same logic. Uncle Chivalry phews and sighs. He is not a County Head, but in our village he is the County Head and King. Now he is considering where he might end up."

"A fart! I won't become a clown," Chivalry grunted.

Grandpa Cloud Forest brayed with laughter and repeated: "Brew tea, brew tea, Plum. Start a fire and brew some tea."

The tea must have been brewed too strong. I drank and gagged and Chivalry too felt giddy and ready to vomit.

In the days that followed, Chivalry busied himself contacting patients and soliciting renters regardless of whether it was day or night. He got noticeably thinner, his cheekbones protruding in a more eye-catching manner. One piece of good news was that the land at Shangqian Village in the north of the Western Capital had been requisitioned to build the third ring-road. The villagers first grew grains and then sold vegetables. Now, their village was suddenly being bulldozed to the ground. They needed temporary shelter where they could settle for a while, and were all solicited to our village by Chivalry.

What's more, the low-lying land to the north of our village was being renovated. A portion of the residents who had been resettled elsewhere returned to the building site to kick up a fuss because their living conditions were too mediocre and the relocation programme was winding on too slowly. Chivalry again took in fifteen households. Because they were all peasants who had lost their home villages, we charged them a peppercorn rent and our village instantly took on the appearance of a refugee camp. So many households swooped down on us, we couldn't be as strict with them as with the other renters.

Gossip intensified daily. The noise from drinking sprees and the clatter of mahjong tiles filled our ears incessantly. Some even pretended to be fat cats before us. They each had a sum of money from the requisitioning of the land, which they shook with a rustle, claiming they had the capital to do business in the city and to speculate, or else to go to the vegetable markets to be wholesale dealers. They even bragged about all their fancy newly-bought TVs, fridges and stereo systems and fished out the working drawings of the new buildings into which they would move and decorate. They appreciated how we had taken them in but, of all things, they pretended to be made of money before us.

Some fellow villagers began to doubt the purpose of protecting the village. Man had only one life, grass had only one autumn, but why couldn't they all strive to live a good life? After the whole village had been razed to the ground, they could each receive a hefty sum of relocation money and, with money, what couldn't they do? Their offspring would be able take care of themselves. Even an emperor couldn't secure his family line for one thousand years, so why should they think that far ahead?

One household in particular had many members but few houses and, worse still, dilapidated buildings. The brothers and sisters-in-law rowed frequently. Chivalry was invited over to settle their family discord. The problems of who should give the main rooms a facelift and who should rebuild the courtyard walls with bricks had already been solved, though later no one was willing to invest and again they went to look for the old Village Head to solve their disputes. Nobody knows how the old Village Head managed it, but the old houses were roofed with only felt sheets and weighted down by bricks and the ramshackle courtyard wall was propped up with rafters alone, which told their own story.

Whether the village could be saved or not still depended on someone else's say-so, so why spend money and manpower in doing the repairs rather than wait for the day when they could move into the new cement buildings? One family did things like this. Nearly ten others, who ought to have repaired their old houses, ceased buying bricks and rafters.

The old Village Head was again in high spirits, sailing through the village with a cigarette tucked behind his ear, playing Chinese chess at the entrance to the football stadium compound, talking and laughing loudly.

The new movements made Chivalry's sense of disgrace give way to mania. He went to that household to kick aside the rafters that propped up the wall, summoned several guys to push down the dilapidated brickwork, ordered the brothers to repair their houses and supervised them personally under the pretence that the safety of the villagers should be guaranteed and that the tumbledown houses were uninhabitable and a blot on the village landscape. After the family had completed the repairs, he again pressed the remaining five to follow suit and held successive meetings. During the meetings, he hurled abuse at those slackers and used Brow as a sobering example, yelling: "Whoever wants to learn from Brow, leave! The rice wok of Benevolent Lenient Village doesn't need and doesn't allow a single mouse crap."

One night, he came to me.

"Plum, I want to shift a load on to you," he said. "The village can't go on like this. I'm the Village Head and while I'm in office, I should do something for the village, something big. I plan to go out and collect some money. When we have the money, we can further the construction of all kinds of facilities. Our village relies on the two fists of medicine and tourism. We should grip them tight. After I go, you should look into the village affairs more regularly and never make excuses for putting it off. Of all my fellow villagers, I have my eye only on you and you should not let me down."

"Where will you go to collect money?"

"You don't need to bother about that. I will bring back a heap of money even if it costs me my life."

I spat skywards three times – *pooh, pooh, pooh.* "Don't spout such ominous words!" He stood up and gave my nose a pinch. I wasn't expecting that, and was scared speechless. "Look at you," he added. "Now, you're the acting Village Head. Put on your gladrags and be decent; find your airs and graces as well."

Chapter Twenty-Three

Five years later, when I was once again exhibiting my Ming and Qing Dynasty furniture in the art museum of the Western Capital, a girl from the distant south of the Yangtze River was among the visitors. Her eyes were large and she had come out of admiration for Fan Jingquan, who introduced her to me. When I spied her slender, soft, long hands, I instantly recalled Chivalry and therefore acted courteously towards her.

After inspecting my emporium, the girl sent me two gifts. One was a round, purple, sandalwood stool with an indented waistline. The legs and the horizontal linking battens all bulged out slightly. The surface of the foot-rest was round, slightly narrow in the middle and looked strangely like a silver nugget. According to surviving records, Ming Dynasty arhat beds and canopy beds usually had a footstool to match, but those that I collected, including the one Chivalry sent to me, never did. The footstool was small, measuring only 60 centimetres long, 30 centimetres wide and about 17 centimetres high, but its design matched that of the arhat bed. It must be a miracle. I never knew if it was just a coincidence or a bond augured by predestination in the great void. Out of my perplexity, I asked her to stay with me for the night.

The second gift turned out to be a picture of a foreigner with elongated eyes, a broad mouth, shaved pate, bare feet and a very serious face. The figure was sitting cross-legged on the ground. The girl observed that this was AC Bhaktivedanta Swami Prabhupada. Such a mouthful of a name, it was simply impossible for me to commit it to memory. She wrote it out on the photo, letter by letter, yet I still didn't know who this foreigner with such a mouthful of a name was. The girl asked me if I knew anything about yoga. I said I didn't. She heaved a sigh and, taking out a tattered book, said: "Let me recite a passage of his writings for you."

We live as if we will live forever, which was the thought of everyone in years past, wasn't it? I mean who has ever thought that we will die.

Nobody ever really wants to die. We all hope that we can live energetically for eternity, free from the visitation of wrinkles, grey hair and arthritis. This is natural because our first and main principle is savouring our happiness, if only we can really enjoy our life forever.

Everyone will die, but I always think that I am the exception and how is it now...

I interrupted her recitation and pleaded that she didn't talk about life and death again. The girl looked at me in puzzlement and asked me why. I didn't disclose why, but at that time my mind was occupied with the question: "Why now?"

This sentence echoed in my mind for ages and the voice no longer belonged to the girl but redounded from an extremely distant place, thundering on my eardrums. The girl was still so young. Why did she like this book? I took hold of her hand – her slender, soft, long hand – to massage it. "My hand is not good," she apologised, her eyelashes fluttering, and tried to withdraw it while staring at me with bemused eyes.

I sat down squarely again and studied a fly on the wall. It was not a fly but a nail. A wind was howling tonight, a yellow wind that every year wreaked havoc in the Western Capital. If rain fell now, the raindrops would also be yellowish and clothes which had been stained with them could not be washed clean. A corner of the windowpane was broken and had been pasted over with a sheet of paper. The wind blew the paper, making it balloon and rustle. The sound lingered, as if the tidewater in the sea was advancing wave by wave, raising a bank of snow and then ebbing to a distant place, very distant, as far distant as the core of the earth, as distant as the bottom of a man's heart, where Chivalry's voice was to be heard.

Human beings are mysterious creatures. I didn't know AC Bhaktivedanta Swami Prabhupada, but I never doubted that a man will die because death is our constant companion, like a candle guttering in the wind. "Does the book relate any omens before a man's death?" I enquired.

"They are not mentioned in this book."

But there are omens before a man's death. Before he left Benevolent Lenient Village, Chivalry announced: "I will bring back a heap of money even if it costs me my life." These words became an augury. A saying that had been around for countless generations in our village related that if a man had been ill for a long, long time and an owl suddenly hooted one night, it was time for him to die. An owl must have an especially sharp sense of smell to pick up the putrid smell of a dying body. Still, when a man spoke an augury, was he perhaps guided by his feelings or was the ready-to-depart soul transmitting its directions to the body.

On which day in which month of which year will I die? And which of my words will become the harbinger of my death?

The girl's large eyes blinked intently. I could see that she sent the photo of that old foreigner to me and read the book, the title of which nobody knew, simply out of curiosity. She hadn't reached the age at which you contemplate life and death; her curiosity was purely academic. While she talked about life and death, with me in all seriousness, death was too far removed from her and she couldn't yet understand its real meaning. I began to tell her the stories about Chivalry.

"Child, many things in this world happen simply because they happen. Man's mistake is that he always complicates the simplest matters and oversimplifies how complicated problems are to be settled. Take Chivalry as an example."

"Who is this Chivalry?" She, of course, didn't know who Chivalry was. I could only brief her about how Chivalry worked diligently for Benevolent Lenient Village and then focus on the reality of his death.

I picked up the story, relating it to her as best I could.

Chivalry left that morning after having spoken those words. Fine white hair was drifting throughout the sky above our village, or perhaps above the whole of the Western Capital like snowflakes. This was, in fact, down from the blossoming willows. The girls had all wrapped their heads with gauze. In this season, a great number of people would be struck by allergic asthma and city slickers, if they could afford it, would stay in the South for a month or two to avoid it. We, however, had grown accustomed to drinking soup made from the roots of the strawberry tree and clay from the kitchen stove. I forced Chivalry to down half a bowlful of soup. He said: "That's fine."

He then hung a pair of old, mud-stained cloth shoes from his feet on a wooden peg in the courtyard wall and changed into alpine rush sandals. All through the summer, such shoes were favoured by the villagers. They were light, convenient, cool and did not give us athlete's foot. I wondered at that moment if the shoes could be worn, since it was still not very hot. Would he be out for a very long time? But I didn't ask him and, sure enough, his soul wasn't seen for three months after that.

Not until summer did I know he had gone to the Museum of the Terracotta Warriors in Lintong County with thievish intent. The alpine rush sandals muffled his footsteps. In fact, his thievery started quite early on. In those few years when we never saw him, he was learning the tricks of the trade from a master robber and had wandered to the four corners of the country before reaching Tibet. To begin, he had planned to steal holy articles from the Potala Palace, but it was fiercely defended and the pious believers worshipped and prayed day and night both in and outside the palace. It was impossible for him to make it.

He then heard about the Kingdom of Kugê in the Ali area on the far side of Tibet. There he would find the ruins of the palace built at the time of the Ming Dynasty. They had always been well-preserved because the snowy plateau was at such a high elevation above sea level. He disguised himself as a traveller so as to sweet-talk a transport soldier at the local military depot. He got in his vehicle and hit the road. After three days of the bumpiest of rides, during which he forced down fried wheat flour, gnawed at ice blocks, bedded down in the local military depots, spewed out green foam when he was attacked by altitude sickness and almost died in a stone room, he finally glimpsed the stone Buddhas at the peak of the mountain where the kingdom had once stood.

He came as a thief, but what he gleaned was a statue of the Buddha. Illuminated by the halo of the Buddha, he cleansed his heart to reform and stay clear of theft. Hating himself so much, he even dashed off his right hand with a stone while swearing his vow. With one hand missing, he came back to Lhasa, where he lost consciousness in a hotel because the wound was festering and had become inflamed. He was sent to a local hospital to have a woman's hand surgically transplanted.

He kept these experiences shrouded in darkness for many years and never mentioned them after coming back home. However, in the interest of Benevolent Lenient Village and owing to his paranoia and insanity, were nurtured by Benevolent Lenient Village, he decided to go back into business one last time.

He sought out a trafficker of cultural relics with whom he had become acquainted back in the day and cut a deal to pay him one million yuan in cash as long as he could procure the head of a terracotta warrior from Lintong. He must have been out of his mind!

On a rainy night, he sneaked into the museum, which was closed. Through making enquiries, he found that a batch of damaged terracotta warriors from the newly-excavated Number Three Pit was hidden out of sight in the conservation room. Displaying preternatural qigong, he entered the storehouse, sawed off the head of one of the clay figures, slid it into a sack padded out with cotton and hair, hung it before his chest and sped away. But when he leapt over the wall of the courtyard, he triggered an iron wire and the alarm bells in the hall rung percussively. By the time he had rolled down on the other side of the wall, the armed security guys were hot on his trail. His qigong proved beyond people's wildest dreams. While hopping across the road, he jumped into a running truck and was able to make tracks back to the Western Capital.

The loss of a terracotta warrior's head was a red hot case.

All the public security forces in the Western Capital had to place it first on their agenda, thus expediting the detection process. All the road junctions in Lintong were put on lock-down, as were those in the Western Capital. Every passing vehicle and suspicious passenger had to be stopped and searched. Knowing a great hermit must lead a life of seclusion in a marketplace, Chivalry lay low in a hotel for a fortnight, daring neither to raise his head nor to go back to Benevolent Lenient Village.

Nevertheless, he still managed to contact the trafficker of cultural relics and made an appointment to conclude the deal in the hotel at midnight. Everything went off at the agreed time and place, but as the trafficker was preparing to leave the hotel room with a rangy leather suitcase, public security officials appeared before their eyes. The trafficker could not have expected that all the some-time traffickers from the province had been taken into custody ten days earlier and ordered to pass on the names of every fence in their game who'd not been brought to book. One of them fingered him, causing him to be put under secret surveillance. The trafficker was pressed down by four policemen and the head of the terracotta warrior was safely recovered.

And yet, Chivalry gave them the slip, leapfrogging out of the window like lightning with the suitcase full of money. He flew to one corner of the building along a several-inch-wide cement ledge outside the window and slid down by hugging a drainage pipe. The policemen keeping guard downstairs hunted him down. That night he played a grand game of hide-and-seek with his pursuers. Whenever he saw a tall building, he simply scaled it rapidly like a monkey without needing a run-up. The jaws of the policemen dropped in wonder. They had never seen or heard anything like it outside the movies and, even then, but those stunts in the films were pulled off by stuntmen.

Was this thief a human being? An idea floated across the mind of the Head of the Bureau of Public Security: since the head of the terracotta warrior was already in their hands and the culprit was such a rare genius, if they could capture him alive and re-educate him into being a detective, wouldn't that be a fantastic job? He ordered that the thief should be taken alive and nobody ought to shoot. Thus, whenever Chivalry found himself cornered, he scooted away and after he had scooted away, he was again cornered. The whole city was under siege, and the people shouted that a superhuman thief had appeared. He had the magical ability to fly and was a very tough nut.

Benevolent Lenient Village was shocked. People all rushed out to watch the clamour, but, afraid that the superhuman thief might suddenly materialise and bring collateral damage on them, they withdrew to their rooms, shut their doors and never went out again. At last, another cohort of military police was deployed to join the line of encirclement and assist with the hunt.

Chivalry was cornered in the southern part of the city. The military police swept every inch of the land, consolidating their ground step by step to tighten the noose, and finally found the superhuman thief who was standing on the top of a building. Gloating over his unique skills and filled with false pride, he leapt on to another building in full view of a large crowd.

He was then on the point of breaking the line of en-circlement. Perhaps the military police and public security were dog-tired as a consequence of horsing around and being teased for the whole night. Or perhaps they harboured a strong hatred after citizens of the Western Capital jeered at how so many chaps couldn't catch a lone robber the whole night long. Or perhaps they were feeling the squeeze like their commander-in-chief. At dawn, the Head of the Bureau of Public Security made up his mind that if he couldn't catch the dog, he wouldn't allow the dog to run away with the leash. He cherished this talent, but he couldn't ignore political duress, so he gave the order that if the thief couldn't be caught alive then he should be shot. Sirens wailed and trumpets hooted to exhort Chivalry to give himself up.

Chivalry, knowing that he could hardly run out of the city after the break of day, descended from a building with the suitcase of money and nimbly ran up to the top of a ruined Ming Dynasty wall. Spotlights turned this way and guns chattered. He dropped down and the suitcase flicked open in mid-air. Banknotes flew everywhere like a flock of birds being flushed out by a detonating bomb. One bullet from the rain-like volley nicked him in the leg and another caught him square on the wrist; the wrist of the transplanted woman's hand. The limb was torn clean off, save for a layer of skin.

Now in a gaol cell, Chivalry found himself a disabled inmate with a broken arm and leg. His life could no longer be spared on the basis of him being a special talent and he received a capital sentence. His execution was scheduled for noon in the late spring, when the plane trees put forth green leaves.

After I finished relating the stories of Chivalry, my newly-made friend, the girl from the south of the Yangtze River, queried: "Do such things really happen under the heavens? Then, what about Benevolent Lenient Village? Could you take me there to have a look?"

I didn't respond.

"Do you still feel sad for him?" she asked. "This is precisely why you should read this book. A man will come back. Really! Listen up. The book puts it like this: 'Some say death ends all, some believe in the existence of Heaven and Hell, and some think this life is only one of the many lives of ours and, in the future, we will live on once again'."

Chapter Twenty-Four

I arranged to meet him in the stadium. I wondered what was happening to the way people conducted relationships? Throughout our lives, we must be predestined to always meet in a hurry, and the scene was the same as our rendezvous at Solitary Tree. Then, we met by a teeming expressway, while now night had fallen and the sky turned leaden. The football stadium hadn't seen a match in yonks and appeared hauntingly empty.

Not far away, the lights in the windows of the guest house, which stood taller than the stands of the stadium, were also on and the bright 'coffins' were hanging in mid-air. The old man who took care of the turf gawped at me from afar. With my hands wrapped around my knees, I smiled at him. The old man, who must not have known my reason, smiled back and walked away. It may have been that he was now watching a war on the chessboard between the States of Chu and Han^{cc} at the gate of the stadium compound while saying: "Looks like a girl from Benevolent Lenient Village. She is going to have a date in the stadium tonight." Or maybe he suspected that I was a thief. After returning to the guest house, he was now looking this way through a telescope from a coffin-shaped window in the building.

I gave the money-bag a press and poked it under my bottom.

I didn't notice Fan Jingquan entering the stadium. He climbed over the guard rails on to the stands from the other side of the entrance. He said he thought that I would be waiting for him in the audience area, but found I was actually sitting on the pitch. He gripped the guard rails of the stand and got ready to jump down.

"Don't jump!" I shouted, after turning my head and catching sight of him. He shrank in on himself and hung in mid-air like a ball, the very picture of what Chivalry had done. But how could Fan Jingquan have Chivalry's kung-fu? Even without kung-fu, Chivalry was as strong as an ox. Could Fan Jingquan survive that nasty fall?

"I will come up there." I scrambled up to the stands from the fencelike gate.

Fan Jingquan still hung there and could no longer haul himself up. His arms were as scrawny as hemp stalks and he didn't have the strength to lift his body. His hands took turns to grip on to the guard rails. When he was on the very point of failing, I bent, grasped one of his arms and drew him up.

"Have you been here for long?" he wanted to know.

"I came just now. I had to shake off the villagers and it's never easy to find a moment when there is nobody around in my house. I can't let them know that I have brought so much money with me."

Fan Jingquan panted.

"Would anyone accept that?"

He didn't utter a word.

"So much money and they are still unwilling to accept it?"

"They say it won't work."

I knew he hadn't found the right man yet. They were afraid to take the money and that's that, but why did they say it wouldn't work? I tossed the money-bag on to the cement steps. "This is money. He is going to lose his life for the sake of money and now money can't save him."

"Calm down," Fan Jingquan soothed me. "Even the lawyers are not willing to defend him. Let me do it. Plum, take the money back. We shouldn't use the money from the pharmacy. If the villagers get wind of it, who knows what will happen. I am not a lawyer yet, I haven't got a lawyer's certificate, but this afternoon I went to look for the judge and compared notes with him."

"What did he say?"

"He said after going through some necessaries, I can appear before the Court as defence counsel. However, he also asked me whether a defence was really needed? I told him Chivalry committed the crime for Benevolent Lenient Village and his motive didn't have its origins in trivial personal desires. Rather, it was a product of the tide of history in which he was caught up. Moreover, reliable sources had it that when Chivalry was being hunted down, the Head of the Bureau of Public Security wanted him alive because Chivalry had superhuman kung-fu and, if he were to be caught alive, he might be rehabilitated and recruited by the police. Therefore, it was necessary that he be taken alive.

"The judge observed: 'He is disabled now so what kung-fu does he have?' In reply, I asked: 'So, if he were not disabled he would be allowed to live, but since he is disabled he should die?' The judge looked at me and smiled and I knew that was because he couldn't answer my question. The judge said: 'This is a capital offence and he has already been sentenced to death in the first session.' I added: 'Is this the law? In your hands, is legislative confirmation carried out like this?'

"The judge replied: 'Yeah, we represent the law!' I said: 'But, you cannot represent the law. If you have harnessed the law, who will harness you?' The judge finally grinned at me and said: 'OK, have a try when the time comes.'"

"Have a try?" I murmured. "What does this mean?"

"Perhaps he is mocking me."

I hadn't seen the judge. I didn't know whether the fellow was old or young, a man or a woman, yet I could feel that the judge must be as self-important and stubborn as Chivalry himself. Chivalry condescended to Fan Jingquan and the judge was also laughing at him. I looked at him and didn't know why, but for the first time I pitied him.

"Do you think you are up to the job?"

"I think I'm up to it."

This was exactly what I had been wanting to hear. While unconsciously pressing my palms together before my chest, I prayed to the stars and the moon in the sky: "You're up to it; Fan Jingquan is surely up to it." I didn't shout this out, though I could hear the booming sound in my heart. I sensed that people were sitting all over the stands and answering my prayers, like they were bawling encouragement and cheering in a football match. I grasped Fan Jingquan's hand and said: "Thank you, Mr Fan."

Fan Jingquan held me in his arms. We were having a genuine date. I didn't struggle or try to extricate myself from his embrace. My body became softer and smaller in his hold. I heard him moan: "Don't cry, Plum. Let's start anew, start to live our lives anew."

Over the next few days, I waited anxiously for Fan Jingquan to come along. He was rifling through the lawyer's formalities with aplomb and preparing the defence materials day and night. He had grown conspicuously black and skinny, dark eyes, dark eyebrows, dark and lean like an iron girder, but he was sprouting more white hair.

On the afternoon of 10th May, he announced he was still yet to appear before a court and, even though his friend was unwilling to be the defence counsel, he was prepared to help him smooth out the articles of the law. For that reason, he needed to go to Magic Farm Tableland and would come back two days later.

A day later, on the afternoon of 11th May, Brow informed me that Chivalry would be executed tomorrow.

In order to alleviate Brow's condition, the policeman Fatty revealed the date of Chivalry's execution in confidence and asked her if she wanted to go and watch it. The one who hung the bell on the tiger's neck could also untie it. She went mad thanks to Chivalry and so Chivalry's death might cure her unfortunate disorder.

Brow thanked Fatty for his solicitude, but she didn't want to spectate. When I visited her, in a moment of clear-mindedness, she let it slip.

"That's impossible!" I cried out. "There must be a public trial first. And we're still waiting for the notice of the public trial."

"He was sentenced to death in the first session. It was said that Chivalry refused to accept and appealed and a second public trial was scheduled. Even so, some senior officials insisted that penal offences should be dealt with harder and faster. So, the second trial wasn't held in public. The original judgement was upheld and the appeal was rejected."

"This, this… even though there might be no public trial and there was no need to inform us, they should have informed the old executioner? He saw me at midday and said nothing."

"These were Fatty's own words. How could he be mistaken?" Brow said. "Fatty said the family of a condemned criminal won't be notified and nor will they be allowed to reclaim the body.

"Before each Spring Festival or red letter day, a batch will be executed. Killing a man is as easy as throttling a chicken, but a chicken with a broken neck can still run. The stupid guy Old Shao tried to kill a chicken at Spring Festival. Somehow, the headless bird still hobbled around with its wings flapping and didn't die until it bumped into a wall. After the gun is fired, the guy won't even be able to kick his leg out and he'll drop dead like this."

Brow's brain became muddled while she was talking and she imitated the body of a slain criminal on the bed, her head tucked in, her buttocks raised up and her red underwear on show.

"It's said the Public Security Bureau will now charge the family of condemned criminals 50 cents for the bullet," I commented.

"How could that be? Possibly in the past, but not now," Brow answered. "Fatty invited me to go and I won't. I'm too scared. Fatty said: 'What's there to be scared about? The criminals are all detained in the prison near the Nanyang Temple. Three days before their execution, they will be fixed on bed planks with iron shackles to keep their hands and feet in place and they sleep there spread-eagled. For three days. On the day of their execution, they will be dragged out and hogtied. When they are being dragged out, every inch of them will have grown soft and the fetters and shackles are so heavy they can't walk. They will then be fed encouraging words and a member of staff will shout: 'Hey, those who come out of the Nanyang Temple are real guys and though they die, they die a neat death. Brace your spirit. Isn't that a death? Twenty years later, you'll be a full-grown man again!'

"Fatty insisted: 'Those words always work. The criminals brace themselves and file out one after another with clanking chains. In the courtyard, after their fetters and handcuffs are removed, they will be hogtied and then the order for execution will be read to them one after another, face to face. They will be asked what their names are, where they live, what their postcodes are, what capital crimes they have committed and the criminals can actually answer fluently. If they are asked if they have anything else to say, mostly probably the answer is no. They then leave their fingerprint on the execution orders, are dragged out and shot.' You ask me, I wouldn't say no. I have something else to say. 'Government'. When the prisoners see any member of the prison staff, they will call them 'Government'. You ask me..."

While saying this, Brow knelt down again and gawked at me.

"What else do you want to say?"

Brow pressed her head against the bed and wailed: "Benevolent Lenient Village – farewell, my home!"

Without warning, my heart ached and I wanted to hold Brow close. Brow was still rambling: "When you shoot me, aim at the back of my head and do it gently. I can't stand the pain."

All of a sudden, I let out a cry.

After saying goodbye to Brow and coming back, I quietly told the villagers about Chivalry's forthcoming execution. They had already heard about it from the mouth of the old Village Head, who said that he had found an acquaintance to take him to the execution ground tomorrow and anybody who wanted could come along with him. Originally, I didn't want to see the old Village Head. But, since he was able to go to the site, I was compelled to look for him and readied myself for swallowing his taunts. He received me hospitably. He was tucking into supper at home and insisted that I have a bowlful. He never said a word about the past and even showed great sorrow over Chivalry's impending death by placing a bowl of food in the courtyard, exclaiming: "This is presented to Chivalry."

"He hasn't died yet." I was a little angry, sensing that he was cursing Chivalry, willing him to die sooner.

"From the very first day he was sentenced to death, I have been presenting food to him," the old Village Head claimed. "As soon as a man is sentenced to death, his soul departs from his body and floats in the air. Haven't you dreamed of him at night? A-Shun's mother said someone knocked at her door for three consecutive days and she felt that the visitor was Chivalry. Once he even told her in her dream that she should not burn touchpaper for him after his death."

I didn't know if his words were true or not, and I expressed no opinion about his presenting food to Chivalry. Perhaps he did it with a true purpose. All I know is that the food being offered up to Chivalry was extremely generous, a huge rough china bowl full of sticky cornmeal jelly.

"He won't be shot in public; the execution site will be the earthen slope in the back yard of the Nanyang Temple Prison. I should go and see Chivalry off. The child grew up before my eyes, but now a white-haired man shall see a black-haired one off. I could never have foreseen that. What a pity he is so capable, but a clay head is being exchanged for the head of a living human being."

I asked him to take me to the execution ground early in the morning, though I hadn't enquired if Fan Jingquan could go too. I had no means of notifying Fan and it wasn't necessary to.

Early the next morning when the old Village Head opened the gate with the intention of calling me, I had already been standing there for ages. His wife wanted to poach eggs for us. I didn't eat and, after glancing at me, the old Village Head didn't eat either. The two of us silently walked out of the village and a car drew up alongside us. The driver was the old Village Head's acquaintance from the Public Security Bureau. We climbed in the vehicle and were ferried to the south of the city.

I didn't know how far we had travelled when the car reached an earthen slope. We could make out an electricity grid standing on the wall of the courtyard, where many armed military sentries were standing guard. Because we were in a police car, we did not have to wait to be allowed in. The car drew up to a small patch of bare earth on the back slope along the foot of the courtyard wall. The old Village Head's acquaintance warned us: "We're late so I can't escort you to see how the prisoners are being marched out. Stay in the car and don't get down. Ordinary persons should stay away from an execution like this." With these words, he climbed out and approached the prison at the foot of the slope.

Not far from the earthen slope stood the taller perimeter wall. What was beyond that? I had no idea. To the left side of the earthen slope was a network of pigsties, which were perhaps tended by the prisoners. The level ground to the right of the sties was far from large, rather like the former wheat threshing ground in our village, which was now thick with blossoms and flowering shepherd's purse. When our village still had its wheat fields, throughout the spring we could eat dumplings, steamed buns and vegetable rolls with shepherd's purse as the filling. But now we couldn't. That particular herb wasn't anywhere to be seen, yet here it was in abundance. Twelve small white flags had been planted along the foot of the perimeter wall. Several police cars came up one by one and the drivers all loitered about chatting, laughing and offering cigarettes to each other. A trio of ambulances waited in a row near the pigsties.

"See? The white flags are where the criminals will kneel today to be shot. Those ambulances are here to harvest the bodies."

"Harvest the bodies?"

"So many patients in this world need kidney transplants and where do they come from? Condemned prisoners. Everything has been arranged well beforehand. After the gun fires, the chosen body will be carried into the vehicle and cut open to have the kidneys removed, while over there in the hospital the patient has been sent into the operating theatre to be prepped for surgery. The kidneys will be transplanted as soon as they arrive. There are also people who need a skin graft, new eyes."

Feeling gripped by a chill, I shivered all over but, not wanting this to be seen by the old Village Head, I pressed myself against the car door, coughed and pretended to be completely at ease. At that moment, I regretted having come here. In the past, death had always seemed so far away from me but, shortly, I would have to witness a dozen exterminations. Who knows how many had been gunned down on this miniscule earthen ground. If their souls were still here, I couldn't even hazard a guess at how much vacant space was still left on the pigsties and underneath and on the top of vehicles.

I wound down the car window. Outside, the sun was shining brightly. Beyond the twelve white flags and on an earthen mound at the foot of the perimeter wall, a cluster of small, white, prickly rose flowers had come into bloom and a small swarm of bees gathered and dispersed abruptly above them.

On the football pitch, the crowd would throng to the centre and then stampede in four directions like the sun giving out its rays. Chivalry bent his body into a ball and got ready to jump down. Uncle Chivalry! Uncle Chivalry! I grasped that dainty, long, soft woman's hand. The hand had only a layer of skin left to link it to the arm. Banknotes showered down in the spotlight like blossoms being shaken from a pear tree. Where was Grandpa Cloud Forest? The old Village Head's acquaintance trotted along the path, pulled the car door open, placed himself down inside and pronounced: "They're coming!"

The old Village Head asked: "Seen Chivalry?"

"Yeah, his legs still couldn't carry him so he had to be dragged by others. None of the other eleven guys said anything after leaving their fingerprints, but he stressed repeatedly that his body should be sold to the hospital and the money be given to Benevolent Lenient Village. The judge nodded his head and replied that they would do as requested, so the hospitals sent out their vehicles. He smiled and even thanked him."

My head buzzed as if that small swarm of bees had all crept inside. This was precisely as he had phrased it before he left: "I will bring back a heap of money even if it costs me my life." He had got the money. Were the ambulances parked over there with the sole intention of dissecting him? After the gun banged, his limbs would become limp and his body would still be slightly warm. After being carried inside, a sharp scalpel would pare his flesh apart, together with the ropes and clothes, his body would be sliced into pieces and then reduced to a pile of minced meat, chunks of which would be priced up by the hospital. I lowered my head and did my damnedest to squeeze against the door of the vehicle, experiencing pain as if a knife were incising a cross on to my body. I was being worked on like cold bean-starch jelly. Two more swishes were added to the cross. Then I would become a birthday cake, ready to be cut into wedges, with bright candles lit.

"You won't go and watch? Then why did you come?" the old Village Head's acquaintance seemed to be interrogating me.

I raised my head. Outside the window, a procession of people was treading from the earthen ground in formation. The armed police had withdrawn and the procession consisted of groups of five with a criminal in the middle, two armed military policemen grasping him from behind and two gun-toting officers standing guard further away. There were a dozen groups in total.

Not a word was breathed and not a sound heard. When I lifted my head, three groups had filed past with Chivalry in the second. Sure enough, he was being tugged by the armed military policemen and stood only half the height of the others. His crown had been shaved clean, but his head was held square, neither twisting nor bending, as if something was sticking out awkwardly from his spine. I immediately felt afflicted by the same disease and the moment I swivelled my neck or looked down, I became dizzy.

I was so overcome with dejection that I ducked my head and so missed seeing Chivalry's face for the last time. I couldn't flash him my friendly sentiments and hated myself acutely as a result. But, every night after that, when I dreamed of how the brain matter splashed following the bang of the gun, I was relieved that I hadn't glimpsed his face. If Chivalry had accidentally tilted his head and seen my face on the other side of the window, perhaps we would have both cried out with the agony of his inevitable death.

When I crooked my head, I overheard the old Village

Head murmur in a low voice: "He is still smiling." I didn't verify who he was talking about, but surmised that it must be Chivalry. I looked at those who followed on. The necks of some prisoners were too listless to support their heads; some prisoners' faces had turned a muddy hue. A 30-something man, in particular, had gone scarlet red in the chops and nape and the veins behind his ears and at the corners of his forehead stood out like earthworms. As he passed our car, a tiny stone tripped him and he shot a glance at our vehicle. I could clearly make out his red rims and how the lower edges of his eyelids were crimson as if caked with cinnabar.

"A forced smile," the old Village Head's acquaintance replied.

"How can he force out a smile? That one, the tenth one, his face and neck are like sauced pork," I winced.

"He is panicking too much and his blood circulating rapidly."

The twelve criminals knelt before their respective white flags, their shoulders secured by the armed policemen and rifles aimed at the back of their heads. Heavens, the muzzles of the guns almost touched their skulls.

The air above the earthen ground was charged: no wind blew, the ants were not festive, a cluster of flowers under the perimeter wall was completely obscured by Chivalry and the small swarm of gathered bees was silent. Abruptly, the commander at the end of the line raised a flag. It was Fatty again! He didn't lower the flag, but strode over instead to adjust the posture of the fifth armed policeman. He was still a green-looking soldier boy, perhaps on his first mission of this kind. He directed his gun at the back of the criminal's head but averted his gaze in dread, his gun-wielding hands shivering and moving the muzzle off target. Fatty twisted the officer's face around, pointed at the back of the criminal's head and instructed: "Here, here."

Bang! A gun growled and the fifth criminal toppled forward. Fatty let out a shrill cry and hopped and bounded over, clamping one hand over the other. The man standing in the centre of the earthen ground – the commander-in-chief perhaps – sprinted over, dragged aside the gun-wielding soldier boy and ordered two armed policemen to assist Fatty. Then, the commander-in-chief raised the flag. When it was brought down, eleven guns growled at the same time and eleven criminals toppled forward together, streams of brain matter spurting out of their heads. They lay in multifarious postures, emitting hot steam.

My stomach churned, I threw up and my vomit sprayed all over the window of the car.

The old Village Head said: "Let's go, I can't stand this either."

The acquaintance added: "If you see more of this, you'll get used to it. Spit out some saliva and don't let the ghosts become stuck to our car." When the vehicle was on its way out, two more gunshots were heard.

"I think those extra bullets must be for the first guy," the acquaintance reasoned.

When the car had gone down the earthen slope and passed the tall wall with an electricity grid standing on top, the old Village Head reflected, while helping me mop the window with paper napkins: "A man who dies like this won't suffer."

I suddenly found a wild bee crouching tight on the other side of the sick-stained window. It must be from that cluster of white flowers. But it was there when the gun discharged.

How could it have flown to our car from the foot of the perimeter wall? "If you are the soul of Chivalry, fly," I prayed in my mind and the wild bee disappeared.

Uncle Chivalry knew that I had come to see him off and he was here to bid farewell. My tears rained down.

Chapter Twenty-Five

Chivalry's death left us bereft. For three days, no one in the village drank, played mahjong or watched TV. Silence reigned. The hospital sent a sum of money for the body, though we didn't know how to use it. Some said burn it. How could we spend money exchanged for Chivalry's body? Burn it as if it were spirit money sent to him by us. Some disagreed and recalled how Chivalry had stressed before his death that the money should be given to the village. If we didn't use it, he would sit heartbroken by the Nine Springs of Hell. These words made sense.

The money was invested in the pharmacy. We bought a batch of medicinal herbs, which would be processed into pills and powder. What was strange was that when the pharmacy received and deposited the delivery in the storeroom, a 'king of ginseng', very big, resembling a kneeling man, was found in one basket of ginseng roots. Chivalry! I immediately thought of Chivalry as he knelt before the white flag on the earthen ground awaiting execution and felt aghast at the wonder of worldly affairs. Chivalry, have you been reincarnated so soon? Or have you entered the ginseng to come back at the behest of the ghosts and gods? I soaked the ginseng in a huge glass bottle of alcohol and then put the container on the counter of the pharmacy. The old Village Head saw it. He must also have recognised the last posture struck by Chivalry in this world but, his mouth agape, didn't say anything.

We tried to suppress the news about Chivalry's execution from being spread, but a city newspaper reported that a group of criminals had been put to death. Chivalry's name was among them. Moreover, it was pointed out that the superhuman thief hailed from Benevolent Lenient Village. Benevolent Lenient Village became the shame of the Western Capital. The district government sent hands to tighten the reins and requested that the old Village Head assume his previous position.

The old Village Head was nothing if not lenient. At the meeting when his re-appointment was ratified, he wore a serious face, spoke earnestly and excoriated himself for his past wrongdoings. That redressed our mental imbalance and won our forgiveness and acceptance. After he resumed his post, save for once again hanging the pennants and certificates of merit on the walls of his office, he made no adjustment to the existing structure of the village. He continued to develop the pharmacy, still revered Grandpa Cloud Forest as a god and still actively solicited renters from outside.

However, the bad news we dreaded most and that the old Village Head took as the gravest and most hopeless headache was still to rear its head. After making a report to the municipal government and gaining their approval, the real estate company reinstated its decision to demolish the village.

The company hired a bunch of non-natives to enter the community and write with brushes: "RESOLUTELY EXECUTE THE PROJECT PLANNED BY THE CITY GOVERNMENT FOR THE RENEWAL OF THE WESTERN CAPITAL"; "WIPE OUT THE DILAPIDATED DEAD CORNERS AND BUILD A NEW CITY"; and, in huge letters, "DEMOLISH", on the gables and courtyard walls of every household. We hated them, yet no one fought back. Many ran out to watch their movements but, without a head man, they beat a retreat to the pharmacy to look for me and fettle out a solution. I didn't know what to do. I went looking for Grandpa Cloud Forest. His teeth had all fallen out and his mouth wrinkled into the likeness of a child's behind. He observed with a smile that this fell within the remit of the old Village Head.

We sought out the old Village Head at home. He was in hospital again. His bald wife complained with a weepy face: "He can't find a way either. What can he do?" I slunk back to the pharmacy and sobbed with that bottle of ginseng liquor in my arms. The wrecking work rolled on step by step. The biggest boss of the company, who sported a red kerchief with oily sweat all over his face, dropped into the village, giving directions while the workmen were measuring up, and nattered about the area and price with every household. Apparently, everything went off smoothly. Moved, he even commented to me in the pharmacy: "How good the masses are. It was only Chivalry who stirred things up. We're men of blood and flesh too. What is money? You can't bring it with you when you are born and can't take it away when you die. This time, I will give an extra ten per cent of the house's worth to each family. I was able to help Brow run an independent shop, and I will also fund more people in the village to become under-bosses. My word is my bond; I will honour my promise."

I didn't respond, instead fixing my eyes on the ginseng bottle. "Chivalry, if your spirit is still here, let the bottle explode. If it does, I will lead the villagers to raise merry hell again." The wine bottle didn't sway and the ginseng man still kowtowed inside.

I committed this day – 19th June – to memory. A huge wrecking crew came into the village and a booming bulldozer butted down our decorated archway. The stone tablet was dug out and crushed into eight pieces by the marauding wheels. Gangs of hired hands gushed into the village to rip down the rafters of the single-storey houses, gouge out the doors and windows in the clay brick walls and fell trees with saws, clangourous as if they were cleaning up the mess on a battlefield.

The villagers had loaded their daily necessities on to carts and tricycles and were ready to go their separate ways to look for temporary lodgings. They bade farewell to each other, left their respective addresses quietly, shook hands and embraced one another's shoulders or heads, managing not to weep out loud. The renters moved on long before, though the patients stayed behind until the last possible moment, hoping to receive one more day of treatment. Now, carrying their bundles and accompanied or supported by their relatives, they were in the pharmacy to get big parcels of medicine.

The pharmacy kept me perpetually busy. When A-Shun and the others were distributing parcels of medicine, I visited the shrine to see Grandpa Cloud Forest.

In the lanes, the company employees were flogging the doors, rafters, purlins and windows from the bulldozed-down buildings to the peasants from the distant suburbs at cheap prices. They were overjoyed, as if they had scavenged treasures, remarking on the quality of the wood and cramming cigarettes and liquor in the hands of the lesser bosses who were doling out orders. Eventually, a used-furniture firm came to scramble for a share of the cake and the two parties squabbled until things got rough.

A peasant intercepted me, beseeching: "Elder sister, please give your judgement. First come, first served is the universal rule. What right do they have to shove a leg in?"

"Why don't you go beat them up?" I asked in reply.

"I'm ready to do that. I can't beat a good guy, but can't I beat a bad arse?"

He legged it in a huff and I shouted at him: "Take this stick with you." Sure enough, he accepted the weapon.

In another lane at the turning in front of Little Wei's house, a wrecking crew were cooking in a wok while shouting and yelling. I didn't have a clue what was in the wok. Someone called from afar: "Another one! Another one!" He fumbled a small switch of twig in his hand, the other end of which was clamped between the jaws of an ancient turtle. Yelling with hilarity, the gang huddled forward to brush and clean the old turtle, then crammed it into the wok together with the switch, nimbly replacing the lid back on, withdrawing the switch and depositing a big stone on top.

"When was this village built?"

"In the Ming Dynasty. It's said that the guys from this village can perform the *Drum Music of the Ming Emperor*."

"Ha, then this is a Ming Dynasty turtle!"

"Shift the pedestal off every pillar. Perhaps they all have old turtles underneath them."

Now I knew the old turtle had been excavated from beneath the pedestal of a pillar. Who knows how many of them were being simmered in the wok? All Ming Dynasty reptiles, these creatures were propping up our village. Now the village would be razed to the ground and they would be interred in human bellies. I stood in a trance, sorrow and indignation stirred the black blood throughout my body, but what could I say to these hired hands? Textbooks claimed that history is created by the people. And still, without Chivalry, Benevolent Lenient Village had obediently allowed itself to be demolished. These navvies were non-native peasants and, for a bit of miserable pay, were tearing down the village with hilarity. As to the disappearance of Benevolent Lenient Village, who was to blame? Feeling my sorrow and indignation to be ridiculous and standing shivering in the wind, I overheard the old turtle's death struggle in the iron wok. After a bit of a racket, there was only the gurgling sound of the boiling water. I knew the old turtle was dead and that the god and spirit of Benevolent Lenient Village had fled. I too found myself as flimsy as a sheet of paper. Everything calmed down.

"The turtle is almost done to a turn and smells really tasty," I opined.

"Are you a villager? You'll come and have a bowl of turtle soup as well?"

I surveyed this gang of rascally, smiling labourers. The old turtle was going to be buried in their bellies. Were they mobile tombs? Or toilets wrapped inside human hides? I smelt a stream of noxious odour that emanated from them and from me as well. I knew I was being buried together with Chivalry and Benevolent Lenient Village.

I tore myself away. But when I turned into another lane, I found I collided with Fatty. In his previous life, the fat policeman must have had a bond with our village. He was clutching A-Bing's lead in his hand. A-Bing refused to follow him. The dog stealthily bit the rope in two and scurried off. Nobody knew why, but the bronze bell fell from his neck and bounced on the ground, letting out a tinkling sound. Fatty shouted at two other policemen to go to an empty courtyard to grab A-Bing. I stopped him.

"Why did you come? Fatty, from now on if a leader gets a disease, there will be no doctor."

"This is my rice bowl," he said. "I'm in charge of the security in this area."

"How many of you are here?"

"A dozen. We shouldn't have been needed. When it came to it, however, the senior officials were uneasy and said, first things first, maintain order. In fact, nothing has gone wrong."

"How can you say nothing has gone wrong? A-Bing can't be hauled away can he?"

Fatty, still feeling embarrassed over the scene that had just unfolded, bellyached while patting the dust from his clothes: "I saved A-Bing, but the little shit will never come near me and bites the hand of his saviour. He was sent to Benevolent Lenient Village by me. Now the village is gone. I say, return the dog to his original owner, but he won't follow me."

"You claim you can capture men, yet you can't even catch a dog. You have a gun on your person. One shot is enough. It won't hurt your fingers."

Fatty's hand had been injured on the execution ground. After the event, I heard the old Village Head remark that the bullet fired by the boy soldier hit the criminal after passing through his middle finger. When he was receiving medical treatment in the hospital, the doctor asked him where the lost piece of finger had gone. His company doubled back. The bodies of the criminals had been transported away. The splashed brain matter and skull splinters hadn't been cleaned up yet. Even so, that half length of finger could not be found – perhaps it had been ricocheted asunder by the bullet. Someone suggested that he should have a criminal's finger transplanted. Fatty thought that would tempt misfortune.

"How did you know that my finger was wounded?" Fatty peered at me in surprise.

"Heard tell," I replied. "Sure, you've lost a finger. Maybe the finger was a condemned criminal in its previous life, or maybe it stole from people, hooked a woman or pointed at the Buddha as blasphemous words were being hurled."

Fatty chuckled and went on: "Plum, you know, I've never gotten much reward money for cracking so many criminal cases. On the other hand, for losing this finger I got several thousand yuan in food vouchers."

"That finger is a martyr," I judged.

I turned my head and went to Grandpa Cloud Forest's shrine. He hadn't touched food for days and his bowl, still half full of noodles with a layer of crust floating on the soup, sat on the windowsill. Grandpa Cloud Forest was huddled on his bed, safe and sound and holding a patient's finger to read the pulse.

The way he checked a pulse was extraordinary. His fingers didn't press on the patient's wrist. Instead, three fingers of one hand pinched the root of the patient's left middle finger and, gripping the tip of the same finger with the middle finger and thumb of the other hand, he murmured the stage of the patient's disease. The patient nodded his head like a pecking chicken and responded continuously with: "Yeah, all your words are right."

I had seen in the movies before how great men displayed their consummate composure on the battlefield. I always thought this was fictional; now I believed it to be true. I stood quietly in the room and stared at Grandpa Cloud Forest. Without warning, I sensed that his body was shining and then became transparent. I could see his heart, lungs, liver, his intestines in his abdominal cavity and, through his body, I could spy the bamboo basket and leather sacks on the wall. Red liquid was circulating about his glassy frame, which caused the halo around him to turn from red to white to yellow.

Shocked, I didn't know how to describe the illusory halo, but, experiencing inexplicable pleasantness and warmth, I was moved to shed tears. I strutted towards the table. Grandpa Cloud Forest didn't greet me. He was still scribbling out the prescription and telling the patient when he should take the medicine, how many days a course of treatment should last and how to go to the pharmacy to buy the medicine. On the statue of the Buddha on the table, beneath the lotus throne of the dignified benign-looking seated bodhisattva, four words were visible: "Weather the Critical Situation." Were the words inscribed there to begin with or had they appeared latterly?

"Have you brought money with you? Buy enough medicine for three months. If you pull through after three months, that's good. Otherwise, go elsewhere to find a better doctor. Plum, is the pharmacy still trading?"

"Yeah," I answered. Grandpa Cloud Forest grinned at me and he was once again his usual self. I rubbed my eyes.

"What's wrong with you?" asked Grandpa Cloud Forest, while still grinning.

"I…"

"The patient is in a critical condition. You escort him and me to the pharmacy to get the medicine."

I nodded my head.

Grandpa Cloud Forest had never escorted a patient to the pharmacy to fetch the medicine before. He did so today and I knew that this was the last patient he would diagnose in the village. I refused to stop him and didn't even carry him on my back. With the help of his small crutches, he clambered down from the bed. His hands paddling against the ground and his body pitching forward, he crawled out of the gate to the earthen ground. All through the village, the tumbling and crackling sound of tiles, ceramic pots and wooden rafters echoed, and motes of floating dust were omnipresent. Grandpa Cloud Forest marched forward in the dusty world and, as his head and body became coated with the residue, he took on the appearance of an adobe brick.

Again, his body shone and became transparent. Honestly. He was transmitting a kind of spiritual charisma and I just followed after him. I didn't know how to describe and explain this phenomenon. Years later, when I told this to many others including renowned biologists, psychologists and philosophers, they were stumped as well.

I followed Grandpa Cloud Forest to the tree beyond the perimeter of the earthen ground and a roar like a wolf's howl came from the cemetery behind the shrine. "Bury me here too! Bury me here too!"

We paused in our tracks. Grandpa Cloud Forest asked: "The old executioner is arguing with others?"

I answered: "Yeah."

"Oh."

I echoed: "Oh."

We stood still at the entrance to the lane for a long time. Fatty and three other policemen were lynching A-Bing on the door-frame of the empty courtyard into which he had crawled. The rope was woven from cowhide. One end of it had been lashed into a noose and placed around A-Bing's neck. The other end was threaded through a bronze knocker and sat in the hands of a policeman. The policeman threw his mettle into it. The two panels of the courtyard gate, however, opened automatically and A-Bing's two hind legs were left touching the ground even as the rest of him was being hauled up.

"Hold the gate steady; hold the gate steady!" Fatty ordered. Another policeman walked over to push the gate panel against the wall. The ground inside the gate was lower and A-Bing's four legs kicked and pumped madly in mid-air. Fatty cursed: "You kick and pump. I asked you to go with me, but you bit my hand. That time I didn't hang you, but this time let me oblige you."

The four limbs of the hauled-up A-Bing quietened down, then his body arched as his hind legs pumped violently again. The rope puller – now a bundle of nerves – tugged the line taut. A-Bing's hind legs pushed against one gate panel and his head butted another.

Fatty instructed: "Give the rope some slack; give the rope some slack." Another policeman struck A-Bing's waist with a club and A-Bing once again dangled, still writhing.

"There is no use beating him. Even if you beat him dead, he will spring back to life again once he touches the ground. Pull the rope taut, pour water and don't let him touch the ground. He will die in no time at all." Fatty went over, wrested the leather rope from the rope-pulling policeman's hand and tethered it to a tree in the lane.

Twice in my life I had witnessed dogs being lynched; this time it seemed like the greatest tragedy. I had felt excited when A-Bing made his first unexpected escape. Now I realised that Fatty, Brow, I and all the Benevolent Lenient villagers had committed a sin. We shouldn't have spared A-Bing back then and let the small running dog, who was as intelligent as a man without being able to speak the language of men, suffer the terror and pain of death twice. If he had died the first time, he might have been reincarnated. In spite of sojourning in the human world, he still couldn't avoid his fate. I beheld both scenes myself. Was the Great

Lord in the blue-grey heavens punishing me again?

We had lost our homeland. A-Bing, who took refuge here temporarily, lost his homeland too – his homeland in name only though – and his life. The real dog had gone and we had become a pack of homeless dogs. Where were we to go? And how would we be treated when we got there? When A-Bing at last quietly drooped beneath the gate frame, I forgot that Grandpa Cloud Forest was alongside me and that we were taking the patient to the pharmacy. All at once, I wanted to see Brow very much. I sensed that Brow was right. We had wronged her too much. I didn't know how or in what way I quit the lane, but I marched straight to the city, thinking only of going to see Brow.

The traffic was heaving on the streets of the Western Capital. The buildings on both sides were seven or eight storeys high, decorated with all kinds of doorplates and neon lights. I forced my way forward against the crowd on the pavement to the left of the road. They slammed into me and I bumped into them. The whole world had become chaotic. I heard someone snarl: "She's violating the traffic rules."

Next came the putt-putting of engines, the hooting of horns, the purring of bike spokes, the tinkling of bike bells and the sound of speaking, crying, coughing and farting. Almost all the parts of all the citizens and all the things on the streets were making a noise. Clothes were rustling, the wind was gurgling, the air was shaking noisily, ants were scrabbling lustily and the shadows of the lampposts were wriggling out loud. I believed that my soul had migrated out of my body. Human souls can leave their bodies. My soul departed from my body and floated in mid-air three metres above my head. I could see that I had sprained my ankle when my body walked past a cracked paving slab. I could see that in the rooms on the second floor of the buildings on both sides, people were handling official business, writing and making telephone calls, their buttocks balancing on the corners of the desks and their legs resting on the back of the chairs and swaying.

Someone in one room had just taken a bath. Now his fat, pig-like body was lying face-down on the bed and a woman was treading on his back. Somebody was reciting something loudly, the words very elegant. The voice was definitely not that of an administrative leader delivering a report or a band of people studying newspaper editorials. But what was he reciting? The window was blocked by a white screen curtain and the silhouettes of three or four people could be seen, though their statuses couldn't be ascertained. A deep booming voice was exhorting:

On the expansive wild lands, grasses and trees thrived with brilliant fragrant flowers, stones stood still in all kinds of postures and water babbled with wavelets mirroring the light of the sky. This was the state of Nature that existed in the Oracle.

One day, several canny men and women came. They built the first house and stoked up the first plume of kitchen smoke and, in order to survive, they tried hard to adapt to and till the land.

Later, more people joined them, more babies arrived and more houses were built. Streets appeared between the houses and the weeds and bushes receded under the assault of fires and axes.

Human communities took form. With the number of inhabitants growing, together with schools, shops, banks, post offices as well as exchange markets, trading buildings and administrative management buildings and cities came into being.

People felt that they had stepped into a civilised age. But the greater the number of people, the farther away the beautiful primitive landscape was pushed. The taller the buildings and the more luxurious the vehicles, the more sophisticated the phony, hypocritical and lowly people became.

With the expansion of the cities, a word appeared, 'pollution' – environmental pollution and psychological pollution. Facing impetuosity, restlessness and all kinds of infectious diseases, people started to return to Nature. On their days off, they went to the fields and mountains and, on coming home, they cultivated flowers. They made lawns on the streets, planted flowerbeds at the crossroads, bought flying birds and running animals, which had been driven away long before, at a price and put them in the urban parks. Plants and animals again existed, but had to adapt to the wiles of humans. If someone shot a wild swan dead in the suburbs with an advanced fowling piece, people would curse at him that he was barbarian and uncivilised.

The second stage of human civilisation had dawned but, with humans having developed to this degree, what should we do next? Nobody could answer this question, though nobody could avoid this question. At this time, one…

"Whose piece this is? Who wrote it? Have a look at the name of the writer," someone shouted.

A voice replied: "Let me see, it is a local writer. Who has torn out the first page? From memory, I think it is a guy whose surname is Fan or Mu." If it was a part of a novel, it must have been written by Fan Jingquan. Only he could write this elegantly. I walked on further. Was this room a restaurant? A number of guys were munching away, a large pile of fish bones, prawn casings and crab shells standing before each one of them. One was thumbing through a newspaper while picking his teeth. He hollered out: "Look, look, the superhuman thief has been shot!"

Another one scoffed: "Ancient news."

It then occurred to me that when Chivalry was being marched to the execution site, his soul might have jumped out of his body long before. What I saw was not Chivalry, only the shell that had accommodated his soul. Had his real soul fled from the scene long before? Or was it standing nearby watching his body being shot and dismembered?

While thinking this, I relinquished my altitude and rejoined the crowd. No more could I see what was happening inside the windows. My soul returned to my body. I bumped head-on into a couple of guys and sent them into a stagger. One of them cursed: "How can you loiter on this side? Do you know how to walk? He has just been discharged from hospital. Will you accept the responsibility if you knock him down?"

I stared at the patient. His face was of an earthen hue, the colour that a patient with a kidney disease would bear. Had he been given a kidney transplant? Received Chivalry's kidney? Into whose sockets did Chivalry's eyeballs go? Was he still looking at the Western Capital?

Chapter Twenty-Six

Grandpa Cloud Forest, Brow and I quit the Western Capital on the third day after our village had been reduced to ruins. On the morning of that third day, blind Grandma Five Springs and Grandpa Five Springs came back hand in hand to the village from their temporary home and sat together among the foundations of their former residence. Their old home had gone and only a few dilapidated walls were still to be bulldozed. The ancient tree had been chopped half away by an axe and nobody knew why it hadn't been felled.

The blind old lady yammered, relating how a fence had stood in front of their home and how a donkey-hitching pillar stuck out in front of the fence back in the year she married into Benevolent Lenient Village; how the donkeys rolled in the courtyard and sent dust flying; how she gave birth to thirteen children, but twelve of them died of infantile tetanus within twenty or twenty-five days of birth and they and their afterbirths were all buried under the steps.

Vexed by her nagging, Grandpa Five Springs decided to head somewhere else; somewhere he could hear people talking. He came across Lianben and Little Wei. Their vehicles were too small to carry their many odds and sods. They didn't bring the drums for performing the music of the Ming emperor. When they came back again, their houses had tumbled down. When they plucked aside the messy brickbats and fragmentary timbers, the drums had been reduced to two patches of cowhide and a pile of wooden shards. Now they were patting the dust off the cowhide, humphing.

Chivalry's grandfather – the old executioner – was bellowing like a howling wolf somewhere faraway: "Bury me here too; bury me here too!" They slanted their ears to listen, though still said nothing, patting off the dirt from the cowhide and humphing.

Grandpa Five Springs went back to his former residence silently, only to find his blind old mate had done herself in by dashing her head against the ancient tree. He asked: "Hi, you want to go or not?" But he didn't shed a tear.

Brow and I wheeled Grandpa Cloud Forest away in a handcart. When we passed the gate of the stadium compound, we took one last look at the village which was no longer even the shadow of a village. We didn't stop. Yesterday, we accepted the invitation of a patient who once boarded at my home. He invited us to practise medicine in his mountainous homeland. Brow blurted out that she felt apprehensive in her heart about entrusting her shop to Old Shao. Now, we were going to a mountain area. It was so far away. Could the cart make it? Her sudden hesitation puzzled me.

I quizzed Grandpa Cloud Forest: "Tell us: shall we go to the mountains or stay in the city? Where shall we go?"

"To where you came from."

At that moment, my soul leapt out of my body again. I had faith in Grandpa Cloud Forest and his words were eternally correct. He told me to go to where I came from. Where did I come from? Benevolent Lenient Village? No, there was no Benevolent Lenient Village anymore. I came from my mother's body. Yeah, I came from my mother's womb. I pictured my mother; her big breasts and broad hips. I entered a tunnel, a dark, moist, slippery, soft and warm tunnel that gave me some comfort. I saw my mother's womb and murmured: "Yes, this is my homeland."

"Sister Plum! Sister Plum, you see! Sister Plum!"

I heard Brow calling me loudly. The dark, moist, slippery and soft tunnel was serene, deep and long, but when I looked back, I glimpsed the other end. My eyes were the portal to the tunnel and I saw my eyes. There, in a patch of white shining light, Fan Jingquan stood in a T-shirt that bore three words printed in large script: "Magic Farm Tableland."

Epilogue

One commercial stretch of Xi'an city is known as the Earthen Gate (*Tu Men* in Chinese). I like this area, partly because I was born in the countryside and didn't come to Xi'an until the age of nineteen. A country cousin must graft and grind and subsist on simple fare; he hasn't seen much of the world and is unkempt in his appearance. For that reason, I am still frequently jeered at by certain city dwellers despite having lived in the provincial capital for more than twenty years. They don't recognise that I am one of them, just as they always perceive that Mao Zedong was a peasant. Apparently, the city belongs to them and their ancestors. However, dipping just once into their genealogy, it becomes evident that their forebears migrated from the countryside a generation or two ago at the most. This is why, after having found my way to the city, I made siring babies my number one priority. I reasoned that my own offspring ought to be acknowledged as bona fide citizens. A second reason is that I, who am not recognised as a citizen myself, do not wish to argue with my neighbours about my status. When all is said and done, twenty years have passed since I last worked the land. In such a large, modernised city, there happens to be a marketplace called the Earthen Gate. It must be a brave spot and poetical as well. As a writer, whose desire is to play around with words, thinking about this place inevitably produces cordial feelings in my heart.

Xi'an is especially hot this summer. In fact, for several straight summers it has been scorching here. In the past, one year consisted of four seasons, but now we are launched into summer as soon as winter has passed and winter follows on directly after summer. I am on my way to being forty-five. Time passes by like flowing water and the Wheel of the Year is spinning faster too. With no garments for spring and autumn, I either wrap myself up tightly from head to foot in a down jacket, leaving only my eyes exposed to watch the world, or else strip myself two-thirds naked. A lone piece of underwear must be retained to cover the leftover third and my expansive belly, thin arms and legs thus remain on show. Winter might send people into hibernation. I don't write in the winter but stay docilely at home. I hang on my door a set of couplets which imitate the calligraphic style of the Buddhist Patriarch Hongyi. These read:

Having tea at home, I entertain my guests simply.
With nothing to do, I thumb through books aimlessly.

It seems the summer is my season for writing. *Turbulence* was written in the summer, *The Abandoned Capital* was written in the summer, *White Nights* was written in the summer and summer was the season I worked on *The Earthen Gate*. Those who know me say I am timid and humble in my life, always keeping a low profile. On the other hand, my works tend to be rampant and wild, always climbing high and dicing with danger. I'm a man of conflicting parts. Thinking about this a while, I find myself agreeing with them.

I'm already forty-four and have been writing for twenty-one years. My writings have brought me both perpetual praise and malicious barbs, but I can always weather a difficult situation. Why? Well, humans have different roles to play in this world. They are like a hive of bees, which consists necessarily of worker bees and soldier bees as well as the queen bee who hogs the best honey for her own exclusive use. It must have been my fate to become a man of letters. Since I am a man of letters and the rules of writing entail flaunting, rising and soaring, I, of course, should unleash my ferocity and impressive power like a tiger in the mountains. But if I don't wield a pen, then I'm a phoenix that has come down from his roost, certainly lowlier than a rooster. When my fellow novelist Lu Yao was still alive, he once commented on my name. He said that the character 平 (*ping*) resembles a man's penis but the character 凹 (*wa*) is like a woman's vagina. My name is a combination of *yin* and *yang*. As a friend, he revelled in poking fun at me. But since my name contains both *yin* and *yang*, they should enhance each other. Why then does illness occupy me all the year round, transforming me into a notorious patient? I am only trying to adapt to the unwieldy climate which has squashed four seasons into two. If a man of letters is neither fond of beating a way to the gates of the movers and shakers, nor willing to dive into the ivory tower to sharpen his writing skills and seek great freedom in writing, he must be adept at enduring suffering.

For a dozen or more years now, I have borne the affliction of a liver disease. Many whose condition has been less serious than mine have died, but I still survive and, what is more, I am on the slow road to remission. My own secret therapy entails regarding malicious remarks as a destiny, uttering no ill words about other people and things and trying to do good for others.

I frequently go to the Earthen Gate street area. Sometimes, I travel by taxi and five stops costs me exactly ten yuan. Or

I ride a bike, humming a tune on the way. The tune is very pleasant to the ears. Such a pity that I don't know how to transcribe the notes; it is like moonlight that flows swiftly across the ground and cannot be retrieved. The street area serves as a venue for all kinds of trades. There I can window-shop for silk and cloth, tea and rice paper, and see restaurants, herbal medicines, soy sauce and liquor, incense sticks and candles, fruits, bronze wares, clothes, green vegetables, lacquered wares, framed pictures, fortune-telling, sewing and darning, lanterns, umbrellas, tooth-filling and foot-manicuring. I look at the men and women.

In the small tea houses, I watch people doing business, seeking the service of working girls and tussling with red faces. At the huge roundabout at the centre of the crossroads, vehicles turn around and people weave in and out of the traffic. I imagine that this is a whirlpool of water, where – *thump* – man and vehicle both plunge in. How did the Earthen Gate get its name? Was it the margin between the city and the country? Or was there once another gate here besides the four main gates of the old city proper? The Earthen Gate has a gate, but the gate panels are shut and I want to push them open to go in.

It must be down to destiny that I came across a stretch of market called the Earthen Gate while I was working on a book with the same title. When I feel tired, I go to hang about at the Earthen Gate and, after coming back home, carry on writing about the Earthen Gate.

When I'm handling my pen, I follow the style of the late politician Lin Biao: the curtains should be shut, no electric fan is needed and there is no air-conditioning. I have *Longjing* tea to drink, noodles to eat and cigarettes to smoke. I disconnect the telephone and lock the door from the inside to write according to my will. What a pleasure it is! Every day, besides strolling at the Earthen Gate, I can write from morning to evening and there is only God in the room – that God is me. Two people govern the world of my novels: one is Jesus and the other is Satan.

A female friend has written to me again. I don't know what she looks like and she has never told me her address in full. For two years, she has been a constant yet mysterious figure for me. She says she has always observed me, but I had better not ask who she is as one day she might pay me an unexpected visit. Her name is Ao Niang. Ao Niang, what a strange but intriguing name! She has only been sending me greetings this particular summer, but what good luck her letter has brought me. Today, as I finish writing *The Earthen Gate*. I push open the window and the smoke inside floats out into the red sunshine. Looking at the wild cloud I have released, I exclaim: "Ao Niang, look how brilliant this summer is!"

Someone is knocking at the door right now. But who?

Acknowledgements

The Earthen Gate was translated by Professor Hu Zongfeng (Northwest University) and He Longping (Changsha Normal University). Dr Robin Gilbank cooperated closely in the editing and preparation of the text.

The author and translators wish to thank Jamie McGarry and Valley Press for bringing this project to fruition. Financial support was provided by the School of Foreign Languages and the Centre for Chinese Literary Criticism at Northwest University. Thanks are also due to Dr J Graham Jones for his assistance in proofreading.

Endnotes

a. *Yep, water and sky were the same colour.* Paraphrased from a poem by Wang Bo (650–76 AD). The original reads: "The setting evening glow flies side-by-side with the lonely vulture. The autumn water shares the same colour as the vast skies."

b. *But far away there were not only single cells and distant shadows.* A paraphrase of a line of poetry by Li Bai (701–62 AD). In the month of March, his friend Meng Haorang left the Yellow Crane Tower in what is now Hubei Province in a sail boat and went to Nanjing in present-day Jiangsu Province. As Li Bai watched, the sail of the boat disappeared before his very eyes, leaving only the ever-flowing Yangtze River.

c. *The East is Red* was an anthem celebrating Chairman Mao and his liberation of the Chinese nation.

d. '*in agriculture we learn from Dazhai Village*' was a propaganda campaign started by Mao Zedong in 1963. The peasants of Dazhai in Shanxi Province were upheld as paragons of industry for working day and night and relentlessly constructing reservoirs, irrigation channels and so forth to boost production.

e. *qi* is the life force or flow of energy said to animate sentient human beings. Learning to cultivate it and harness it through the practices of *qigong* and kung-fu were thought to allow an individual to deploy remarkable powers.

f. *Zhu Yuanzhang* (1328–98 AD), also known as the Emperor Hongwu, was the founder of the Ming Dynasty. His supposed peasant origins were emphasised in later tellings of his life.

g. *The Pass* refers to the strategic Shanhai Pass on the borders of Hebei and Liaoning Provinces. Breaching this route signified the impending victory of the Qing forces.

h. *The Yellow Emperor and Laozi* is an alternative means of referring to the Warring States period (476 BC–221 BC) when these patriarchs lived.

i. *feng-shui* (wind and water) refers to the geomantic conditions of a place. If a man lives or a man's ancestor is buried in a place with good feng-shui, he will be blessed with health, wealth, good luck and talented, promising children.

j. *A Nocturnal Patron God* is the counterpart of a Day-time Patron God. The earliest record of the Nocturnal Patron God appears in *Travels in the Mountains and on the Seas*, which says that there are sixteen gods who take charge of the night for the Heavenly Emperor with their arms joined together. They have "small cheeks and bared shoulders." According to *Huainanzi* in the Han Dynasty, the Nocturnal Patron Gods appear in the southwest of China who "shout loudly at night and patrol the lands with their arms joined together." There were no such gods in the heartland of China at that time. The Ming Dynasty had many legends about the Nocturnal Patron Gods. According to the folk description, they are fair and kind. After doing their patrolling duty at night, they often report the grievances of the common people to the Heavenly Emperor so that justice is served and evildoers are punished. According to the *Creation of the Gods*, the Nocturnal Patron God's name is Qiao Kun.

k.   *Qin Hui* (1090–1155 AD) was twice prime minister in the Southern Song Dynasty. Because the emperor persisted in surrendering to the northern Jurchen regime, Qin Hui and several other wily ministers framed and murdered the renowned anti-Jurchen general Yue Fei. Later, the wrong was put right. White iron was forged into the images of the four ringleaders in a kneeling position and put before Yue Fei's tomb forever. Qin Hui's wife was the granddaughter of Wang Gui (1019–85 AD) and the foster daughter of Tong Guan (1045–1126 AD), two wily, talented ministers.

l.   *Concubine Yang* (719–56 AD), or Yang Guifei, was the ultimately ill-fated consort to the Tang emperor Xuanzong (reigned 712–56 AD). She was celebrated for her full and curvaceous figure and artistic depictions of the lady show her beauty putting the flowers to shame.

m.   *Wu Zetian* (624–705 AD) was the only widely-recognised woman monarch in the history of China.

n.   *Qigong* literally means "health energy cultivation." It is an ancient healing and relaxation therapy considered complementary to the practice of kung-fu. It involves learning to control the circulation of the life-force *qi* (commonly manifested in the breath) through the body. Acolytes who attain a high level of discipline may find themselves able to accomplish seemingly superhuman feats such as withstanding blows to the chest without injury or being capable of breaking bricks with their bare hands.

o.   *Interrogating the Maiden Servant* is a scene from *Romance of the Western Chamber* (also known as *The Story of the Western Wing*), a notable play by the dramatist Wang Shifu (1250–1307 AD). A scholar Zhang Sheng became infatuated with Cui Yingying, the daughter of a late prime minister. Yingying's maiden servant escorted Yingying to Zhang Sheng's study for a secret liaison, which was detected by Yingying's mother, Lady Cui, who summoned the maiden servant to be interrogated and blamed her that she had dragged the name of the ministerial residence through the mud. The maiden servant argued vehemently with just cause and Lady Cui finally had to consent to the marriage between Zhang Sheng and her daughter.

p.   *A household registration card* (*hujika* or *hukou*) is a document issued by the Chinese government to all its citizens. It lists the holder's place of birth and the place where they live and work. A *hukou* is of great importance. If an individual moved to another place, especially to the city, not having a local *hukou* would make it virtually impossible to gain official employment and access to services.

q.   *Six Records of a Floating Life* was written by Shen Fu (1763–1825 AD) in an autobiographical style. The book records the sourness, sweetness, bitterness and spiciness, and sorrow, happiness, partings and reunions of the author's life in a vivid bold and flowery language. It describes the mysterious marital bliss and the everlasting conjugal love, narrates in detail his bizarre experiences overseas and includes the health-preserving secrets of the Confucian, Taoist and Buddhist schools.

r.   *Yun* is a character in *Six Records of a Floating Life* and the wife of the author.

s.   A "*broken shoe*" is an indirect way of saying prostitute.

t.   *Du Fu* (712–70 AD) was a Tang Dynasty poet hailed as the "Poet Saint" and considered to have had a profound influence over both Chinese and Japanese literature.

u.   *Chen Yonggui* (1915–86) was the major beneficiary of the Dazhai campaign (see note iv, above). A native of that village, he led his fellow peasants to build stacked terraces in the foothills of the mountains and helped improve the efficiency of their agricultural production. Despite having no formal education, he went on to be elected a member of the Politbureau of the Central Committee of the Communist Party of China and was appointed a vice premier of the State Counsel of the People's Republic of China.

v.   *Wu Song* was one of the protagonists in *Outlaws of the Marsh* written by Shi Naian (1296–1372 AD). He ranked fourteenth among the one hundred and eight greenwood heroes who gathered in Liangshan Marsh to rob the rich and deliver the poor. His major feats included pummelling a tiger to death with his fists on the Jingyang Mountain after drinking eighteen bowlfuls of hard liquor.

w.   *The Art of War* by Sunzi was written by Sun Wu (544 BC–496 BC) and divided into thirteen chapters. It is the most ancient and most outstanding book on military strategies in China.

x.   *Red eggs* are eggs first boiled and then dyed red with a pigment for auspicious congratulatory purposes, frequently used to celebrate a marriage, a new arrival in a family, a birthday and other festive occasions.

y.   *The First Emperor* (259 BC–210 BC), or Qin Shihuang, was a great statesman, strategist, tactician and reformer. Historically, he first united China proper and founded the Qin Dynasty. He made many unprecedented contributions: created the emperor system, enforced the three dukes and nine ministers system in the government, divided China proper into districts and counties, united the usage of characters, currencies, weights and measures, and so forth. He established the basic pattern of China's more-than-two-thousand-year-long political system.

z.   *The Gang of Four* refers to a political clique formed in the Cultural Revolution, which included Jiang Qing (the final wife of Mao Zedong), Zhang Chunqiao, Yao Wenyuan and Wang Hongwen. Their fall in 1976 marked the end of the Cultural Revolution.

aa. The *Kun Diagram* is the name of one of the fundamental terms of the Eight Trigrams (*Ba Gua*) which represent the basic principles of reality within the Taoist system of cosmology.

ab. *The Yellow Emperor* (2717 BC–2599 BC) was the chieftain of all the tribes and the lord of all the peoples in ancient China. He was hailed as the "Earliest Humanistic Ancestor" of the Chinese people. His major inventions include: houses, clothes and hats, carts and boats, orders of battle, music, utensils, and square fields.

ac. *Li Shizhen* (1518–93 AD) was the most esteemed medical scientist, pharmaceutical scientist and naturalist in the history of China. His masterpiece, the *Compendium of Materia Medica*, which took him twenty-nine years to compile, exercised great influence over later generations' research into medical science and natural history. The book records 1,892 kinds of herbal medicines, among which 374 were original to him, collected 11,096 remedies, and included 1,160 delicate illustrations.

ad. *Frost's Descent* is the eighteenth term that marks the twenty-four divisions of the solar year in the traditional Chinese calendar and generally falls on 23rd or 24th October.

ae. *two hundred and fifty* insinuates a fool.

af. The *Eight Trigrams* (*Ba Gua*) represent the basic principles of reality within the Taoist system of cosmology. The names of the fundamental terms are *Qian* (referring to the heavens); *Xun* (wind); *Kan* (water); *Gen* (mountain); *Kun* (earth); *Zhen* (thunder); *Li* (fire); *Dui* (lake).

ag. The story of *Zhang Lian Sells the Cloth* concerns Zhang Lian, a once-well-off peasant, who got hooked on gambling, lost all his family property and had to scrape a living off the cloth woven by his wife Fourth Sister. Only the sobering intervention of their neighbour Aunt Wang, persuaded him to reform. A certain far-sighted gentleman recorded this story to urge and enlighten his fellow villagers. Its influence purportedly expanded beyond the local countryside.

ah. *Mei Lanfang* (1894–1961) was an outstanding performing artist in modern China who played the female protagonist in the Beijing and Kun operas and a world-famous Chinese operatic master who ranked first among the "Four Greatest Artists of Beijing Opera."

ai.   *Lu Xun* (1881–1936) was the outstanding essayist, revolutionary provocateur and controversialist of early twentieth century China.

aj.   *'female' ginseng (angelica sinensis)* has this unusual common name because it is a staple ingredient in gynaecological medicines.

ak.   *Yue Fei* (1103–42 AD) was a strategist, tactician, crack horseback archer, poet and calligrapher and the leader of the four reviver generals of the Southern Song Dynasty. In a dozen or more years, he led his army to fight and always crushed the northern Jurchen army. When he was on the point of taking the enemy capital and rescuing the two former emperors who had been taken captive earlier, he was pressed to come back to the Court by the then reigning emperor, who issued twelve gold tablets in one day. Later, he was framed and executed under the charge of "plotting treason".

al.   *The Queen Mother* used to be a goddess who took charge of disasters, plague and punishment. Later as her legends circulated, she became a kindly, aged goddess who ruled over all the other goddesses in the Heavenly Palace and held sway over anything feminine between Heaven and earth. Legend has it that she lives by the Jade Pool in the Kunlun Mountains and immortality peach trees are planted in her garden.

am.   *Chen Sheng* (?–208 BC) was the one of the co-leaders (the other one being Wu Guang) of the first large-scale peasants' rebellion at the end of the Qin Dynasty.

He was a hired hand when he was young. Once while labouring in the field, he said to his partners: "If we become wealthy and dignified later in the future, we shouldn't forget each other." His partners all laughed at his wishful thinking. Chen heaved a long sigh and said: "How can a swallow or sparrow know of the ambition of a roc?"

an. *Zhang Liang* (3rd century BC–186 BC) was a strategist under the service of the first Han Dynasty emperor Liu Bang and one of the three talents at the beginning of the Han Dynasty together with Xiao He and Han Xin. His main achievements include helping Liu Bang establish the Han Dynasty and helping the crown prince preserve his crown princeship. After the founding of the Han Dynasty, he lived a life of seclusion and died of a disease while many of his colleagues were butchered by Liu Bang.

ao. *Han Xin* (died 196 BC) was a generalissimo, strategist, tactician and military theorist who left behind many textbook battle examples of strategies and tactics. But he was also suspected and looked upon as a potential threat by the emperor. Finally, he was lured to the palace by his benefactor Xiao He and executed by the Empress Lü Zhi.

ap. '*He has one bosom friend in death and life; Survive or not, that's down to two wives.*' The bosom friend refers to Xiao He, who caught up and brought the deserter Han Xin back to the barracks on a moonlit night so that Han could reach the glorious heights of his life later on, but who also helped the Empress Lü Zhi lure Han to the palace to be executed. One of the two wives was an old lady washer who gave Han Xin some porridge to eat and saved him from starving to death. The other wife was Empress Lü Zhi.

aq. *Golden Altar Boy and Jade Girl* refers to the boy and girl servants-in-waiting who stand on either side of an immortal.

ar. *Zhong Kui* is the god of exorcism and banishing evil in Chinese folklore and the "Saintly Lord Who Confers Blessings and Protects the Residence" in traditional Chinese culture. According to ancient books, he hailed from the Zhongnan Mountains at the beginning of the Tang Dynasty and had an awe-inspiring appearance – a leopard's head, ring-like eyes, an iron face and bristling whiskers. But he is righteous, upright, honest, sincere and learned.

as. *Little Cabbage* is a story of murder which occurred in the twelfth year of the reign of the Emperor Tongzhi (1873). Bi Xiugu – a woman nicknamed "little cabbage" because of her green and white attire – was seduced by a paramour who then poisoned her husband.

at. *Cold Kiln* relates the early life of Lü Mengzheng (944 or 946–1011 AD), whose in-laws considered him so lowly that they drove him out together with their daughter. After weathering destitution, cold, hunger, and suspicion the couple's love grew deeper than ever and Lü defied the odds to serve three terms as prime minister.

au. *The Three Kingdoms* refer to the Kingdom of Wei (220–66 AD) established by Cao Pi, the Kingdom of Shu (221–63 AD) established by Liu Bei, and the Kingdom of Wu (229–80 AD) established by Sun Quan.

av. *Plight Mutual Faith in the Peach Garden* refers to a fictionalised incident in which the figures Liu Bei (161–223 AD), Guan Yu (died 220 AD) and Zhang Fei (unknown–221 AD) each pledged to become blood brothers in a peach garden.

aw. *Three Visits to the Cottage* refers to how Liu Bei visited Zhuge Liang three times to invite him to leave the mountains and become his Director General.

ax. *Liu Xuande* was the style name of Liu Bei. He was a prominent statesman born in Baoding City, Hebei Province in the Three Kingdoms Period. In 221 AD, he proclaimed himself Emperor (until the title Zhang-wu) in Chengdu and founded the Kingdom of Shu.

ay. *Cao Cao* (155–220 AD) was a celebrated statesman, strategist, poet, essayist and calligrapher from the end of the Eastern Han Dynasty. He united Northern China by cracking down on separatist regimes and subduing the ethnic minorities. This and his economic and social policies laid the foundation for his son Cao Pi to establish the Kingdom of Wei.

az. *Sun Quan* (182–252 AD) was a statesman in the Three Kingdom Period, who in spite of his decidedly odd physical appearance excelled in both letters and martial deeds and in 229 AD declared himself Emperor in Wuchang, Hubei Province and founded the Wu Kingdom.

ba.   *The Southland* refers to Sichuan Province.

bb.   *Zhang Fei* (?–221 AD) was a prestigious general in the Three Kingdoms Period. When Liu Bei was defeated by Cao Cao at Changbanpo, he led twenty mounted warriors to bring up the rear. No enemy dared to venture close. In the end, he was murdered while sound sleep by his two lieutenant generals because he wanted to avenge his sworn brother Guan Yu and pushed them too hard.

bc.   *Guan Yu* or Lord Guan (162–220 AD) was an important general around the transition between the Eastern Han Dynasty and the Three Kingdoms Period. In Chinese culture, his name symbolises loyalty and valour.

bd.   *The Cowherd and the Girl Weaver* is a tale of forbidden love. As punishment for refusing to end their relationship the pair was cast into the sky and became the stars Altair and Vega at the opposite ends of the Milky Way respectively. On the same day every year, they are granted a brief reunion. On 7th July numerous magpies are believed to fly into the heavens to build them a bridge across the "silver river" (the Milky Way). In commemoration of them, that day of the calendar has come to be celebrated as the Chinese version of Valentine's Day.

be. *The Stories of Twenty-four Filial Sons* is generally attributed to Guo Jujing in the Yuan Dynasty (1260–1368 AD). It consists of: 1. How the legendary King Shun showed kindness to his blind father, stepmother and half-brother in the face of their murderous plots 2. How the Emperor Wen of Han (202 BC–157 BC) tasted his mother's medicine personally before giving it to her. 3. How Confucius's student Zeng Shen (505 BC–435 BC) felt his heart ache telepathically in the mountains when his mother bit her finger back home, then returned to entertain a guest with brush-wood. 4. How Confucius's student Zilu (542 BC–480 BC) carried back home rice from more than thirty-three miles away to serve his parents while he himself subsisted on wild vegetables. 5. How Confucius's student Min Shun (536 BC–487 BC) begged his father not to dump his stepmother though she maltreated him and gave him a reed-flower-padded garment to wear in winter. 6. How Tanzi in the Spring and Autumn Period (770 BC–476 BC) was almost shot to death by a hunter when he camouflaged himself with a deer hide in order to obtain milk from a doe to cure his parents' eye disease. 7. How the septuagenarian Laolaizi (599 BC–479 BC) acted the fool to humour his ancient parents. 8. How Dong Yong in the Eastern Han Dynasty sold himself to cover the cost of his father's burial. 9. How Ding Lan in the Eastern Han Dynasty carved wood into the images of his late parents and served them as if they were alive, even valuing these effigies over his wife 10. How Jiang Ge in the Eastern Han Dynasty hired himself out to earn money for his mother's upkeep. 11. How Lu Ji

(187–219 AD) hid oranges in his chest at a banquet and wanted to bring them back for his mother when he followed his father to pay Yuan Shu (?–199 AD) a visit. 12. How Guo Ju in the Jin Dynasty wanted to bury his own son so that he could save some grain and feed his mother. 13. How Huang Xiang (18 –106 AD) fanned his widowed father's pillow and mattress in summer and warmed his quilt in winter. 14. How Cai Shun in the Eastern Han Dynasty put the black and red mulberries he picked into different baskets, leaving the black ones for his mother and the red ones for himself. 15. How Jiang Shi and his wife were so kind to their mother that spring water spurted out of their courtyard and two gold carp (her favourite fish) leaped out of the spring water every day. 16. How Wang Pou (unknown–311 AD) would go to his mother's tomb on thundery days to reassure her that she had nothing to fear. 17. How Lady Tang, the grandmother of Cui Shannan in the Tang Dynasty, breastfed her toothless mother-in-law every day for several years and Cui treated Lady Tang with the same measure of filial affections. 18. How Wang Xiang (185–269 AD) lay on the ice to catch fish for his disease-stricken stepmother even though she often badmouthed him in front of his father. 19. How Wu Meng (265–420 AD) stripped himself to the waist and sat before his father's bed on summer nights so the mosquitoes would bite him rather than his father. 20. How Yang Xiang in the Jin Dynasty jumped on the back of a ferocious tiger and wrestled with its throat to save his father from its jaws. 21. How Meng Zong (unknown–271 AD) cried in a bamboo grove in the depths of winter and prayed that bamboo shoots would sprout so he could make them into soup to cure his mother's disease. 22. How Yu Qianlou in the Southern and Northern Dynasties tasted his father's faeces to discern the severity of the old man's disease. 23. How Zhu Shouchang (1014–83 AD) abandoned his official post to look for his birth mother, finally finding her after fifty years of separation. 24. How Huang Tingjian (1045–1105 AD) cleaned his mother's chamber pot personally every night though he was a high-ranking government official.

bf.   *Jia Wansan* is a cipher for the historical figure Shen Wansan (1296 or 1328 or 1330–76).

bg.   *Xiezhi* is a legendary beast which can tell right from wrong and use its horn to butt an evildoer whenever there is a fight.

bh.   *Hou* is a legendary doglike man-eater.

bi.   *The Three Sage Kings* refers to Suiren, Fuxi and Shennong. *The Five August Emperors* refers to Huang Di, Zhuan Xu, Di Ku, Tang Yao and Yu Shun. The Three Sage Kings and the Five August Emperors led the masses to create the ancient Chinese civilisation.

bj.   *Shi Qian the Flea on the Drum* was a supporting role in *Outlaws of the Marsh* and ranked one hundred and seventh among the one hundred and eight greenwood heroes who gathered in Liangshan Marsh to rob the rich and help the poor. He was a *qinggong* master and a thief wizard able to fly over eaves and walk up walls.

bk. *Wu Guang* (unknown–208 BC) was one of the co-leaders (the other one being Chen Sheng) of the first large-scale peasants' rebellion at the end of the Qin Dynasty.

bl. *The Huai River*, together with the Qinling Mountains, is traditionally said to form the boundary between Northern and Southern China.

bm. The Peach Blossom Spring was a Utopian earthly paradise invented by the poet Tao Yuanming (c. 365–427 AD). Class division and exploitation were eradicated there so everyone savoured a peaceful life supported by their own labour.

bn. *The Yan'an Rectification Campaign* was a political and cultural campaign launched in 1942 and lasting for about three years. The main content of the campaign included: opposing subjectivism to rectify the learning style, opposing factionalism to rectify the Party style, and opposing hollow long-winded "eight-part" essays to rectify the academic style. The campaign fortified Mao Zedong's position in the Central Committee of the CPC and strengthened the leadership of the CPC over the Party cadres and the common Party members.

bo. *Zeng Guofan* (1811–72) was a statesman, strategist, neo-Confucianist and man of letters born in Shuangfeng County, Hunan Province. His major achievements included: creating the Xiang army, crushing the Taiping Rebellion and initiating the Westernization Campaign. His willingness to slaughter disobedient peasants also earned him the monickers "Butcher Zeng" and "Barber Zeng."

bp.   *Zizhan* was the style name of the outstanding poet and artist Su Shi (1037–1101 AD).

bq.   *Zheng Banqiao* (birth-name Zheng Xie) (1693–1765 AD) was an artist who rose to become an official calligrapher, poet and painter to the Emperor Qianlong. He was especially famed for his depictions of b a m b o o ,   o r c h i d s ,   s t o n e s ,   p i n e s   a n d chrysanthemums.

br.   '*The birds all get paired up in the trees... Husband and wife together return...*' are lines from the classic Huangmei Opera, *The Fairy Couple*. It elaborates on the story of Dong Yong, the eighth of the *Twenty-four Filial Sons*. The youngest daughter of the Jade Emperor was willing to forsake her status as an immortal to marry this worthy pauper, but her father ultimately forced them apart leaving the faithful Dong to suffer eternal regret.

bs.   The *Pipa* is a plucked string instrument with a fretted fingerboard.

bt.   *Zhuge Liang* (181–234 AD) was a statesman, strategist, essayist, calligrapher and inventor who played a decisive role in forming the Liu Bei-Sun Quan alliance and establishing and defending the Kingdom of Shu.

In traditional Chinese culture, he is seen as a paragon of loyalty and wisdom.

bu. *Ma Su* (190–228 AD) was a minister in the Kingdom of Shu. Having helped Zhuge Liang to pacify the southern barbarians, his master thought very highly of him. Ma's downfall came when a tactical mistake of his led to defeat at the Battle of Jieting and Zhuge Liang had no choice but to tearfully order him to be beheaded.

bv. *The God of Thunder* in Chinese mythology has a red monkey's face, a bird's beak, two wings on his back and claw-like feet. He holds a hammer in his right hand, an awl in his left hand and several drums are hung about his person. Thunderbolts are created when he beats these drums.

bw. *The Six Kingdoms* refer to the Kingdoms of Han, Zhao, Wei, Chu, Yan and Qi. They were wiped out by the Kingdom of Qin.

bx. Known by the title *jinshi* in Chinese.

by. *Eight-treasure porridge* or *Laba* porridge is a kind of rice porridge mixed with nuts and dried fruits eaten on 8th December according to the lunar calendar.

bz. *Wuliangye* is the brand name of a kind of top-grade liquor produced in Yibin, Sichuan Province. The liquor (*ye*) got its name because it is made of the five (*wu*) kinds of grains (*liang*): wheat, rice, corn, sorghum, and sticky rice.

ca.   The title of *Three Drops of Blood* is a reference to the actions of the County Head Jin Xinshu in the opera. Thrice he deploys a spurious method when asked to determine kinship, each time with drastic consequences for those involved. In ancient times, some people believed that if spots of blood from biological relatives were placed together they would spontaneously blend together. Jin's misguided faith generates much anger and leads to his downfall.

cb.   A *Ward Head* was the administrative, military and educational head of a ward. During the Qing Dynasty and the Republic of China, the *bao jia* system was carried out to rule the common people. Generally, a village consisted of three wards (*bao*) and a ward consisted of thirty households. If one man or household committed a crime, the other households must report. Otherwise, they would be implicated.

cc.   *The War between Chu and Han* refers to a large-scale war that lasted from 206 BC to 202 BC for the supreme power between Liu Bang, the King of Han, and Xiang Yu, the Hegemon-king of the Western Chu. The war ended with the failure and death of Xiang Yu and the founding of the Western Han Dynasty by Liu Bang. But here it refers to a Chinese chess game.

www.ingramcontent.com/pod-product-compliance
Lightning Source LLC
Chambersburg PA
CBHW021132090426
42740CB00008B/757